1990

Women, Sex, and the Law

New Feminist Perspectives Series
General Editor: Rosemarie Tong, Davidson College

Beyond Domination: New Perspectives on Women and Philosophy
edited by Carol C. Gould

Claiming Reality: Phenomenology and Women's Experience
by Louise Levesque-Lopman

Dehumanizing Women: Treating Persons as Sex Objects
by Linda LeMoncheck

Gendercide: The Implications of Sex Selection
by Mary Anne Warren

Manhood and Politics: A Feminist Reading in Political Theory
by Wendy L. Brown

Mothering: Essays in Feminist Theory
edited by Joyce Trebilcot

Uneasy Access: Privacy for Women in a Free Society
by Anita L. Allen

Women and Spirituality
by Carol Ochs

Women, Sex, and the Law
by Rosemarie Tong

Women, Militarism, and War: Essays in History, Politics, and Social Theory
edited by Jean Bethke Elshtain and Sheila Tobias

Toward a Feminist Epistemology
by Jane Duran

Is Women's Philosophy Possible?
by Nancy Holland

Evidence on Her Own Behalf: Women's Narrative as Theological Voice
by Elizabeth Say Virgili

WOMEN, SEX, and the LAW

ROSEMARIE TONG

Rowman & Littlefield Publishers, Inc.

In memory of my mother,
Lillian Nedved Behensky

ROWMAN & LITTLEFIELD PUBLISHERS, INC.

Published in the United States of America
by Rowman & Littlefield Publishers, Inc.
8705 Bollman Place, Savage, Maryland 20763

British Cataloging in Publication Information Available

Library of Congress Cataloging in Publication Data

Tong, Rosemarie.
  Women, sex, and the law.

  (New feminist perspectives series)
  Includes bibliographical references and index.
  1. Women—Legal status, laws, etc.—United States.
2. Sex discrimination against women—Law and legislation—
United States. 3. Sex and law—United States. 4. Common
law. 5. Sexism—United States. 6. Sex role. I. Title.
II. Series.
KF478.T66   1983   346.7301'34   83–16001
ISBN 0–8476–7230–1   347.306134
ISBN 0–8476–7231–X (pbk.)

CONTENTS

Acknowledgments   vii

Introduction   1
  Notes, 5

1 Pornography   6
  The Traditional Concept of Pornography in Anglo-American
      Law, 7
  Toward a Definition of Women-Degrading Pornography, 9
  The Search for an Appropriate Legal Response to Gyno-
      Thanatica, 13
  Conclusion, 27
  Notes, 32

2 Prostitution   37
  The Traditional Image, 38
  Arguments for Criminalization, Legalization, and
      Decriminalization, 39
  Feminist Concepts of Prostitution, 48
  Feminist Legal Approaches to Prostitution, 55
  Conclusion, 59
  Notes, 61

3 Sexual Harassment   65
  The Ubiquitous Phenomenon, 67
  Standard Legal Responses, 71
  Feminist Legal Responses: Antidiscrimination Law, 77
  Extralegal Remedies, 83
  Conclusion, 87
  Notes, 88

4 Rape 90
Traditional and Contemporary Definitions, *91*
The Effect of Misogynistic Images on Legal Theory and
Practice, *98*
Recent Reforms in Rape Law, *104*
Conclusion, *119*
Notes, *120*

5 Woman-Battering 124
Definition and Causes, *125*
Traditional Legal Doctrine, *127*
Civil and Criminal Remedies, *128*
The Search for More Effective Legal Remedies, *141*
The Connections Between Woman-Battering and
Spouse Murder, *145*
Conclusion, *149*
Notes, *150*

6 Black Perspectives on Women, Sex, and the Law 153
Pornography, *155*
Prostitution, *159*
Sexual Harassment, *162*
Rape, *166*
Woman-Battering, *169*
Conclusion, *171*
Notes, *172*

7 Lesbian Perspectives on Women, Sex, and the Law 175
Pornography, *179*
Prostitution, *181*
Sexual Harassment, *186*
Rape and Woman-Battering, *189*
Conclusion, *190*
Notes, *190*

8 Conclusion 193
Common Connections, *193*
Differences of Perspective, *200*
The Limits of the Law, *203*
Notes, *207*

Index 209

ACKNOWLEDGMENTS

I am indebted to numerous people and wish to thank them for whatever contribution this book may make. In particular, I owe my thanks to Mr. and Mrs. Willcox B. Adsit, whose generosity provided me with financial assistance to take a semester off from my teaching responsibilities, and to Williams College. I am also indebted to Robert Fullinwider of the Center for Philosophy and Public Affairs at the University of Maryland; to William Puka, Department of Philosophy at Rensselaer Polytechnic Institute; and to Mary Vetterling-Braggin for copious comments. I am also grateful to Kim Carpenter, Jane Appling, and Sarah McFarland for editorial assistance. Many thanks to Eileen Sahady for typing the manuscript and Rosemary Lane for supervising its completion. Finally, I wish to thank my husband, Paul K. K. Tong, and my sons, Paul S. M. Tong and John Joseph Tong, who have encouraged me in my effort.

An earlier and abbreviated version of Chapter 1 was published under the title "Feminism, Pornography, and Censorship" in *Social Theory and Practice,* vol. 8, no. 1, Spring 1982.

INTRODUCTION

Although feminist scholars have written many excellent books and articles on pornography, prostitution, sexual harassment, rape, and woman-battering, there have been few systematic efforts to analyze the legal theories and practices that bring these diverse issues under the same scrutiny.[1] Neither have there been many sustained attempts to raise in detail questions of perspective—questions that involve conflicts within as well as between gender, sexual preference, race, and class division.[2] One begins with some stereotypical differences of perspective between genders: Why is it what a man describes as "aggressive bird-dogging" a woman describes as sexual harassment? what a man terms consensual intercourse, a woman terms rape? what a husband terms a heated argument, a wife terms a brutal brawl? Having stated these real or contrived differences, one immediately notes that some men and some women break rank with their respective genders. Some men have little trouble distinguishing consensual sexual conduct from coercive sexual conduct, and some women, those who join organizations such as HOW (Happiness of Womanhood) and MOM (Men Our Masters) for example, not only conflate consensual and coercive sex but pride themselves on being sexually submissive. When it comes to questions of female sexual submission, dominance, and equality, blacks may disagree not only with whites, but with one another. Lesbians may argue not only with heterosexuals, but among themselves. And women of the lower class may challenge not only middle-class women, but each other.

To fail to address these crucial differences of perspective is to speak to a limited audience, such as only to white, heterosexual, middle-class women. But to focus exclusively on these differences is to risk remaining silent for fear of misrepresenting a point of view that needs to be expressed. The general aim of this book is to avoid both extremes. It is to ask, as simply and straightforwardly as possible, why different kinds of women have suffered in different sorts of ways at the hands of Anglo-American law for the same reason: their sexuality.

Sex or sexuality is of course not an unambiguous concept. It refers to at least four separate but related sets of data: (1) *biological sex,* constituted by six characteristics (chromosomes, gonads, internal genitalia, external genitalia, hormones, and secondary sexual manifestations; (2) *gender identity and behavior* (masculine/feminine); (3) *sexual identity and behavior* (heterosexual/homosexual); and (4) *reproduction.*[3] Significantly, Anglo-American law has largely accepted the traditional view according to which biological sex determines not only one's reproductive functions but also one's gender identity and behavior. Biological females will think and act in feminine modes unless they are reared to think and act in masculine modes. In turn, gender identity and behavior is supposedly correlated with one's sexual identity and behavior: The "normal" woman will not only exhibit culturally selected feminine characteristics (gentleness, modesty, humility, supportiveness, empathy, sensitivity, unselfishness), but she will also typically pursue men as the object of her sexual needs and wants. In contrast, the "abnormal" woman— even if she exhibits culturally selected feminine characteristics as opposed to culturally selected masculine characteristics (strength of will, ambition, courage, independence, assertiveness, aggression, hardiness, the ability to think abstractly and analytically, and the ability to control emotion)[4]—will typically pursue women as the object of her sexual needs and wants.

If one contrasts "normal" women with their "abnormal" counterparts, it becomes clear that a woman will be classified as abnormal unless she abides by the rules of what Adrienne Rich terms the institution of compulsory heterosexuality.[5] This institution mandates a unilateral arrangement according to which "female sexuality cannot be lived or spoken or felt or even somatically sensed" apart from its definition as that which has the "capacity to arouse desire" in men.[6] In other words, female sexuality has no meaning or use apart from male wants and needs. Therefore, according to the code of compulsory heterosexuality, if women fail or refuse to nurture men, to fulfill their erotic wants and needs, or to bear and rear their children (reproduction), then men may punish women by degrading, harassing, raping, or beating them.[7]

At first glance, the ethos of compulsory heterosexuality seems to be diametrically opposed to that of Anglo-American law, which promises to protect each person from the harms others would unjustifiably or inexcusably inflict upon him or her. Clearly, when a husband batters his wife, he harms her; when a boyfriend rapes his girlfriend, he harms her; when a male employer harasses a female employee, he harms her. Nevertheless, the law has frequently chosen to trivialize these harms, to redescribe them as lovers' quarrels, as healthy excesses of male sexual prowess, as mere flirtations. Where harm has resisted such facile trivialization, the law has frequently sought to blame the victim for her plight. Supposedly, the battered woman had it coming, the raped woman wanted it, and the harassed woman encouraged it.

In sum, women seek out the sexual abuse they receive. Women are temptresses who arouse men's seething passions only to complain when men cannot control these "irresistible" forces. When women argue that they do not tempt the men who freely choose to sexually abuse them, they are dismissed as liars. The extent to which the image of woman as lying temptress is woven into the texture of Anglo-American law is remarkable. Long before Freud claimed that women show less sense of justice than men, that they are less ready to submit to the "great necessities of life," and that they are more often influenced in their judgments by feelings of affection or hostility,[8] Anglo-American legal theorists and practitioners convinced themselves that women were morally deficient. As a result, they adopted an overly critical attitude toward female victims of crime, insisting that the testimony of all women must be taken with a large grain of salt to correct for female prejudice and bias.

Fortunately, the image of woman as lying temptress, as moral nerd, is being exposed by feminists for what it is: a pernicious myth that has no substance in reality. Woman's character is no more deficient than that of man, and vice appears to be distributed equally among the males and females of the human species. As contemporary society gradually overcomes its misogynism, police officers, prosecutors, and judges are beginning to take the rights of women seriously. Less often is the victim of rape put on trial alongside her rapist; less often is the victim of woman-battering told to love, honor, and obey her assailant; and less often is the victim of sexual harassment told that big girls can take a little pawing and patting. In addition, there is less sympathy for the view that prostitution and pornography are always harmless and more sympathy for the view that they sometimes constitute complex social harms that affect women severely.

That feminists should have come to rely on the law as an instrument of social reform is not surprising. In a pluralistic society where moral and cultural diversity is not only tolerated but celebrated, and where institutions such as religion, education, and the family are relatively weak, increasing emphasis is placed on the law both as a means of social control and as a vehicle for social transformation. When a justice of the Supreme Court speaks, his or her words are listened to with the same care and respect that at other times and in other cultures met the utterances of the priest, prophet, or sage. Consequently, women have attempted to improve their social position by legal means. Regarding pornography, prostitution, sexual harassment, rape, and woman-battering, women have turned for succor to the police departments, to the courts, and to the legislatures. Although their entreaties have not always been heard in the past, they are being heard today. Reforms are being enacted and enforced.

But legal reforms are not always the only or the best answer to women's social problems, especially when these problems have sexual dimensions. The law is a paradoxical instrument of social control. It is a minimalist institution that prevents and punishes only manifest or serious harms. It does not censor or sanction those hidden or less blatant harms that plague us more routinely. Nor does it encourage or reward positive behavior that benefits or improves society. In short, the law is not a substitute for morality, and legal reform is not the same as moral transformation.

But even if the law is a minimalist institution, it has certain maximalist tendencies—tendencies to impose uniformity where diversity ought to prevail. When women encourage the law to be more active on their behalf, they tread a potentially perilous path. Support can mutate into control, and a gain on one front can represent a loss on another. A "Catch-22" situation can develop only too rapidly. Women have argued, for example, that the right to privacy covers their respective decisions to marry, to divorce, to use contraceptives, and to have abortions: "Goings-on" in the marital bed or in any bed are private matters. But if what goes on in the bedroom is all that private, then, or so begins the counterargument, the law's agents should not be snooping around a man's castle, looking for evidence of pornographic fiestas or seeking out victims of sexual harassment, rape, or woman-battering. If women respond to this argument by suggesting that, after all, sexual relations are not absolutely private, that no woman is an island, then either they must prepare for the probable—encroachments on their hard-won reproductive freedoms—or they must provide criteria for warranted as opposed to unwarranted invocations of the right to privacy.

That the law can backfire on women does not mean that women should not invoke it. Without the law, women's condition would be substantially worse than it is. However, the law is not a panacea for women's woes. If feminists wish to create and maintain a sexual morality that liberates women, men, and children of all races, classes, and sexual preferences, they will have to transform not only law, but education, religion, and the family. Although this may strike some as an overwhelming task, women have the strength to accomplish it.

This book is a tribute to those women who have worked to reform the law so that no woman need suffer *simply* on account of her sexuality. If the law can be transformed, so can other social and cultural institutions. One day woman's work will be done, and the future will see the achievement of such crucial feminist goals as the elimination of gender, race, and class barriers, the construction of a society in which each person is provided with the concrete means to take advantage of bona fide educational and occupational opportunities, and the creation of a human community based on mutual respect and concern. For now we can celebrate the progress that women have made on the legal front. That there is more to be done is no reason not to applaud the gains that have already been made.

Notes

1. Catherine A. MacKinnon promises to offer such a jurisprudence in the Summer 1983 issue of *Signs: Journal of Women in Culture and Society.*

2. One of the few sustained attempts to raise in detail questions of perspective is that of Angela Davis in *Women, Race and Class* (New York: Random House, 1982).

3. For a similar listing, see Ethel Spector Person, "Sexuality as the Mainstay of Identity: Psychoanalytic Perspectives," in *Signs: Journal of Women in Culture and Society* 5, no. 4 (Summer 1980):606.

4. Mary Vetterling-Braggin discusses these characteristics in her introduction to *"Femininity," "Masculinity," and "Androgyny": A Modern Philosophical Discussion* (Totowa, N.J.: Littlefield, Adams, 1982).

5. Adrienne Rich, "Compulsory Heterosexuality and Lesbian Existence," *Signs: Journal of Women in Culture and Society* 5, no. 4 (Summer 1980):631–60.

6. Catherine A. MacKinnon, "Feminism, Marxism, Method, and the State: An Agenda for Theory," *Signs: Journal of Women in Culture and Society* 5, no. 4 (Summer 1980):533–34.

7. Dorie Klein, "Violence Against Women: Some Considerations Regarding Its Causes and Its Elimination," *Crime and Delinquency* 27, no. 1 (January 1981):64.

8. Sigmund Freud, *Sexuality and the Psychology of Love,* Philip Rieff, ed. (New York: Collier Books, 1963), p. 193.

CHAPTER 1

PORNOGRAPHY

In 1979 Women Against Pornography (WAP) organized a march of 7,000 people through Times Square and held a conference with about 800 attendees. After the conference, an editor of *Playboy* called a woman participant he knew, angered that she had addressed the meeting. "How could you do that?" he demanded. "Don't you know that if the forces of censorship win, they will get you too?"[1] Like many others, this woman admitted that the editor had a point. Increasingly, feminists are concerned that a stance against pornography may be used to justify censorship. Their concern is not without warrant. For example, in parts of the country where regional censorship ordinances have been enforced, officials have classified feminists works such as *Our Bodies, Ourselves, Fear of Flying,* and *The Joy of Sex* together with "Jane Birkin in Bondage," "Chester the Molester," and "The Joy of Pain." As a result of instances where fundamental differences between works on female sexuality have gone unrecognized, more and more feminist writers have been arguing that the antipornography campaign is a "hot and dangerous" issue for feminists,[2] not only because it is perilously in alliance with the New Right, but because it may be mistakenly viewed as "antisex." At a recent feminist conference, Alice Echols argued that the antiporn movement (as practice) and cultural feminism[3] (as ideology) may detrimentally "re-inforce and validate women's traditional sexual conservatism and manipulate their sense of themselves as culture's victims as well as its moral guardians."[4]

Echols and others have not dissuaded some feminist theorists from writing antipornography treatises or some feminist activists from organizing marches, boycotts, and teach-ins against pornography, but they have caused them to try to clarify their precise motives and exact aims. First, this chapter will schematize the position of feminist antipornographers, contrasting it

The genesis of this chapter first appeared, in a much shorter version, as "Feminism, Pornography and Censorship," *Social Theory and Practice* 8, no. 1 (Spring 1982).

with more traditional antipornography positions. Second, it will ask whether it is possible to shape legal remedies for women-degrading pornography that fit the contours of a pluralist democracy. Finally, it will be suggested that before any woman condemns all pornography, she should decide to what extent sexually explicit material plays a salutory as well as deleterious role in women's lives.

The Traditional Concept of Pornography in Anglo-American Law

Groups such as Women Against Pornography, Take Back the Night (TBTN), and Women Against Violence in Pornography and the Media (WAVPM) insist that their concept of pornography is not to be confused with more traditional concepts of pornography, especially those embedded in Anglo American law, which conflate the notion of pornography with obscenity. As David A. J. Richards notes, the term "pornography" (from the Greek *pornographos*) initially meant "writing of harlots." In this sense, pornography is indeed sexually explicit material consisting in graphic depictions of sexual organs and various modes of coitus. It is important that pornography not be equated with obscenity. The notion of sexually explicit depictions (pornography) is not the same idea as that of the abuse of a bodily/personal function (obscenity) that causes one to react with disgust (such as coprophagy).[5]

Significantly, and not without serious consequences, pornography and the obscene were equated in Christian culture because theologians defined proper sexual functions in a particularly limited way: All sexual acts are improper except those in which the aim is procreation. Not only are extramarital and male homosexual or lesbian intercourse prohibited, but all "unnatural" forms of intercourse within conventional marriage as well as oral or anal sex. Furthermore, all depictions and descriptions that will lead to "illicit genital commotion" (masturbation) are prohibited. Thus, pornography is obscene not only in itself, but because it leads to extramarital sex, to non-vaginal intercourse within marriage, or to masturbation, which, according to the traditional Christian view, are "independently obscene acts" because they supposedly violate "minimum standards" of appropriate sexual functions, thereby causing "disgust."[6]

Richards points out that fear of "unnatural" sexuality probably accounts for the rash of obscenity legislation in England and the United States in the mid-nineteenth century. This legislation reflected a curious Victorian view that linked sexual indulgence, in general, and masturbation, in particular, to insanity and even to death. Since it was thought to aid and abet human sexual fantasy and subsequent sexual activity, pornography was condemned for medical as well as theological reasons. For example, Anthony Comstock, leader of the Committee for the Suppression of Vice, argued that those who read pornography invariably engaged in masturbation, and that those who masturbated either went crazy or died at a tender age. He never tired of noting pathological cases such as the one in which a thirteen-year-old girl supposedly wasted away to the shell of her former self after reading too many dirty books.[7]

Although our courts are no longer preoccupied with the evils of autoeroticism, they do continue to identify the pornographic with the obscene. However, unlike their nineteenth-century predecessors, today's courts do not automatically classify sexually explicit material as obscene/pornographic. As a result of several controversial cases involving massive public support for works of literature such as *Ulysses, Lady Chatterley's Lover,* and the *Memoirs of Fanny Hill,* the courts have had to distinguish between sexually explicit material that is obscene/pornographic and sexually explicit material that is not. In order to make these distinctions, the courts have proposed more or less unsuccessful definitions of obscenity, and therefore, in their terms, of pornography. The test currently employed is the one that was articulated in *Miller* v. *California* (1973). In deciding whether or not, an instance of sexually explicit material is obscene/pornographic, the trier of-fact (judge or juror) must ask himself or herself:

(a) Whether "the average person, applying contemporary community standards," would find that the work, taken as a whole, appeals to the prurient interest

(b) Whether the work depicts or describes, in a patently offensive way, sexual conduct specifically defined by the applicable state law

(c) Whether the work, taken as a whole, lacks serious literary, artistic, political or scientific value[8]

If a work appeals to the "prurient interest," is "patently offensive," and "lacks serious . . . value," it is obscene/pornographic.

According to many critics, including some feminists, the *Miller* test is seriously flawed not only because it is difficult to operationalize phrases such as "prurient interest," "patently offensive," and "lacks serious . . . value," but also because it is not certain which, if any, of these criteria suggest a legitimate reason for legal restriction of sexually explicit material. That something appeals to prurience, which the dictionary defines as a lustful, itching desire, is not necessarily a reason to control it legally. Unless it can be empirically established, for example, that occasionally giving into one's prurient interests is more enervating than rejuvenating, more socially destructive than socially creative, then the law has no good reason to restrict this form of self expression. Likewise, that something "lacks serious . . . value" is not necessarily a reason to control it legally. To ban sexually explicit material simply because it has no serious value is not only to make an arrogant, global judgment about its worth, but also to forget that even if such material is not of serious value it may still serve a social function. Finally, that something is "patently offensive" is not necessarily a reason to control it legally. Since the sensitivities of persons vary enormously, what one person finds patently offensive, another will find manifestly unoffensive. Therefore, unless a sexually explicit depiction is likely to offend persons whose sensitivities are neither under- nor overdeveloped, and unless those who take offense at the depiction are unable to avoid it without disrupting their own lives, the law has no good reason to restrict its discreet production, procurement, and enjoyment.

If the *Miller* test is as flawed as its critics insist, then what, if anything, does make or would make sexually explicit material somehow morally objectionable and/or legally restrictable? Feminists have found it difficult not only to distinguish between those modes of pornography they think are objectionable (women-degrading) and those modes of pornography they think are unobjectionable, but also to suggest appropriate legal remedies for the former.

Toward a Definition of Women-Degrading Pornography

In a searing critique, Deirdre English takes to task Women Against Violence in Pornography and the Media's attempt to distinguish between pornographic modes that supposedly degrade women (hard-core porn and soft-core porn) and pornographic modes that supposedly do not degrade women (erotica). According to WAVPM, erotica is not women-degrading because it is "personal, emotional; has 'lightness'; is refreshing; has an element of trust or caring or love; is natural, circular."[9] In contrast, hard-core porn and, to a lesser extent, soft-core porn[10] is women-degrading because it "is defined by penis, men, is for the titillation of men; shows a power imbalance; suggests violence; is heavy; [depicts] bodies contorted; [shows] no reciprocity between people, gratification at someone's expense; is voyeuristic, linear, something you can buy and sell."[11]

Deirdre English comments: "Can't you buy and sell erotica? Is looking at sexual representations voyeuristic? The penis is pornographic; the 'circle' is erotic? Hmm."[12] As a result of this and related criticisms, the general public as well as some feminists have come to believe that degradation is in the subjective eye of the beholder, and that attempts to provide criteria for objectionable (women-degrading) pornography are doomed. Such pessimism, however, may be premature. Feminists have advanced at least two plausible tests for identifying women-degrading pornography: It depicts disrespect for women's wishes as sexual beings and it falsely portrays women's wishes as sexual beings.[13] A close examination of these tests will reveal why feminists have regarded women-degrading pornography as a real and serious problem rather than a manufactured and trivial issue.

The type of pornography to which feminists are most opposed is best termed gyno-thanatica (from the Greek words for "woman" and "death or a destructive principle").[14] Unlike gyno-erotic pornography (from the Greek words for "woman" and "love or a creative principle"), which depicts women being integrated, constituted, or focused by creative sexual forces, gyno-thanatic pornography depicts women being disintegrated, dismembered, or disoriented by destructive sexual forces. When gyno-thanatic pornography first appeared, feminists called attention to the way in which it displayed men disrespecting women's ends as sexual beings. The standard way to indicate disrespect for another person's ends (such as happiness and perfection) is deliberately to ignore that person's wants and needs in one's transactions with him or her; and the usual means of calling attention to this fact is to point out that person x has not secured person y's consent to action z. Along this line of reasoning, depictions of sexual exchanges in which men do whatever they please to women without taking into account their interests, needs, and wants as sexual beings are portrayals of men failing to respect women properly. Comments Gloria Steinem:

> Look at any depiction of sex in which there is clear force, or an unequal power that spells coercion. It may be very blatant, with weapons of torture or bondage, wounds and bruises, some clear humiliation, or an adult's sexual power being used over a child. It may be much more subtle: a physical attitude of conquerer and victim, the use of race or class to imply the same thing, perhaps a very unequal nudity, with one person exposed and vulnerable while the other is clothed. In either case, there is no sense of equal choice or equal power.[15]

Therefore, any time a man is portrayed as foisting himself sexually upon a woman as proof of his superiority, he is depicted as degrading her.

Interestingly, feminists have recently deepened their critique of gyno-thanatic pornography. Although they continue to object to its coercive—especially violent—features, they are also objecting to its tendency to depict women as creatures who welcome or seek out male sexual abuse. Whereas the feminists anthologized in Laura Lederer's *Take Back the Night*[16] concentrate on magazines like *Bondage,* which feature depictions of men torturing women (businessmen systematically applying hot irons, scissors, torches, and knives to the breasts and vaginas of their secretaries), in *Pornography and Silence: Culture's Revenge Against Nature,*[17] Susan Griffin concentrates on the connections among pornography, anti-Semitism, and sadism, arguing that in the same way that Jews did not volunteer to be gassed, women do not volunteer to be sexually abused. Whatever their focus, however, feminists agree that gyno-thanatic pornography is women-degrading not only because it typically suggests that "sexuality and violence are congruent"[18] and that what women *want* as sexual beings is irrelevant, but also because it often relays pernicious lies about *what* women want as sexual beings, suggesting that "for women sex is essentially masochistic, humiliation pleasurable, physical abuse erotic."[19]

Significantly, critics chastize feminists for focusing on gyno-thanatic pornography. In general, these critics are of two sorts: the type who thinks that feminists should not object to any kind of pornography, including gyno-thanatica, and the type who thinks that they should object to every kind of pornography, no matter how slightly it degrades, objectifies, or trivializes women.

The first type of critic is epitomized by Jean Bethke Elshtain, who argues that members of Women Against Violence in Pornography and the Media have frightened women, plunging them ever deeper into the psychic terrors of female victimization. By setting up men as brutal enemies, as "implacable foes", feminists have increased women's incipient fears that they, too, will be victims of male violence or already are.[20] However, as Elshtain sees it, the *rise* of violence against women is a largely trumped-up issue. She notes, for example, that FBI statistics, as well as those available from the U.S. Justice Department's Bureau of Justice, show little overall change in the rate of reported forcible rapes from 1973 to 1978. This rate holds at two-tenths of 1 percent of households (an estimated 75,989 reported rapes in 1979 and an estimated 82,088 reported rapes in 1980).[21] Nevertheless, Elshtain observes that women have become increasingly preoccupied with and unnecessarily worried about their personal safety. Therefore, she concludes, to the extent that it contributes to women's perceptions of themselves as victims and to the degree that it causes women to limit their sexual contacts with men, the feminist antipornography movement must ask itself whether it is serving to lengthen rather than to shorten women's sexual oppression.

The second type of critic is epitomized by disillusioned members of WAP, TBTN, and WAVPM who regret that the feminist antipornography movement has shriveled from an all-inclusive campaign against soft-core as well as hard-core porn to a narrowly focused attack on the most violent and most women-degrading modes of pornography. As these critics see it, everyone knows that women do not want to be tortured and killed, even if it is in the name of sexual expression. What everyone does not know, however, is that women are not by nature sexually voracious and indiscriminate creatures, always yielding gladly and responding orgasmically to the most perfunctory male advances. So what is needed is not so much a campaign against gyno-thanatica as a campaign against soft porn (sentimental soap operas, gushy romantic novels, "macho" spy films).

Although most feminist antipornographers admit that their critics' objections are not without merit, they do not think that they are unassailable. First, feminist antipornographers are not at all convinced that violence against women is a largely manufactured issue. They note, for example, that arguments such as Elshtain's reply on statistics of reported instances of rape. Such *reported* instances of rape must be balanced against *unreported* instances of rape, woman-battering, and sexual harassment. Despite certain improvements in the criminal justice system, most women still think twice or three times before they report a sex-related crime. These same women, however, may not be reluctant to communicate their woes through informal women's networks. As in the past, women today have their own lines of communication—the coffee-break chat, the casual conversation at the laundromat, the extended phone talk—and if the reports of those who work in battered-women's shelters and rape crisis centers are any index, violence against women is definitely on the rise. Second, although feminist antipornographers were originally convinced that soft porn was telling as many lies about women as hard porn, they have come to doubt the truth of their initial claim. Given women's continuing penchant for sort porn, some feminists are wondering whether the first antiporn movement was launched before women had had an opportunity to ascertain the "truth" about female sexuality and to decide how many, if any, lies about female sexuality were being told in soft-porn favorites like *Charlie's Angels* (a television series in which three female detectives, dressed for the most part in bikinis, pursue law, order, and attractive men); Harlequin or Silhouette romances (pulpy novels in which it takes about 50 pages for a reluctant first kiss and another 150 or so to get married); and *James Bond* thrillers (movies in which a "macho" spy alternates his time between pursuing heinous criminals and chasing curvacious women).

Of these two responses, the second is by far the most controversial. Only a few years ago, feminists would have chided any woman who dared to read, for example, a Silhouette romance, and not without some cause. The typical plot of a Silhouette romance features a "poor, orphaned young woman of beauty and integrity who meets and falls for a powerful, wealthy, and slightly older man."[22] Although this man dominates the heroine throughout the book, "mocking her emotions" as he arouses her seething passions, in the final pages she learns what the reader has known all along, namely, that he has always loved her.[23] In short, the classic formula of a Silhouette romance is one of female sexual submission and male sexual dominance—scarcely a feminist theme. Although feminists are still inclined to agree with Ann Douglas that "it is a frightening measure of the still patriarchal quality of our culture that many women of all ages cosponsor male fantasies about themselves and enjoy peep shows into masculine myths about their sexuality as the surest means of self-induced excitation,"[24] they are increasingly willing to confront the possibility that Silhouette romances and other types of soft porn may not be presenting an entirely false view of female sexuality. Indeed, they observe that the relative place of responsiveness and initiative in women's sex lives is likely to remain an open question until women define themselves not only sexually but also ontologically. Comments Catherine MacKinnon:

> If women are socially defined such that female sexuality cannot be lived or spoken or felt or even somatically sensed apart from its enforced definition, so that it is its own lack, then there is no such thing as a woman as such, there are only walking embodiments of men's projected needs. For feminism, asking whether there is, socially, a female sexuality is the same as asking whether women exist.[25]

But even if women do not have all the answers to the questions "what is a woman" and "what is female sexuality," they do have some of the answers. It may make sense for women to discuss whether an issue of *Playboy* displaying a Great White Hunter disrobing a quivering "bunny" down to her itsy-bitsy cottontail is women-degrading, but feminist antipornographers are confident that it does not make sense for women to discuss whether an issue of *Hustler* displaying a woman being ground into meat is women degrading. This is perhaps the reason why most feminists have decided to concentrate on blatant examples of women-degrading pornography (gyno thanatica) rather than on more ambiguous instances of it. A woman may dream of her lover stripping her bare, but a vision of him reducing her to a bloody pulp can only strike her as a nightmare.

The Search for an Appropriate Legal Response to Gyno-Thanatica

Hard as it is to convince people that at least gyno-thanatic pornography is women-degrading, it is even harder to convince people that anything should be done about it. Feminist antipornographers have been severely criticized because of their search for appropriate legal as well as extralegal remedies (consciousness-raising conferences, seminars, and teach-ins) for gyno-thanatic pornography. According to the critics, there are sound legal grounds for restricting, say, gyno-thanatic *behavior*, but these grounds cannot be invoked to restrict mere *depictions* and *descriptions* of such behavior. A person's liberty to do as he or she pleases or sees fit—in this instance his or her liberty to engage in gyno-thanatic fantasies—may be limited only if it constitutes a violation of at least one of the four principles that this society generally accepts as legitimate reasons to restrict a man's or a woman's liberty.

In order of decreasing social acceptance, these principles are:

1. The harm principle—A person's liberty may be restricted to prevent physical or psychic injury to other specific individuals; likewise, a person's liberty may be restricted to prevent impairment or destruction of

institutional practices and regulatory systems that are in the public interest.

2. The offense principle—A person's liberty may be restricted to prevent offense to other specific individuals, where "offense" is interpreted as behavior that causes feelings of embarrassment, shame, outrage, or disgust in those against whom it is directed.

3. The principle of legal paternalism—A person's liberty may be restricted to protect himself or herself from self-inflicted harm, or, in its extreme version, to guide that person, whether he or she likes it or not, toward his or her own good.

4. The principle of legal moralism—A person's liberty may be restricted to protect other specific individuals, but especially society as a whole from immoral behavior, where the word "immoral" means neither "harmful" nor "offensive," but something like "against the rule of a higher authority" (God) or "against a societal taboo."[26]

According to most liberals, acts such as sexual harassment, rape, and women-battering are clear violations of the harm principle, if not also of the offense, legal paternalism, and legal moralism principles. In contrast, mere depictions or mere descriptions of such acts do not constitute any violation of the harm principle; and if they do constitute some sort of offense to others, harm to self, or social "immorality," it is so slight as not to warrant the restriction of any individual's liberty to see, read, or hear what he or she pleases.

Like their liberal critics, feminists are not eager to restrict the liberty of any person. However, unlike their liberal critics, they think that two liberty-limiting principles—the harm principle and the offense principle—apply at least in the case of gyno-thanatica.[27] As they see it, these two principles can be invoked successfully when it comes to constructing a case not for the outright censorship of all forms of women-degrading pornography, but for the imposition of certain legal restrictions on the public display and public dissemination of the worst of this material (gyno-thanatica). Indeed, censorship has never been the *essential* goal of feminist antipornographers. Says Susan Brownmiller, one of women-degrading pornography's most vehement foes: "We are not saying 'Smash the presses' or 'Ban the bad ones,' but simply 'Get the stuff out of our sight.'"[28] What has been and remains one of the *peripheral* aims of feminists however, is the exploration of legal remedies aimed at putting a damper on the celebration of gyno-thanatica not in the *privacy* of a man's or a woman's castle, but in the *publicity* of an open marketplace. Although members of organizations such as WAP, TBTN, and WAVPM have not, to date, advanced an entirely acceptable legal remedy for gyno-thanatica, their arguments are illuminating and worth the measured consideration of those who oppose any legal restrictions on pornography whatsoever, as well as those who advocate limited legal restrictions of the worst and most conspicuous forms of it.

ARGUMENTS INVOKING THE HARM PRINCIPLE

According to some feminists, gyno-thanatic pornography is harmful in one or both of two senses: (1) Although gyno-thanatic pornography may not be harmful per se, it causes men to engage in harmful behavior toward women; or (2) gyno-thanatic pornography is harmful per se since it consists in the defamation of women. Related as these two arguments are, they make substantially different points and should be considered separately.

1. *Argument One:* The first argument—that there is a causal connection between viewing gyno-thanatic pornography and engaging in corresponding forms of behavior—is based on the commonsense belief that there is an intimate relationship between thought and action. In 1970 the Commission on Obscenity and Pornography denied the truth of this relationship insofar as pornography/obscenity is concerned, concluding that there is "no evidence . . . that exposure to explicit sexual material plays a significant role in the causation of delinquent or criminal behavior among youth or adults."[29] That the commission came to such a conclusion is not surprising. Traditionally, two working models have guided researchers in their study of pornography and aggressive behavior: the catharsis model and the imitation model. When applied to any kind of pornography, including gyno-thanatic pornography, the catharsis model assumes that pornography is a harmless outlet for sexual aggressions. The imitation model assumes that pornography is a propaedeutic for sexually unacceptable behavior, especially sexual violence.

Most of the research done for the Commission on Obscenity and Pornography was guided by the catharsis model. Derived from psychoanalytic theory, the catharsis model predicts that women-degrading pornography serves society by allowing men to release, in a nonviolent manner, their instinctual sexual aggressions against women. Using this model, Donald L. Mosher found that "sex-calloused" attitudes, manifested in *verbal* approbation of the sexual exploitation of women, decreased among men who were exposed to pornographic films. That is, the men who saw these films were less likely—at least for twenty-four hours—to fill in the blank in "When a women gets uppity, it's time to _____ her" with words such as "rape" or "smack." Mosher attributed this phenomenon to the fact that seeing pornography in the company of only men satisfies the need for "macho" behavior— that is, it satisfies the need for endorsing "sex- calloused" attitudes on paper and for boasting about one's sexual prowess.[30]

On the basis of Mosher's study and other similar studies, the commission drew the conclusion that men who view any kind of sexually explicit material, be it gyno-erotic or gyno-thanatic, are less inclined to sexually abuse women after seeing such material than before seeing it. This conclusion was unwarranted for several reasons. In very few, if any instances, had Mosher exposed his audience to gyno-thanatic pornography. In fact, Mosher himself admitted that he usually used as test material a "better-than-average" pornographic film (that is, a gyno-erotic film) because it showed "more affection and fewer genital close-ups" and because it appealed more to "sexually uninhibited, experienced adults of both sexes" than "kinky," exclusively male-oriented films.[31] This suggests that if Mosher proved anything it was that men who are exposed to erotic pornography—to sexually explicit descriptions and displays that show the involved parties caring about each other's desires and experiences as sexual beings—are less inclined to make women-degrading statements after seeing such material than before seeing it. But even if Mosher did prove this, he did not also prove, as the commission thought he had, that men who are disinclined to make women-degrading *statements* are also disinclined to engage in women-degrading *behavior*. There are always significant gaps between a subject's guarded statements in a scientist's laboratory and a subject's spontaneous behavior at home or on the street. And even if, contrary to fact, Mosher had proved everything the commission had hoped he would prove, it should have checked Mosher's hypotheses, data, and conclusions against those put forward by the competing, imitation model.

Unlike the catharsis model, the imitation model suggests that people learn patterns of violence from role models. Aggression and anger are behaviors that are learned from the environment like any other social behavior. A child, for example, is not naturally militant. He learns warlike behavior from the games he plays, from the stories he reads, from the television programs he sees, and especially from the heroes he emulates. Using this model, recent researchers of gyno-thanatic pornography have suggested that the rapist, a pervasive figure in contemporary gyno-thanatica, functions as a role model for porn devotees. For example, in a paper entitled "Pornography Commission Revisited: Aggressive-Erotica and Violence Against Women," Professor Ed Donnerstein reported that angered males who had watched "aggressive erotica" (gyno-thanatica) displayed aggression to females but not to males. Donnerstein explained this phenomenon of "selective aggression" toward females by noting that in the typical gyno-thanatic film, the female plays the role of victim. Because she is observed to be the object of male violence in the fantasy world of depictions and descriptions, the female takes on what is called "aggressive cue value" in the real world. That is, she becomes an aggressive stimulus that, given certain conditions such as work-related anger on the part of the male spectator, can elicit aggressive responses in him. In short, once a woman is seen as a scapegoat, she will be the target for male aggression when that aggression seeks release.[32]

Should studies such as Donnerstein's be confirmed, the causal link between viewing gyno-thanatica and perpetrating sexually abusive acts against women would be more firmly established. More credence could be given to Susan Brownmiller's view that the anti-female propaganda that permeates our nation's cultural output "promotes a climate in which acts of sexual hostility directed against women are not only tolerated but ideologically encouraged."[33] But even if empirical evidence of Donnerstein's sort were to increase, it would have to increase dramatically to support the claim that some early feminist antipornographers made: that gyno-thanatica constitutes a "clear and present danger" to women, that it causes men to rape, beat, and even murder women.

According to Wendy Kaminer, a feminist lawyer, not only would it be difficult to support such a claim, but the clear-and-present-danger standard would in fact give greater legal protection to gyno-thanatica than contemporary obscenity law.[34] Under contemporary obscenity law, sexually explicit material that is judged obscene is classified as nonspeech on the grounds that there is no speech without thought, and that thought is not behind mere depictions and descriptions, especially those that appeal only to the prurient interest.[35] As many feminists see it, however, thought is reflected in the images of filmmakers, photographers, painters, dancers, and musicians no less than it is reflected in the words of journalists, essayists, novelists, and speechmakers. Therefore, if sexually explicit depictions and descriptions, including instances of gyno-thanatic pornography, communicate thought, then they constitute speech. But if gyno-thanatica constitutes speech, it has the prima facie protection of the First Amendment; and if it has this protection, it will be very difficult to establish that any instance of it presents a clear and present danger to society in general and to women in particular. In order to prove, for example, that *Snuff*, a film in which a sexually aroused man gives a "bitch" what "[she] wants" (supposedly, a death worse than being drawn and quartered),[36] the prosecution would have to show that as a result of viewing this horror, some male viewers would, as soon as the opportunity presented itself, sexually assault or even brutally murder women. But it is not at all certain whether viewing *Snuff* has the same sort of behavioral effect on an audience as yelling "Fire" in a crowded theater does. It may, however, have some sort of suggestive effect on viewers.

The fact that three schoolgirls raped a nine-year-old girl with a beer bottle only four days after *Born Innocent*, a film in which several schoolgirls used a "plumber's helper" to rape a girl, was aired on television does not seem to have been pure coincidence.[37] Nonetheless, courts are loathe to admit that there is a direct causal relation between adult persons seeing something and their acting out what they have seen. Even in the case of adolescents, courts are reluctant to recognize such causal connections. When 15-year-old Ronald Zamora argued that he had killed an aged neighborhood woman as a result of "prolonged, intense, involuntary, subliminal television intoxication,"[38] his defense fell on deaf ears. The jury convicted him of murder, not at all convinced that viewing *Kojak* and other violent television programs could have caused Zamora to act violently in real life. No one is quite sure how, or even if, fantasy may influence action; and even those who are convinced there is some causal relationship between the two tend to think that it is usually within a person's power to separate his real life from his fantasy life. This being the case, it is difficult to convince jury members that heinous sights and sounds can immediately propel persons to perpetrate heinous deeds.

2. *Argument Two:* Given, then, that there is so much confusion about whether or not seeing x is causally related to doing x, feminists have advanced a second argument against gyno-thanatic pornography. Like the causation argument, this one is based on the harm principle. Unlike the causation argument, this one claims that in and of themselves certain sexually explicit depictions and descriptions (such as gyno-thanatica) constitute a harm to women akin to defamation. Defamatory communications are those that damage a person's reputation by expressing thoughts to third parties that either diminish the esteem in which the defamed party is held or excite adverse feelings or opinions against him/her.

The law of defamation covers not only verbal statements (written or oral) but also nonverbal representations (cartoons, sketches, drawings, photographs, gestures), as well as modes of communication that combine verbal statements with nonverbal representations (most films, television programs, magazine articles). Defamatory communications belong to that class of speech acts that do not have the protection of the First Amendment. Included in this category are, as Helen Longino points out, "the incitement to violence in volatile circumstances, the solicitation of crimes, perjury and misrepresentation, slander, libel, and false advertising."[39] According to Longino and other feminist antipornographers,

> that there are forms of proscribed speech shows that we accept limitations on the right to freedom of speech. The manufacture and distribution of material which defames and threatens all members of a class by its recommendation of abusive and degrading behavior toward some members of that class simply in virtue of their membership in it seems a clear candidate for inclusion on the list [of proscribed speech acts][40]

In short, if it can be shown that gyno-thanatic pornography defames women, then it will be possible for women as a group to bring, for example, civil suit against pornographers for damages to their reputation.[41]

a. *Objection One:* There are several problems with this novel, legal approach to gyno-thanatic pornography. First, it is not at all clear that pornographers flash images of sexually abused women across the screen in order to make statements, defamatory or otherwise, about women. According to many students of film, the typical pornographer does not mean to *state* anything in particular when he creates images of women who plead to be tortured or killed during sexual exchanges with men. That is, he does not intend the depiction of these gross images to produce specific effects in his audience (the excitation of adverse feelings or opinions against women, for example) *by means* of their recognition of his intention to make them have these specific, negative feelings or opinions about women.[42] Supposedly, he does not intend this because he realizes that people who patronize porn films come not to be educated, but to release or relieve their sexual tensions. Says Deirdre English: "Pornography is not understood to 'teach' anything, but to provide mechanisms that carry off the effluvia of socially banned sexual expressions."[43]

Cogent as this objection is, some feminist antipornographers note that there could exist, for example, a Bertolt Brecht of pornography.[44] Such a pornographer would refuse to entertain his audience, insisting instead on educating them. By means of flashing images of sexually abused women across the screen, he would intend to excite women-degrading feelings in his audience, and he would, as Brecht did, try to force his audience to recognize his intentions. In such a case, a group-defamation suit would be possible, and a Brechtian pornographer would have but two defenses: (1) that what he said about women is in fact true, or (2) that his audience misunderstood what he said.

Truth of course is a defense in standard defamation cases, whether the defamation is libelous (written or depicted) or slanderous (oral). If I publicly charge Smith with buggery and he sues me, I can defeat the suit by showing that he is indeed a buggerer. If the same rules prevail in group-defamation suits, then a Brechtian pornographer would be allowed to defend himself by establishing the truth of some proposition such as "all women are masochists and they like being masochists." This means that judges and jurors woud be called upon to determine the truth of what amounts to an ideological claim.[45] They would be asked to decide whether it is Theodor Reik who is correct when he exclaims, "Feminine masochism of the woman? Sounds like a pleonasm. It is comparable to an expression like, 'the Negro has dark skin.' But the color of the skin is defined simply by the term Negro; a white Negro is no Negro,"[46] or whether it is instead Andrea Dworkin who is correct when she insists that women are not willing masochists but persons whose bodies have been "sexually colonized" and who are routinely forced to "volunteer," against their best interest, for male sexual abuse.[47] (Note that the term "masochist" is used here to denote not a women who freely chooses to engage in sadomasochistic practices because they fulfill *her* sexual wants and needs as well as those of her sadist partner, but a woman who has been socially encouraged or conditioned to submit to sexual abuse, and even to risk her own physical and psychic destruction, if by so doing she is able to satisfy a *man's* gyno thanatic impulses.)

Assuming that it is wise to let judges and jurors arbitrate the truth of general philosophies, a Brechtian pornographer would have difficulty proving that "all women are masochists and they like being masoschists." But prove this he would have to. In a defamation suit the burden of proof would fall upon his shoulders, since "out of a tender regard for reputations the law presumes in the first instance that all defamation is false, and the defendant has the burden of pleading and proving its truth."[48] In short, women would not have to disprove that they are willing masochists; rather, the pornographer would have to prove that women are willing masochists.

Since this would be no easy task, a Brechtian pornographer might prefer to argue in his defense that his audience misinterpreted his message. He might claim that although his audience took him to say that "It's great that all women are masochists—nothing must be done to alter this wonderful state of affairs," what he intended to say through his film was that "It's a shame that all women are masochists—something must be done to alter this lamentable state of affairs." If this were the case, it would be unfair to accuse him of defamation. Why not instead accuse his audience of defamation?

Along these lines, B. Ruby Rich relates a story. One of her friends worked as an artist's model. Usually she refused to model for photographers because, with photographers, models have little control over who sees their bodies. Once, however, she violated her rule and modeled for a photographer friend who did a series of nude photographs of her that she thought were beautiful. Unfortunately, one of these photos was stolen from the photographer. The model went into a depression, tormented by the image of an unknown man masturbating to her photo. Ruby Rich asks: "Was that photograph erotic or pornographic?"[49] On the one hand, if the viewer's perceptions determine whether a depiction is "erotic" or "pornographic," then the photo of the woman was "pornographic." On the other hand, if the intentions of the photographer determine whether a depiction is "erotic" or "pornographic," then the photo of the woman was "erotic." But if, as suggests Rich, there is no way to decide whether a photographer's intentions or a viewer's perceptions determine the message of a photo, then there is no way to decide whether a photo is essentially "erotic" or essentially "pornographic." Indeed, continues Rich, there is no reason to think that any photograph has an essential meaning. Rather, there are as many interpretations and/or uses of a photograph as there are interpreters and users. The photographer's viewpoint is but one among many; and he should not be held responsible for viewpoints that diverge from his.[50]

Although this is probably the most accurate way to articulate complex issues of perception and intention, if we are talking about standard defamation law, then the pornographer's intended statements—and not a specific audience's interpretations of them–determine whether defamation has been perpetrated or not. This being the case, our Brechtian pornographer will have to be given an opportunity to establish that his message was misunderstood, for example, by an exceptionally "hypersensitive" or "prudish" audience. If the largest majority of his audience takes him to be communicating a gyno-thanatic message, this will of course count against his defense. Nonetheless, our Brechtian pornographer will escape liability, if he can show that a "reasonable man,"[51] that is, a person of ordinary sensibilities, would not have interpreted his film as conveying gyno-thanatic ideas.[52]

b. *Objection Two:* Even if it could be established that most pornographers intend to communicate women-degrading messages to their audiences—that they mean to activate the brains as well as the penises of their audience against women—the objection will be made that Anglo American law simply has no way to handle cases of group defamation.

Traditionally, the law of defamation is concerned with the protection of an individual's reputation and not with the protection of a group's reputation, especially an unwieldly and huge group like women. John Salmond, the sage of torts, for example, dismissed as ridiculous any notion of a suit against someone for saying that all clergymen are hypocrites or all lawyers dishonest. According to Salmond, as the number of a defamed group swells, the extravagance of the defamer's assertions will discredit him or her. It is one thing to convince a person that some clergymen are hypocrites, that some lawyers are dishonest, and that some women are masochists. It is quite another matter to persuade a person that *all* clergymen are hypocrites, that *all* lawyers are dishonest, and that *all* women are masochists. And even if a few people were convinced by such global generalizations, would this fact actually hurt any or all clergymen, lawyers, and women; and could this fact support anything but the most "speculative claim" for damages, either material or psychic?[53]

Once again this is a forceful set of objections to which feminists have responded more or less convincingly. Although there are no precise precedents for *civil* group-defamation suits in the United States, feminists note that the Supreme Court has upheld *criminal* statutes that protect groups from harms akin to defamation; such as from contempt, derision, or obloquy. For example, in a 1952 case, *Beuharnis* v. *Illinois,* the Supreme Court sustained the constitutionality of a state statute that made it unlawful to disseminate or display publicly any "lithography, moving picture, play, drama or sketch" portraying "depravity, criminality, unchastity, or lack of virtue of a class of citizens, of any race, color, creed or religion" thereby either exposing these citizens to "contempt, derision or obloquy" or producing a "breach of the peace or riots."[54] Given that the criminal law is a more onerous legal sanction than the civil law (it is, for example, more disgraceful to stand criminal trial than to be sued in a civil court), feminists point to *Beuharnis* not because they want to send pornographers to prison for publicly displaying and disseminating gyno-thanatica, but simply because the *Beuharnis* case sought to remedy the harms that *groups* sustain. Therefore, the case is a precedent for a civil group-defamation suit only in the weak sense that it encourages legal theorists to think in terms of collective harms—the type of harms that an entire race or an entire gender is likely to sustain.

If feminists have found only weak precedent for the concept of group defamation, they have found strong legal support for their claim that statements like "all women are masochists" cause harm to women as a group as well as to women as individuals. In a lengthy article on group defamation, David Reisman argues that statements like "all lawyers are dishonest" have had a negative effect on the legal community:

> The legal profession has suffered in esteem and influence from such reiterated remarks (it is noteworthy that Hollywood usually portrays lawyers as obfuscators or crooks. . .), and its members have directly suffered in pocket, for many persons are deterred, as we all know, from resorting to lawyers out of fear of excessive fees and other sharp practices.[55]

Reisman concludes by observing that no member of a racial or cultural minority—blacks, Jews, American Indians, Poles—escapes "some psychic or material hurt as a consequence of the attacks upon the group with which he is voluntarily or involuntarily identified."[56]

Taking their cue from Reisman, some members of WAP, TBTN, and WAVPM have argued that statements like "all women are willing masochists who both want and need sexual abuse" do indeed cause harm to women as a group and to women as individuals. When pressed to specify the harm done to women by gyno-thanatic statements, however, feminists hesitate. Either an act of defamation causes material damage (loss of business, opportunity, income, physical security) or it causes psychic distress. A claim that gyno-thanatic pornography does the first sort of harm to women requires some form of the causal argument—that is, some appeal to the notion that if men see gyno-thanatic visions and hear gyno-thanatic statements they will engage in gyno-thanatic acts (sexual harassment, rape, women battering). But as noted in Argument One, this causal relationship is tenuous and unlikely to support a claim for material damages.

The second possible avenue, that pornography is harmful because it causes psychic distress (insomnia, agitation, fear and trembling, hysteria) seems more promising. For example, feminist antipornographers claim that gyno-thanatic images have a profoundly upsetting effect on them. Nevertheless, a significant number of women insist that the "pornophobia" of feminist antipornographers is a largely manufactured syndrome, an overreaction to sexually explicit fantasies that should not bother real women in the least. Interestingly, Reisman accounts for such divergent reactions by observing that adults who claim that nasty generalizations about their group (race, class, religion) are "mere idle blathering" remind him of children who chant "Sticks and stones can break my bones, but names can never hurt me" precisely because they are hurting.[57] Sometimes this may be so, but it is also possible for women not to be psychically distressed by gyno-thanatica. Indeed, this is why at least some women have joined the anti-antipornography movement. If this is the case, the persuasiveness of a civil suit on behalf of *all* women seems questionable.

c. *Objection Three:* Even if it could be established that women as a group and women as individuals were materially damaged and/or psychically distressed by gyno-thanatica, a third objection to the group defamation approach remains: That it opens the flood gates to all manner of lawsuits. If women can sue the creators and purveyors of gyno-thanatic pornography for depicting and describing women as sexually warped masochists, then they can sue the producers of television commercials that portray women as rather unintelligent housewives who spend their days agonizing over what laundry detergent to use. That is, if women can sue pornographers for spreading deep and vicious lies about females as *sex* objects, then they can sue commercial artists for manufacturing falsehoods or half-truths about women's *gender* roles. And if women can initiate such suits, then industrialists can sue leftists who claim "all capitalists are bloodsuckers," and Italian-Americans can sue the producers of "The Untouchables" for conveying the impression that most Italians belong to the Mafia and spend Saturday nights machine-gunning whole neighborhoods.

In response to this objection, feminists admit that a society such as ours cannot survive if not only individuals but also groups sue each other at a drop of a hat. If a constitutional democracy is to remain stable, both the virtue of democratic tolerance and that of mutual respect have to be practiced. The one cannot be sacrificed for the other. Therefore, potential litigants needs tests to which they can appeal as they decide whether or not to bring suit against their defamers.

One such test may be the following: Defamatory statements are more or less harmful to the extent that they attack the core of a person. As Carolyn M. Shafer and Marilyn Frye point out:

> In dealing with persons, one is dealing with behaving bodies, and it is these that have domains. . . . Since biological life and health are prerequisites for the pursuit of any other interests and goals whatever, everything necessary for their maintenance and sustenance evidently will fall very close to the center of the domain. Whatever has a relatively permanent effect on the person, whatever affects its relatively constant surroundings, whatever causes it discomfort or distress—in short, whatever a person has to live with—is likely to fall squarely within its domain.[58]

If Shafer's and Frye's analysis is correct, then defamatory depictions and descriptions directed against one's race or sexuality violate the center of a person's domain more grievously than those directed against one's national origin or gender role. One's race is not escapable in the same way that one's national origin is. Blacks stand out in a white population in a manner that Italian-Americans do not stand out in an American population. Similarly, a woman cannot transcend her biological sex as easily as she can belie gender stereotypes. Therefore, to defame persons on account of their race or sexuality, to suggest that those characteristics which constitute their essential persons are precisely those characteristics which make them less than fully human, is to do something more harmful to persons than to attack them on account of their national origin or gender role. If this is so, when courts are faced with the problem of balancing democratic tolerance against mutual respect, they may decide to tip the scales in favor of the former when it comes to civil suits involving ethnic group, gender role, religion, or profession and in favor of the latter when it comes to civil suits involving race or sex.

But even though this test is available, feminists realize that the group defamation approach is not likely to work unless Objection Two above can be answered; and this is precisely the objection that cannot be met unless women *as a group* come to share the same negative reactions to gyno-thanatic pornography. If recent arguments between feminist antipornographers and feminist anti-antipornographers are any indication, however, a consensus will not be achieved tomorrow, if ever.

ARGUMENTS INVOKING THE OFFENSE PRINCIPLE

Realizing that it is difficult to convince society as a whole, women in general, and every feminist in particular that gyno-thanatica is harmful either in the sense of causing men to engage in harmful behavior toward women or in the sense of constituting a group defamation to women, some feminist antipornographers have argued that gyno-thanatica is legally restrictable on other grounds; namely, on the grounds that it constitutes an offense to many onlookers. That is, the state may restrict the public display and dissemination of gyno-thanatic pornography not because such exhibitions harm all women, but simply because they give offense—cause responses of shame, disgust, embarrassment, or "boiling blood"—to many onlookers, especially women.

The main problem with this approach is that the offense principle is one of the weaker liberty-limiting principles. Ever since John Stuart Mill's time, there has been considerable debate as to whether any principle other than the harm principle can constitute a sufficient reason for limiting the liberty of a citizen. In general, the overwhelming sentiment has been that each citizen may do as he or she pleases, provided that he or she causes no other person harm. This being the case, the law may not restrict a person's liberty merely because he or she harms himself or herself, gives offense to others, or engages in "harmless" immoralities.

Significantly, it is not clear that Mill, who is usually regarded as the main advocate of the preceding point of view, really espoused it in every detail. He seems, for example, to have conferred some validity upon the offense principle. At times, Mill relates harm to the violation of personal or property rights and offense to the violation of something less stringent than rights, such as aesthetic sensibilities. Whereas harms violate the law, offenses violate good manners, propriety, or custom. Nonetheless, offenses do not always fall entirely outside the scope of the law. Says Mill:

> There are many acts which, being directly injurious only to the agents themselves, ought not to be legally interdicted, but which, if done publicly, are a violation of good manners, and coming thus within the category of offenses against others, may rightfully be prohibited. Of this kind are offenses against public decency.[59]

But why may a "harmless" offense such as public nudity, be validly restricted? Is it not an instance of symbolic speech, a nonverbal or primarily nonverbal expression of opinion about the artificiality of clothing, entitled to the same protection that safeguards theological, philosophical, and political arguments that are verbal or primarily verbal?

Those who are not impressed by the merits of *offensive* symbolic speech argue that, to the extent that it is really a commentary on obsolete social taboos, it is a mere *form* (and a second-rate one at that) of saying something that can be equally well said without using that form. In other words, nudists do not have to resort to self-exposure to get their message across; supposedly, they can get their message across better by giving a speech when fully clothed or by writing a book in the privacy of their own nudist colony. Mill suggests as much when he says that public indecencies that aim to communicate opinions in nonverbal modes are not as valuable as assertions, criticisms, advocacies, and debates.[60]

But this is not always true, especially in an age when nonverbal modes of communication are intermingled with verbal modes of communication and when some entirely nonverbal modes of communication are understood to convey ideas and attitudes in a powerful manner not to be rivaled by verbal modes of communication. Indeed, the general direction of the Supreme Court has been to recognize these developments and to lend increasing First Amendment protection to modes of art, such as films, whose meaning cannot be conveyed through words at all or through words alone. This concession suggests that unjustified prohibitions on art forms such as punk music, modern dance, and mime would be unconstitutional.[61] In short, the First Amendment protects all *communications,* nonverbal as well as verbal; and it does not assign primacy of value to any specific mode of communication.

But if verbal modes of communication are not necessarily more valuable than nonverbal modes of communication, then the main justification formerly given for legally restricting certain public indecencies evaporates. However, there may be another, better reason to restrict legally some offensive behavior; namely, that a pluralistic society can withstand only so much in the way of denigrating and degrading speakings, writings, soundings, and depictings before its viability is threatened. There are certain moral virtues or character traits, such as democratic tolerance and mutual respect, that citizens must exhibit if the democracy is to remain stable over time.[62]

This is probably the intuition behind Joel Feinberg's attempt to add credence to the offense principle as a liberty-limiting principle. He argues that offensive expression may be restricted provided that it is universally offensive, publicly flaunted, and imposed on the beholders. An offense is of the universal sort when it can be expected to evoke reactions such as shame, embarrassment, repugnance, repulsion, or disgust in almost any person simply because he or she is a person, and not because he or she belongs to the Moral Majority, the Black Panthers, or the Society for Prevention of Cruelty to Animals.[63] Almost anyone would be disgusted by the sight of a man who defecated in public and then ate his feces in front of passersby. An offense is publicly flaunted when individuals can avoid it only by unreasonably inconveniencing themselves.[64] For example, someone would be unreasonably inconvenienced if the only way he could avoid blatantly offensive sights would be by foregoing his forays into the public marketplace except between the hours of 2:00 A.M. and 3:00 A.M. Finally, an offense is imposed on beholders when they have not voluntarily assumed risk of offense upon themselves. For example, a person would be so imposed upon if she were misled to think that a movie theater was featuring Walt Disney's *Bambi*, a sentimental tale about a fawn, when in fact it was featuring some pornographer's version of *Bambi*, where Bambi is a woman upon whom sexual abuse is heaped.

If Feinberg is correct, the implications are these. Considering almost any account of women-degrading pornography, at least gyno-thanatica is universally offensive. Most women and perhaps most men are offended by depictions of men treating women as pieces of meat ready to be branded or butchered on the altar of male sexual entertainment. And even if the population as a whole is not offended by such depictions, some feminists note that Feinberg's standard of universality can be supplemented with the doctrine of retaliatory violence, a doctrine meant to offset such insensitivity. According to this doctrine, expressions like public cross-burnings, displays of swastikas, and "Polish jokes" may be curtailed if they are bound to upset, alarm, anger, or irritate those whom they insult in ways that will cause them to vent their anger in retaliatory aggression.[65]

An example will clarify the import of this doctrine. In a 1939 prosecution for using disorderly, threatening, or insulting language/behavior in a public place, a strict orator named Ninfo was convicted for shouting from a soap-box, "If I had my way, I would hang all the Jews in this country. I wish I had $100,000 from Hitler. I would show those damn Jews what I would do, you mockies, you damn Jews, you scum."[66] Significantly, Ninfo was convicted on the grounds that a reasonable Jew could not be expected to listen to his words passively. If a reasonable Jew in Ninfo's audience were to lose his temper, then Ninfo and not the Jew would be responsible for the Jew's aggressive behavior. Therefore, to prevent such justified but nonetheless violent outbursts, the law demands that Ninfo either tone down his rhetoric or speak in a more private location where Jews are not likely to be in attendance. Analogously, whether or not gyno-thanatic pornography offends the entire population, provided that it is upsetting enough to prompt reasonable women to militant action, as it has in some cases where women have "trashed" gyno-thanatic displays, there may be cause for legal intervention. In such a case, it is not the women who should be prosecuted for the damage they cause, but the displayers of gyno-thanatic pornography for prompting such retaliatory violence.

Still, if those who take offense at gyno-thanatica can easily and effectively avoid them, then such depictions and descriptions may not be legitimately restricted. In other words, no matter how universally offensive a gyno-thanatic film is and no matter how conducive to retaliatory violence it is, provided that it is not publicly flaunted or foisted upon unwilling spectators, it may be viewed in private no matter how many nonviewers are repulsed, embarrassed, shamed, or angered at the mere thought that others are viewing it. This seems to have been behind the Supreme Court's thinking in *Stanley* v. *Georgia,* the decision that held that Georgia could not convict Mr. Stanley merely for possessing in his home an obscene film for his own viewing.[67] After citing the First Amendment right of Mr. Stanley to receive information and ideas, the Court appealed to the constitutional right of privacy: "For also fundamental is the right to be free, except in very limited circumstances, from unwanted government intrusion into one's privacy."[68] Therefore, if gyno-thanatic pornography violates neither women's interests nor rights, if it simply wounds women's sensibilities, then, provided that it is not publicly displayed and disseminated, feminists must live with the knowledge that it is being viewed in the recesses of the so-called private realm.

Conclusion

Apparently, there is no ideal legal remedy for gyno-thanatic pornography in particular or for women-degrading pornography in general. To date, all of the legal remedies advanced by feminist antipornographers have proved to be somehow flawed or limited. Still it is possible to rank them in order of increasing cogency. The clear-and-present-danger approach is the most problematic. If gyno-thanatic pornography presents a threat of this magnitude to society, then it is not enough to restrict it when it appears in the *public* domain. It must also be restricted when it emerges in the *private* realm. If those who view gyno-thanatic material are caused to sexually abuse women, then as far as the law is concerned, it matters not whether they view it in public or in private. In either case, it is extremely dangerous and must be extirpated. But there is little consensus on just how dangerous gyno-thanatic pornography is. Although feminists are confident that gyno-thanatic images shape the way people think and act, they do not know how they do this or to what extent. And until they know the how and why of gyno-thanatica, the clear-and-present-danger approach should be resisted. After all, to invoke a test that ensnared antidraft protestors in both world wars and alleged "Communists" during the Cold War is to risk depriving citizens of their liberty unnecessarily; and it is extremely doubtful that feminists wish to add to such injustices if they can avoid it.[69]

Better than the clear-and-present-danger approach is the group defamation approach; but it, too, is fatally flawed. What seems to be central in the group-defamation approach is the "lie" that gyno-thanatica tells about women and their sexuality: That women love to be sexually abused by men. But lies about female sexuality are not confined to *Snuff, The Devil in Miss Jones,* and *Deep Throat.* Silhouette romances may be telling lies about female sexuality that encourage women to accept as natural their inferior status in the social structure. Moreover, all sorts of religious, psychological, and philosophical works tell "lies" about female sexuality. What is incoherent about the group-defamation approach is that it comes close to losing the connection between its principle of regulation (prevention of "lies" about female sexuality) and its object of regulation (control of sexually explicit material).[70] If feminist antipornographers want to prevent *lies* about women, then they must take on Freud as well as Hugh Hefner and the producers of *Snuff.* After all, the lies that stimulate the brain are more powerful than those that stimulate the penis—unless, of course, I am hopelessly misguided to think that men of Freud's stature have had a deeper effect on the way we think than men of Hefner's talents.

More adequate than either of the preceding legal approaches is the offense-principle approach. Assuming that a gyno-thanatic depiction or description is either universally offensive or sufficiently gross to make the blood of at least feminists boil, and provided that it is publicly flaunted or foisted upon unwilling spectators who have no reasonable way to avoid it, then the state may drive this material out of the public domain. Unfortunately, it is not that clear either where the public domain ends, or how blatant, brazen, and/or blaring a gyno-thanatic display must be before it constitutes an unavoidable assault upon an unwilling spectator's sense.

In this connection, the so-called Skokie crisis is instructive. In 1979 the

National Socialist Party won the court's permission not only to march in the predominantly Jewish community of Skokie, but also to wear their swastikas, and this despite the fact that their message of anti-Semitism was all too familiar, their action was offensive to Gentiles as well as to Jews, and their mode of presentation deliberately unavoidable.[71] Although the court did not deny "that the proposed demonstration would seriously disturb, emotionally and mentally, at least some, and probably many, of the village's residents,"[72] it nonetheless proclaimed:

> It is better to allow those who preach racial hate to expend their venom in rhetoric rather than [for us to] be panicked into embarking on the dangerous course of permitting the government to decide what its citizens may see and hear. . . . The ability of American Society to tolerate the advocacy even of the hateful doctrines espoused by the plaintiffs without abandoning its commitment to freedom of speech and assembly is perhaps the best protection we have against the establishment of any Nazi-type regime in this country.[73]

As it so happened, the Nazis did not march in Skokie. Fearing retaliatory violence on the part of the Jews, they marched around Chicago's Grant Park instead. But what if the Nazis had marched that day in Skokie? Or what if they wanted to march every week in Skokie or to schedule systematically a march in a different Jewish community every weekend? Or what if, as Susan Brownmiller speculates, "the bookstores and movie theaters lining Forty-Second Street in New York City were devoted . . . to a systematized, commercially successful propaganda machine depicting the sadistic pleasures of gassing Jews or lynching blacks?"[74] Faced with such incidents, would not the courts reconsider their stance on democratic tolerance, stressing instead this nation's need to strike a better balance between the freedom to speak and the freedom not to listen? If so, feminists ask, should not the courts also attend to the fact that many bookstores and movie theaters are currently devoted "to the humiliation of women by rape and torture?"[75] In any event, even if the courts did do something about gyno-thanatic pornography, if only to restrict its *public* celebration to the Forty Second Streets of this nation, little would be gained. Pornography is a four-billion dollar a year enterprise; and as the years pass, it is becoming an increasingly slick business. Less of it is being publicly disseminated and displayed as more of it finds entrance into the home via video cassettes, cable television, and 16 mm. home films. Were laws against gyno-thanatica's *public* appearances passed and enforced, the process of its "privatization" would be accelerated. More and more video cassettes, for example, would be produced; and far from withering away, gyno-thanatica would thrive as men discovered the pleasures of watching it at home rather than in some shabby center-city theater.

Indeed, it is this last point which has persuaded many feminists largely to abandon the search for legal remedies. More of them are agreeing with Wendy Kaminer that "it makes little sense for feminists to focus on a legal 'war' against pornography or to direct much energy to reformulating obscenity prohibitions."[76] Not only does the effort seem disproportional to the outcome, but the outcome is one frought with danger, since, as Kaminer also points out, legislative or judicial control of pornography may not be possible without jeopardizing the legal principles and procedures that are essential to feminists' right to speak and, ultimately, feminists' freedom to control their sexual destinies.[77]

Realizing that Anglo-American law is such that it cannot provide remedies for every blight that poisons the human community in general and male-female sexual relations in particular, feminists are relying on extralegal means of persuasion—book writing, filmmaking, and consciousness-raising. Although feminists have been criticized for even these efforts, the criticisms seem excessive. To call a feminist "a moral prude," "a sexually repressed woman," or "an enemy of freedom" simply because she is not prepared to praise any and all sexually explicit material is to castigate someone because of her desire to make reasoned distinctions.

Admittedly, a few feminist antipornographers have on occasion bombarded their captive audiences with the horrors of gyno-thanatica, appealing more to their "guts" than to their minds and forcing them to hasty conclusions. Amber Hollibaugh, for example, complains about the manner in which WAVPM has constructed its antiporn slide show:

> There will be an image from a porn magazine of a woman tied up, beaten, right? And they'll say, *Hustler* magazine, 1976, and you're struck dumb by it, horrified! The next slide will be a picture of a woman with a police file, badly beaten by her husband. And the rap that connects these two is that the image of the woman tied and bruised in the pornographic magazine *caused* the beating that she suffered. The talk implies that her husband went and saw that picture, then came home and tried to re create it in their bedroom. That is the guilt by association theory of pornography and violence. And I remember sitting and watching this slide show and being freaked out about both of those images. And having nowhere to react to the analysis and say, what the hell is going on? I found it incredibly manipulative.[78]

For similar reasons, Gayle Rubin condemns a WAVPM tour of New York's porn strip:

> When I went on the WAVPM tour, everybody went and stood in front of the bondage material. It was like they had on blinders. And I said, look, there's oral sex over there! Why don't you look at that? And they were glued to the bondage rack. I started pulling out female dominance magazines, and saying, look, here's a woman dominating a man. What about

that? It was like I wasn't there. People said, look at this picture of a woman being tied up![79]

But even though Hollibaugh and Rubin have a point—that the presentations they describe left no room for discussion—most feminist antipornographers are not as dogmatic as the ones they encountered. On the contrary, like those feminists who currently support pornography, those feminists who currently oppose it wish to explore its liberating as well as its enslaving features.

Of course, it is difficult to decide when sexually explicit material is a source of sexual liberation and general freedom for humans and when it is a source of sexual oppression and general unfreedom. Although many feminists who endorse pornography admit that it can be a "bastion of sexism," they hasten to add that ordinarily it is a "vehicle of rebellion" against repressive, oppressive, and depressive sexual and moral norms. Indeed, these women claim that society has the pornographic imagination to thank for the "new openness about, say, nudity, lesbianism, oral-genital sex or even non-marital sex";[80] and they insist that anyone who is for sexual liberation must also be for pornography. Therefore, to be a liberated woman is to enjoy sex is to enjoy pornography.

But *must* a liberated woman enjoy all sexual experiences and *must* she enjoy all types of sexually explicit material? Susan Sontag is one woman who answers this question with a definite 'no.' As she sees it, the question to ask women is: What kind of sex are women being liberated to enjoy?

> Merely to remove the onus placed upon the sexual expressiveness of women is a hollow victory if the sexuality they become freer to enjoy remains the old one that converts women into objects. . . . This already "freer" sexuality mostly reflects a spurious idea of freedom: the right of each person, briefly, to exploit and dehumanize someone else. Without a change in the very norms of sexuality, the liberation of women is a meaningless goal. Sex as such is not liberating for women. Neither is more sex.[81]

As usual, Sontag has made a profound observation. The path to freedom is not through *Playgirl* or through male striptease joints; that is, women will not come into touch with their own sexuality by exploiting and dehumanizing men, or by trading the role of masochist for that of sadist, or by creating men-degrading pornography. Rather, if women are to understand what female sexuality means apart from men as well as in relation to men, then they must shatter the old sex roles and drown out this society's dominant, if not exclusive, discourse on sexuality; namely, sex = violence = death. But if women are to succeed, they must say something more than sex = nonviolence = life; for to say this is only to negate what men have said in the past.

It is difficult to say something new about sexuality and about its vehicle, the body. It will take time for women to free their imagination from the definitions and concepts men have, because of certain social conditions, constructed for it. But free it they can. And when women achieve this feat, they will drown out gyno-thanatic discourse not with andro-thanatic discourse, but with multiple voices celebrating the incarnation of woman as woman. In this connection, Deirdre English describes one of the more "erotic sights" she ever saw:

> It was a hot summer day in Pennsylvania, and during a break in the weekend-long conference we gathered at an outdoor swimming pool. There were no men around, so we all stripped and swam naked—dozens of women, most of them perfect strangers. I had never really been struck before by how *different* women's bodies are from how they're "supposed to be," and how woman's body is unique.[82]

The more women learn to love their bodies, the less power men will have over women. Once women revere their bodies, and once they rejoice, revel, and relax in them, they will refuse to hand them over to anyone who would treat them cruelly and contemptuously. And once men as well as women realize that woman's sexuality is not "for-man," a real sexual liberation will be effected. At last, men and women will be able to relate to each other as sexed beings whose sexuality is an expression of personal uniqueness, rather than the reflection of any unilateral vision or universal prescription of how one sex should relate to the other.

Notes

1. Deirdre English, "The Politics of Porn: Can Feminists Walk the Line?" *Mother Jones,* April 1980, p. 20.

2. Judith R. Walkowitz, "The Politics of Prostitution," *Signs: Journal of Women in Culture and Society* 6, no. 1 (Autumn 1980):123–35.

3. Cultural feminism is a school of thought that equates women's liberation with the development and preservation of a female counterculture. It advocates separatism from male values rather than men.

4. Deborah Sherman and Harriet Hirshorn, "Feminists and Sexuality: Background to a Debate," *WIN* 18 (October 15, 1982):9.

5. David A. J. Richards, *The Moral Criticism of the Law* (Encino, Calif.: Dickenson Publishing Co., 1977), p. 64.

6. Ibid., p. 64.

7. Ibid.

8. *Miller* v. *California,* 413 U.S. 15, 24 (1973).

9. English, "The Politics of Porn," p. 23.

10. I take the distinction between hard- and soft-core pornography to be this: Although both of these pornographic modes suggest male sexual domination and female sexual submission, only the former is tinged with violence.

11. English, "The Politics of Porn," p. 23.

12. Ibid.

13. I owe this distinction to Robert Fullinwider, Center for Philosophy and Public Policy, University of Maryland.

14. Rosemarie Tong, "Feminism, Pornography, and Censorship," *Social Theory and Practice* 8, no. 1 (Spring 1982):1–17.

15. Gloria Steinem, "What is Pornography?" *Take Back the Night*, Laura Lederer, ed. (New York: William Morrow, 1980), p. 39.

16. Lederer, ed., *Take Back the Night*.

17. Susan Griffin, *Pornography and Silence: Culture's Revenge Against Nature* (New York: Harper & Row, 1981).

18. Adrienne Rich, "Compulsory Heterosexuality and Lesbian Existence," *Signs: Journal of Women in Culture and Society* 5, no. 4 (1980):641.

19. Ibid.

20. Jean Bethke Elshtain, "The Victim Syndrome: A Troubling Turn in Feminism," *The Progressive* 46 (June 1982):43.

21. Ibid., pp. 42–43.

22. Martha Nelson, "The Sex Life of the Romance Novel," *Ms.*, February 1983, p. 97.

23. Ibid.

24. Ibid., p. 99.

25. Catherine A. MacKinnon, "Feminism, Marxism, Method, and the State: An Agenda for Theory," *Signs: Journal of Women in Culture and Society* 7, no. 3 (Spring 1982):534.

26. For a complete explanation of these four liberty-limiting principles, see Joel Feinberg, *Social Philosophy* (Englewood Cliffs, N. J.: Jersey: Prentice-Hall, 1973), pp. 36–55.

27. Feminists have eschewed the principle of legal paternalism, except to suggest that some women who view gyno-thanatica may harm themselves to the extent that they think less of themselves as persons or let themselves be treated as less than persons. Feminists have not, however, gone on to argue that women should be denied access to gyno-thanatica. There is little, if any, empirical evidence to establish the hypothesis that women who view women-degrading pornography in general or gyno-thanatica in particular lose their sense of self-respect. Indeed, the opposite may be true. Most women who willingly view such pornography may, after awhile, become so outraged by the sight of brutalized female flesh that their sense of self-respect is either retrieved or comes alive for the first time. Insofar as women are concerned, "Enough is enough" is a more probable response to *Snuff* than "Wow! What a turn-on." Likewise, regarding other issues, feminists have shunned the principle of legal moralism. Of all the purported liberty-limiting principles, the principle of legal moralism is the most problematic. It aims to restrict legally actions, descriptions, and depictions that are immoral, where "immoral" means something other than either "harmful" or "offensive." But because it is difficult to conceive what the term "immoral" can mean other than "harmful" or "offensive," feminists have not, like the Moral Majority, argued that women-degrading pornography in general and gyno-thanatic pornography in particular should be legally restricted simply because it is immoral—where "immoral" means "against the rule of a higher authority" (God) or "against a societal taboo."

28. Susan Brownmiller, "Let's Put Pornography Back in the Closet," in Lederer, ed., *Take Back the Night*, p. 255.

29. United States Commission on Obscenity and Pornography, *Report of the Commission on Obscenity and Pornography* (Washington, D.C.: U.S. Government Printing Office, 1970), p. 27.

30. Donald Mosher, "Sex Differences, Sex Guilt, and Explicitly Sexual Films," *The Journal of Social Issues* 29, no. 3 (March 1973):95–112.

31. Pauline B. Bart and Margaret Jozsa, "Dirty Books, Dirty Films, and Dirty Data," in Lederer, ed., *Take Back the Night*, p. 209.

32. Sarah J. McCarthy, "Pornography, Rape, and the Cult of Macho," *The Humanist* 40, no. 5 (September/October 1980):19.

33. Irene Diamond, "Pornography and Repression: A Reconsideration of 'Who' and 'What,'" in Lederer, ed., *Take Back the Night*, p. 191.

34. Wendy Kaminer, "Pornography and the First Amendment: Prior Restraints and Private Action," in Lederer, ed., *Take Back the Night*, p. 245.

35. Speaking for the majority in a decision that vindicated states' rights to ban publicly disseminated and/or publicly displayed obscenity, Justice Berger said: "We have directed our holdings, not at thoughts or speech, but at depiction and description of specifically defined sexual conduct that states may regulate within limits designed to prevent infringement of First Amendment rights." *Paris Adult Theater I* v. *Slaton*, 413 U.S. 49 (1973).

36. For a full description of *Snuff's* plot, see Beverly LaBelle, "Snuff—*The Ultimate in Women-Hating*" in Lederer, ed., *Take Back the Night*, pp. 272–74.

37. Diana E. H. Russell with Laura Lederer, "Questions We Get Asked Most Often," in Lederer, ed., *Take Back the Night*, pp. 25–26.

38. Hugo A. Bedau, "Rough Justice: The Limits of Novel Defenses," *Hastings Center Report* 8 (December 1978):8.

39. Helen Longino, "Pornography, Oppression and Freedom: A Closer Look," in Lederer, ed., *Take Back the Night*, p. 50.

40. Ibid., p. 51.

41. Criminal statutes against *threatening* defamation are another possibility.

42. H. P. Grice, "Meaning," *Philosophical Review* 66 (1957):385.

43. English, "The Politics of Porn," p. 44.

44. Bertolt Brecht was an innovative German playwright who transcended the parameters of Greek theater. He did not believe that the primary function of tragic theater was cathartic; rather, he believed that it was didactic.

45. For a thorough discussion of the impact that sexist and racist language use has on women and minorities, see Part IV of Mary Vetterling-Braggin, ed., *Sexist Language: A Modern Philosophical Anaylsis* (Totowa, N.J.: Rowman and Littlefield, 1981), pp. 249–318.

46. Andrea Dworkin, "Pornography's Exquisite Volunteers, *Ms.,* March 1981, p. 96.

47. Ibid.

48. William C. Prosser, *Handbook of the Law of Torts,* 2d ed. (St. Paul, Minn.: West Publishing Co., 1955), p. 631.

49. B. Ruby Rich, "Anti-Porn: Soft Issue, Hard World," *The Village Voice* 20 (July 1982):17.

50. Ibid.

51. The "reasonable man" test is a standard test for liability applied to Anglo-American tort law. It is meant to serve as an objective check on the individual subjectivities of men and women who are not perfectly reasonable.

52. But all this is quite beside the point. Most pornographers are neither as artistically skilled nor as politically aware as Bertolt Brecht, and most consumers of porn would balk at attempts to intellectualize gyno thanatic films. Does this mean that pornographers cannot be sued for defamation because they usually do not intend to say anything slanderous/libelous about women when they flash across the screen images of bruised and bloodied women, or because porn devotees do not usually link their feelings about women during a gyno-thanatic film with any didactic intentions they think the film's writers, producers, distributors, or displayers had? Does the magic of catharsis relieve the porn establishment of any causal responsibility for the

exacerbation of women-despising attitudes in real life? I think not. If images reach into the lives of an audience, a point we stress when we discuss the impact of media violence on children's psyches, then they probably reach into the lives of any audience, young or old.

The law of defamation could be adopted in ways that would ascribe liability to members of the porn industry for publicly displaying gyno- thanatic material that is known, as the result of empirical tests on substantially similar material, to lessen the esteem in which women are held or known to excite adverse feelings and opinions against women; and this, even though most porn consumers go to gyno-thanatic films, say, to be entertained and not to be educated, and even though most pornographers make gyno-thanatic films to entertain their audiences and not to educate them. In other words, there is no reason to insist that all defamations have to be intentional anymore than that all homocides have to be intentional. Just as the harmful effect counts more in cases of manslaughter than the lack of intent to kill, so, too, the harmful effect may count more in "negligent defamation" than the lack of explicit intent to damage the reputation of women.

53. David Reisman, "Democracy and Defamation: Control of Group Libel," *Columbia Law Review* 42 (May 1942): 770.

54. *Beuharnis* v. *Illinois*, 343 U.S. 250, 725 S. Ct. 725, 96 L. Ed. 918 (1952).

55. Reisman, "Democracy and Defamation," p. 770.

56. Ibid., p. 771.

57. Ibid.

58. Marilyn Frye and Carolyn M. Shafer, "Rape and Respect," in *Feminism and Philosophy*, Mary Vetterling-Braggin, ed., (Totowa, N.J.: Rowman and Littlefield, 1977), p. 337.

59. John Stuart Mill, *On Liberty*, David Spitz, ed., (New York: W.W. Norton, 1975), chap. 5, par. 7.

60. Joel Feinberg, *Rights, Justice and the Bounds of Liberty: Essays in Social Philosophy* (Princeton, N.J.: Princeton University Press, 1980), p. 71.

61. Richards, *The Moral Criticism of the Law*, p. 69.

62. Ibid., p. 25.

63. Feinberg, *Rights, Justice and the Bounds of Liberty*, p. 88.

64. Ibid., p. 89.

65. Ibid., p. 88.

66. Reisman, "Democracy and Defamation," p. 751.

67. *Stanley* v. *Georgia*, 405 U.S. 113 (1973).

68. Ibid.

69. Wendy Kaminer points out that "the standard was first enunciated by the Supreme Court in 1919 after the First World War, to allow for prosecutions for anti-draft pamphleteering under the Espionage Act; it was used in the early 1950's to uphold convictions for allegedly 'subversive' speech under the Smith Act; it has recently been invoked unsuccessfully by the government in an attempt to restrain the publication of the Pentagon Papers." Kaminer, "Pornography and the First Amendment," Lederer, ed., *Take Back the Night*, p. 245.

70. I owe this distinction to Robert Fullinwider.

71. Nat Hentoff, *The First Freedom* (New York: Delacorte, 1980), p. 312.

72. Ibid., p. 322.

73. Ibid.

74. Brownmiller, *Against Our Will: Men, Women and Rape*, p. 395.

75. Ibid.

76. Kaminer, "Pornography and the First Amendment," Lederer, ed., *Take Back the Night*, p. 246.

77. Ibid., p. 247.

78. Deirdre English, Amber Hollibaugh, and Gayle Rubin, "Talking Sex: A Conversation on Sexuality and Feminism," *Socialist Review* 11, no. 4 (July-August 1981):58.

79. Ibid.

80. English, "The Politics of Porn," p. 44.

81. Susan Sontag, "The Third World of Women," *Partisan Review* 40, no. 2 (1973):180 –206, esp. 188.

82. English, "The Politics of Porn," p. 50.

CHAPTER 2

PROSTITUTION

Pornography and prostitution have always been linked. *Pornographos* were sexually explicit depictions drawn by prostitutes on the walls of caves, in which they proffered their services. A potential patron could literally see which of his sexual fantasies a prostitute could, for a price, make real for him.

Although there are male as well as female prostitutes, and although we are seeing a dramatic increase in males offering their sexual services to other males,[1] the type of prostitution that concerns feminists as feminists is female prostitution. Next to pornography, prostitution is the most difficult, sex-related legal issue for feminists to address. This is because there is considerable confusion as to whether prostitutes are the paradigm of sexual liberation, the epitome of sexual oppression, or something in between. Coupled with the fact that society in general has treated prostitution as everything from an utterly condemnable evil to an unfortunate but unavoidable reality, we begin to see why so few of us understand either what prostitution is and what, if anything, should be done about it. Is a prostitute an evil and immoral woman, a victim of unjust social and economic opportunity structures, or an enterprising business woman? Is she a criminal from whom society needs protection, or a provider of an essential service whose work should be actively supported by the State? Should the law criminalize, legalize, or decriminalize her activities? And so on.

This chapter first will consider the image of the prostitute that continues to dominate the psychology of Anglo-American law. Second, it will examine several standard, arguments for the criminalization of prostitution, showing how each of these arguments, based on the legal moralism, harm, legal paternalism, and offense paternalism, and offense principles, can be countered by those who favor its decriminalization with or without regulation and/or licensing (legalization). Third, two competing feminist concepts of prostitution will be considered. One position states that prostitution is profoundly degrading to women who are forced into it either because of economic discrimination or sexual exploitation. The other position suggests that prostitution is an acceptable profession that many women would choose to enter were it not for the pressures of modern society's still-Victorian morality. Fourth, feminist arguments in support of prostitution's legalization (the minority view) will be contrasted with those in support of its decriminalization (the majority view). Finally, it will be suggested that no legal remedy—whether it is criminalization, legalization, or decriminalization—is likely to benefit prostitutes unless we first determine whether or not prostitution is in line with a woman's sexual identity as she understands it, and with a woman's sexual activity as she wishes to pursue it.

The Traditional Image

Society has many beliefs about the prostitute, but one stands out above the rest: The prostitute is the quintessential bad girl. According to the common mythology, there are two sorts of women—bad girls and good girls. The bad girls meet men's need for sexual objects; the good girls meet men's need for nurturers. It is significant that bad girls are no less indispensable than good girls. The early Church Fathers, for example, viewed prostitution as a necessary evil God permitted in order to prevent male lust from running rampant and destroying society: "Sewers," it was noted "are necessary to guarantee the wholesomeness of palaces."[2] In this connection, Simone de Beauvoir observes that "it has often been remarked that the necessity exists of sacrificing one part of the female sex in order to save the other and prevent worse troubles . . . a caste of 'shameless women' allows the 'honest woman' to be treated with the most chivalrous respect.[3] In other words, were it not for prostitutes, husbands would force their wives to make real their Saturnalian sexual fantasies.

So powerful is the good-girl/bad-girl myth that some men even suffer from what has been termed the "madonna-prostitute complex." These men differentiate between women who must be respected and therefore not sexually used, and women whom one can "lay" with carefree abandon. Since the respected woman—one's wife, for example—represents the mother, sex with this woman would create too much anxiety because of its incestuous overtones. Therefore, if one wishes sex at all, one must seek out the services of a woman who does not represent the mother—the prostitute, harlot, or whore.[4]

Although few men suffer from clinical versions of the "madonna prostitute complex," many men do distinguish between promiscuous girls and nonpromiscuous girls. The popular literature, especially magazines aimed at the teen population, is full of short stories about the girl who wears neither a bra nor panties, who sleeps around, and who "goes all the way" on the first date. This literature is also full of stories about boys who fool around with "easy" girls only to abandon them in favor of "choosy" girls. These literary accounts are bolstered by everyday experience, which suggests that men feel free to take liberties with women they perceive as promiscuous. A man on the prowl will not hesitate to approach a woman in a singles' bar who is dressed in a slinky black dress. He will, however, mind his manners in the presence of a nun or a uniformed nurse. Nevertheless, in the latter cases as well as the former he is, according to some feminists, likely to assume that these women exist for him. The good sister is there to minister to his spiritual needs, the nurse is there to bind his wounds, and the prostitute is there to spice up his bland sex life.[5]

The fact that men tend to conceive of women as persons who exist to serve them helps explain not only the long history of prostitution but also the law's strange ambivalence about prostitution. On the one hand, Anglo-American thought is dominated by the image of prostitutes as bad girls, as temptresses who lure men away from their duties and who cause them to walk other than the straight and narrow path of virtue. On the other hand, Anglo-American thought has always expressed special sympathy for the sexual wants and needs of men, and the law's desire to punish bad girls has often been moderated by its wish to save nice boys from harm, inconvenience, or embarrassment. Indeed, standard arguments both for and against the criminalization, legalization, and decriminalization of prostitution are heavily skewed in ways that favor men over women.

Arguments for Criminalization, Legalization, and Decriminalization

Individual liberty may not be justifiably restricted unless one's actions violate at least one of the principles that have been advanced as legitimate liberty-limiting principles. Traditionally, those in favor of the criminalization of prostitution have relied primarily on the principle of legal moralism and only secondarily on the harm, legal paternalism, and offense principles. In contrast, those in favor of the decriminalization of prostitution either with licensing (legalization) or without have relied primarily on the harm principle and to a lesser extent on the offense principle. In both cases, however, the arguments are influenced by an image of the prostitute as a bad girl.

ARGUMENTS IN FAVOR OF CRIMINALIZATION

1. *Arguments Invoking the Principle of Legal Moralism:* Given the power of the bad-girl image, it stands to reason that the principle of legal moralism— individual liberty may be limited to prevent immoral behavior—has loomed so large in arguments for the criminalization of prostitution. Invocations of this much controverted principle are based on two assumptions: (1) that a social consensus on what is immoral can be reached; and (2) that the health

of a society rests on its firm adherence to a binding moral code. In the latter case, the entire system of conventional moral beliefs may in principle be subject to legal enforcement, even when violations of these moral beliefs are neither harmful nor offensive in any straightforward way.

Not surprisingly, both of these assumptions encounter serious philosophical obstacles. First, it is highly unlikely that a melting-pot society could produce a consensus on what is moral or immoral, especially regarding prostitution and other so-called morals offenses (homosexuality, lesbianism, drinking, gambling). Second, and more crucially, even if there were a consensus about the immorality of prostitution—even if 90 percent of the population agreed that prostitution was immoral—it is not clear that society has a right to punish conduct simply because its members strongly disapprove of it or believe it is wrong. Of course there are those who insist that society does have this right. Lord Patrick Devlin, for example, argues that although there are some moral principles we may adopt for our own private guidance, there are other moral principles we must adopt for public guidance. That is, a society that does not have a public, shared morality, limiting and illuminating the personal moralities of its members, is charting a perilous course. Devlin insists that no society can survive for long without some degree of moral conformity. Therefore, since every society has a right to preserve its own existence, every society also has the right to insist on some moral conformity, and to enforce legally that conformity: "Society may use the law to preserve morality in the same way it uses it to safeguard anything else if it is essential to its existence."[6]

As Devlin sees it, the common morality of a society at any time is "a blend of custom and conviction, of reason and feeling, of experience and prejudice."[7] Indeed, he goes farther than this: What makes x immoral is that reasonable persons feel or believe that x is immoral. Says Devlin: "If the reasonable man believes that a practice is immoral and believes also—no matter whether the belief is right or wrong . . . —that no right-minded member of his society could think otherwise, then for the purposes of the law it is immoral."[8] If Devlin is correct, then what makes prostitution immoral is not its intrinsic "wrongness," but the fact that the community of "right-minded" persons feels or believes that it is wrong.

But against Devlin it may be reasonably argued that morality is not a matter of mere belief or feeling, and that what makes a position moral is not the fact that it is "passionately and sincerely held." It is not that a position has "a certain emotional depth," or that it is "the view of one's father or mother," or that it is "conventional" that gives it its steering authority, but rather that one can provide reasons for holding such a position.[9] Plausible reasons presuppose or invoke some general moral principle (treat others as you would like to be treated in comparable circumstances) or some general moral theory (utilitarianism, contractarianism, deontology). If a man's reasons are sound, he should be able to convince any other rational, open-minded, unbiased person that his reasons are more viable and consistent than those of his opponents. Therefore, even *if* society does have a right to enforce a public morality, each item of that morality must be rationally defensible.

Most of those who insist that prostitution is immoral have advanced not reasons, but pseudoreasons for their claim: expressions of prejudice ("prosti-tutes are fallen women"), or expressions of emotion ("prostitutes make me sick"), or instances of rationalization ("acts of prostitution render prostitutes sterile"), or instances of parroting ("everyone knows that prostitution is sinful").[10] In particular, some have advanced the argument that prostitution is immoral because it is an instance of nonprocreational sex. A long tradition of moralists have argued that the purpose of sexuality is the procreation of children within marriage. All other functions of sexuality—the expression of love or the experience of pleasure—are abuses of sexuality, which will lead to the decay of one's rationality and the emergence of one's previously controlled animality. But this argument may be turned on its axis: It seems that procreational sex rather than nonprocreational sex represents an abuse of human sexuality. Unlike animal sexuality, human sexual activity is not bound to the female reproductive cycle. Human sexuality is a "continually available resource, upon which are built longstanding and intense personal relationships resting on reciprocal sensual delight."[11] In short, the procrea-tional model is a description not of the human world, but of the animal world, and if anything is wrong with prostitution, it is not that it is nonpro-creational.

Other proponents of criminalization have argued that what makes prosti-tution immoral is that it violates the norms of romantic love, where the term "romantic love" is shorthand for an overly stylized ritual of dating involving swooning, starry-eyed evenings, sentimental poetry writing, and so on. But even assuming that prostitutes and their patrons never achieve romantic love, it is inarguable that the only fully human form of sexual expression is this rarified form of love.[12] In many cultures, romantic love is unheard of, and even in this culture some view romantic love as so much narcissistic nonsense. Seemingly, once sexual expression is freed from its procreational *telos*, it is freed from any unidimensional *telos* whatsoever, romantic love included. Sexual expression becomes unique to each individual, assuming as many specific forms as there are individual human beings. As a result, it seems that nonromantic sex, provided that it is not straightforwardly harm-ful or offensive to others or to self, is just as legitimate as romantic sex; and if anything is wrong with prostitution, it is not that it is nonromantic.[13]

Still other advocates of criminalization have suggested that what makes prostitution immoral is that it is degrading. (Note that a version of this standard view is advanced by those feminists who perceive prostitution as the ultimate degradation of women into sexual objects or commodities.)

According to the degradation argument, a woman is the object of shame if she personally fails to live up to standards of conduct that are valued by society as essential to the integrity of the self. Traditionally, one of the norms of behavior Anglo-American women have been judged by is chastity. Women in England and America (as well as elsewhere) have been taught that only bitches in heat are unable to control their sexual impulses, and that proper young women restrain their sexual desires until they are married. Whatever the social benefits of enforced female chastity may be (for example, men can be reasonably certain that their heirs are the product of their sperm), this standard has clearly caused individual harm to many women.[14]

In the nineteenth century Freud observed that a "strict demand for abstinence before marriage" produces harmful results in women's nature, most notably the "artificial retardation" of her sexual development. Contemporary psychoanalysts and psychologists reinforce Freud's observations, noting that many emotionally crippled women would have been psychically sound had they been allowed to confront their sexuality as developing children and adolescents. For these and related reasons, the norm of female chastity is evaporating. Society as a whole and women in particular have a more relaxed attitude about female sexual exploration and experimentation. Most contemporary women who engage in extramarital sex, especially premarital sex, tend to view their actions as the product of rational decision-making rather than the outcome of irrational lack of control. And if present trends continue, it is likely that society will permit more and more in the way of female promiscuity. In any event, large segments of society are already smiling indulgently upon female fornicators ("girls will be girls"), so much so that it is becoming increasingly odd for anyone to castigate prostitutes *simply* on account of their lack of chastity.[15]

According to some social commentators, however, there are other reasons to castigate the prostitute. What is degrading about prostitution is not that it violates an admittedly debatable behavioral ideal (female chastity), but that it violates society's standards about what may be justly sold in the marketplace. In a lengthy discussion of commercial sex and the alienation of moral personality, David A. J. Richards points out that no less an authority than Immanuel Kant claimed that persons were not entitled to sell their teeth let alone their limbs. As Kant saw it, the body was part of the self and in its togetherness with some sort of immaterial self it constituted the total person. Thus according to Kant, the body is the foundation of personal integrity and the condition of the possibility of all ethical relationships and rational decision-making. To sell one's body is to sell one's self–a kind of moral slavery. And because this is exactly what happens in prostitution, this manner of satisfying sexual desire is not permitted by the rules of morality.[16]

Despite the initial force of this argument, it is not without flaws, according to Richards. First, it suggests that prostitutes do in fact sell their *bodies.* Strictly speaking, however, all that the prostitute sells is her *sexual* services in much the same way as the mover sells his muscles, the model sells her beauty, and the lawyer sells his legal talent. Second, and more important, it is not possible to distinguish adequately commercial sex from other forms of service that people need and pay for. This is to say, prostitution seems no more empty, alienating, or socially unproductive than many other service occupations—for example, poodle clipping. And even *if* it is not only possible to regard prostitution as a sale of body parts but also to distinguish it in an uncomplimentary manner from other forms of service, taken together these two facts do not necessarily establish the immorality of commercial sex. Those who argue that they do insist that prostitution is always wrong because by selling one's body one sells, at least temporarily, one's person (for the body and the person are the same). When one sells one's person, one lets some other person have control over one's mind, over one's ability to make one's own decisions. To give someone such control over one's self is a form of moral slavery; one is no longer an autonomous agent, but the passive instrument of another person.[17]

Conceptually, such an argument is plausible, but it is empirically flawed. Putting the matter bluntly, when the prostitute hires out her genitals, she does not lose control over her person any more than the person who hires out his body to a football team. Like the woman who agrees to be a surrogate mother, the prostitute accepts certain limitations on her liberty, but these constraints do not destroy her autonomy. She agrees to accept these constraints on her body in exchange for money, and provided she receives fair payment for the services she renders, she is no more alienated from her person than millions of other persons who sell their nonsexual services for money. Indeed, it may be immoral to prevent her from engaging in prostitution. In other words, there may be something morally wrong about condemning prostitution, since the prohibition of it seems to be an unwarranted abridgment of sexual autonomy.[18]

2. *Arguments Invoking the Harm Principle:* If none of the standard reasons advanced to justify the claim that "Prostitution is immoral" is convincing, the claim fails and prostitution may not be criminalized on the grounds that it is immoral. However, the argument that prostitution should be criminalized on the grounds that it is harmful to others remains to be tested. It has been argued, for example, that prostitution contributes significantly to venereal disease, and that prostitution is the cause of a number of crimes, such as theft and assault of patrons, beating and raping of prostitutes, trafficking in heroin, and the enlarged scope of organized crime activities.[19]

As it turns out, however, none of these claims is empirically substantiated. First, recent studies indicate that prostitution accounts for less than 10 percent of the current incidence of venereal disease. Moreover, the venereal disease rate is the highest in those age groups (fifteen to thirty) in which patronage of prostitutes is rather low.[20] Consider for example, the current herpes epidemic. Prostitutes are not being blamed for spreading this disease; rather, sexually-active middle class men and women are being chastized— although gently—for bringing this disease upon themselves. Second, prostitution's links with organized crime have been exaggerated. In 1967 the President's Committee on Law Enforcement and the Administration of Justice reported that prostitution plays "a small and declining role in organized crime operations."[21] As for ancillary crime, much of it arises from the fact that prostitutes and patrons cannot report crimes perpetrated upon them without admitting their involvement in prostitution. Were prostitution decriminalized, prostitutes and patrons would be more likely to report ancillary crime and, as a result, the rate of ancillary crime would decrease. In short, it seems that prostitution is not in itself harmful to others and therefore cannot be legitimately restricted by invoking the harm principle.[22]

3. *Arguments Invoking the Principle of Legal Paternalism:* Those who continue to favor the criminalization of prostitution may invoke yet another purported liberty-limiting principle: the principle of legal paternalism. According to this principle, the law rightfully serves in the role of a benevolent father who restricts his child's liberty in order to save the child from self-harm. Those who accept this principle begin their argument by pointing out that prostitutes are subjected to all types of physical as well as psychological harm. Depending on how much business a prostitute does, she may contract certain diseases that otherwise she would not contract, as well as unwanted pregnancies. Her hours can be long and exhausting, and she runs the risk of assault, battery, and even permanent injury or death either from customers with sadistic or homocidal tendencies or from pimps unsatisfied with her job performance or displeased by her attitudes. On the psychological side, many prostitutes are said to suffer from depression, neurotic impulses, and self-degrading—even self destructive—behavior. Therefore, or so the argument goes, the state should criminalize prostitution in the same way as it criminalizes self- maiming. Arguably, society would do some prostitutes a favor by criminalizing prostitution. As M. Anne Jennings puts it, "To the extent that arrest does allow prostitutes to receive medical attention, counseling and a respite from the rigors of their life, it may have positive effects."[23]

But, queries the objector, is prostitution really harmful to the prostitute herself? On the one hand, if one answers this question by focusing on the image of a haggard streetwalker who has just been brutally beaten by her pimp for refusing to engage in sadomasochistic sex with her clients, then one will probably conclude that prostitution is harmful to self. On the other hand, if one answers this question by focusing on the image of a beautiful call girl who has just been wined and dined by a carefully-screened and enormously wealthy politician, then one may not know what to say. In any event, since most prostitutes are of the streetwalker variety, it is safe to assume that most prostitutes do harm themselves. Yet this is not to articulate it precisely enough. What prostitutes do is to *risk* harm to themselves, for not all prostitutes are physically or psychologically harmed during the course of their activities. So the question becomes: Is the state warranted in preventing a woman from assuming these risks to self? If it is, then it should consider criminalizing dentistry (dentists have the highest suicide rate of all professions) as well as assembly-line work (people who work on assembly lines are more prone to depressions caused by tedium than are people who are challenged by their jobs). Indeed, the state should contemplate criminalizing many other jobs that are taken at great risk to oneself— police work, bomb-squad work, contagious-disease work—but are nevertheless needed by the public to preserve it from harm.

According to many legal theorists, however, the principle of legal paternalism does not generate such ludicrous and disastrous programs of action. The state is not warranted in preventing a person from assuming any or all risks to self. If it were, it could prevent each of us from getting out of bed in the morning. What the state is warranted in preventing is personal assumptions of risk that are either unreasonable or the reflection of choices that fail to meet the criteria for full or nearly full voluntariness.[24]

Whether the assumption of a risk is reasonable or unreasonable depends on several factors. Joel Feinberg articulates at least five of these factors:

> (1) the degree of probability that harm to oneself will result from a given course of action; (2) the seriousness of the harm being risked; (3) the degree of probability that the goal inclining one to shoulder the risk will in fact result from the course of action; (4) the value or importance of achieving that goal, that is, just how worthwhile it is to one; and (5) the necessity of the risk, that is, the availability or absence of alternative, less risky means to the desired goal.[25]

A woman could come to the conclusion that if she played her cards right—if she got a fairly decent pimp or madam and obeyed his or her instructions faithfully—she could make a lot of money as a prostitute without risking anything near the injuries a professional athlete risks. Of course, even if a life of prostitution is one of *reasonable* risk, the state may still intervene if a woman has entered this profession as the result of a choice that is neither fully voluntary nor nearly fully voluntary.

As Feinberg sees it, what makes the assumption of a risk fully voluntary is that one assumes it with informed consent—aware of all relevant facts and known contingencies, and without any external coercive pressure or internal compulsion. Among the factors that tend to defeat ascriptions of full responsibility are: "neurotic compulsion, misinformation, excitement or impetuousness, clouded judgment (as, from alcohol or drugs), or immature or defective faculties or reasoning."[26] Given that virtually every person lacks something in the way of knowledge and power, it is doubtful that any choice is *fully* voluntary. Nevertheless, this does not make it impossible for us to distinguish between nearly fully voluntary choices and those that are nearly involuntary. So, for example, it is possible to distinguish between a half-starved, teenaged runaway who "decides" to be a prostitute because she is fed a steady diet of alcohol and narcotics by a ruthless pimp, and a college-educated, reasonably well-employed woman who decides to be a prostitute because she can make a lot of money quickly. In the former case, most persons are inclined to think that the state may intervene, at least temporarily, for the teenager's own good. In the latter case, however, many persons are inclined to think otherwise, observing that a competent, well-informed, calm, mature, unconstrained, adult woman is the best judge of her own good.

4. *Arguments Invoking the Offense Principle:* If the arguments made so far are correct—if prostitution is neither immoral nor harmful to others and/or to self—then the act of prostitution itself may not be criminalized. However, it still may be the case that *public* solicitation for prostitution may be criminalized on the grounds that it is offensive. In the same way that citizens should not have to confront public displays of pornography (at least its gyno-thanatic varieties), they should not have to confront public, street solicitation.

The success of this argument depends on whether public solicitation is, first, universally offensive—likely to evoke reactions such as shame, embarrassment, repugnance, repulsion or disgust "from almost any person chosen at random"[27]—or productive of retaliatory violence; and second, whether public solicitation is not reasonably avoidable—flaunted in such a way that one can neither easily nor effectively avoid it without a major effort or inconvenience on one's part.[28] Obviously, if prostitutes set up business in front of family restaurants, universities, churches, and offices at high noon, and if they make it perfectly clear what their line of business is, then many persons will not be able to avoid exposure to unwelcome solicitation. And even in these supposedly sexually liberated times, it seems likely that many men would be embarrassed were they approached by a prostitute as they prepared to enter or leave their places of work or worship. Therefore, assuming that the offense principle is a legitimate liberty-limiting principle to the degree that public, street solicitation is universally offensive and not reasonably avoidable, it may be restricted by the criminal law.

ARGUMENTS IN FAVOR FOR DECRIMINALIZATION WITH REGULATION OR LICENSING

Those who favor the decriminalization of all modes of prostitution— public (streetwalkers soliciting pedestrians) as well as discreet (call girls booked by "agents" who bring customers to their apartments)—may ask: If the offense principle is such a weak liberty-limiting principle, then why insist on *criminalizing* solicitation? After all, criminalization is the appropriate response to violations of interests and rights and not to woundings of mere sensibilities. What is more appropriate to the latter woundings is state *regulation* of solicitation, especially public solicitation. Instead of incarcerating prostitutes for solicitation, the state could respond either by adopting an English or European system of regulation or by expanding the Nevada system. Whereas solicitation takes place through ambiguously worded advertisements in England, in continental Europe the form of regulation is some form of zoning, whereby solicitation is confined to certain well-known urban districts.[29] In Nevada, the form of regulation consists in confining prostitutes to brothels.[30] Any one of these approaches would solve the offense problem without invoking the criminal sanction. No one whose sensibilities are likely to be wounded or aroused need read the advertisements for prostitution, go to the "red-light" districts, or patronize the brothels.

If uncertainty about the harmfulness of prostitution to others renders any imposition of the criminal sanction unwarranted, the state may still be justified in licensing prostitution if there is a *risk* of harm to others. That is, it may not be overstepping its bounds by demanding that in order to engage in commercial sex a woman must secure a legal permit that entails having her name entered in a public record, various regulations of dress, price, and place of business and solicitation, and even regular medical inspections for venereal disease. In short, proponents of regulation/licensing argue that an ounce of prevention is worth a pound of cure.

ARGUMENTS FOR LAISSEZ-FAIRE DECRIMINALIZATION

In response to this cautious approach, those in favor of a laissez faire regime of decriminalization argue that neither licensing of prostitution nor regulation of public solicitation is necessary. Licensing is unnecessary because the risk of contracting venereal disease from prostitutes is relatively slim, and because were prostitutes offered cheap and noncoercive medical inspections, they would *voluntarily* take advantage of them. Similarly, regulation of public solicitation is not necessary either. Comments David A. J. Richards:

> For all practical purposes, solicitations for prostitution occur in familiar locations where no reasonable person can claim surprise. Furthermore, the presence of prostitution is, on balance, one of the colorful amenities of life in large urban centers. It should not be hidden and isolated, but robustly accepted as what in fact it is: an inextricable part of human life.[31]

However, most feminists struggle with the suggestion that prostitution is a "colorful amenity" that should be "robustly accepted," if not by all, then by the liberal and the rational.[32]

Feminist Concepts of Prostitution

What is remarkable about twentieth-century feminists is their desire to avoid the implicit moralism of their nineteenth-century predecessors. During the last century, feminists mounted an attack on the institution of prostitution and the double standard of sexual morality that they perceived to underlie it. According to the formidable Englishwoman Josephine Butler, men, like women, should be compelled to observe the same sexual standard, which she assumed to be chastity or sex in marriage alone.[33] For this reason, so-called purity reformers in England and America worked hard to block attempts at government licensing of prostitution.[34] As they saw it, state-run brothels would only facilitate and perpetuate the double standard. Moreover, women working in these public houses of prostitution would be subjected to various indignities, including mandatory medical examinations inflicted by callous physicians equipped with "iron penises" (speculums).[35]

Although nineteenth-century feminists were right to challenge what they considered the manhandling of prostitutes, they never bothered to ask them whether they preferred life in a relatively orderly brothel to life on the rough-and-tumble back streets of England and America. Nor did these early feminists, in their fight against the double standard, ever "investigate the potential of sexual expression for women rather than continence for men."[36] Aware of these past shortcomings, twentieth-century feminists have approached the issue of prostitution with considerable humility. Nevertheless, because most contemporary feminists find it difficult to understand why any woman would freely choose to be a "sex object" (prostitute, pornography model, go-go girl, *Playboy* bunny), they have sometimes constructed barriers between themselves and women who engage in commercial sex. In this connection, one porn model complains:

> I've never had anybody from a poor or working-class background give me the "How could you have done anything like that?" question, but middle class feminists have no consciousness about what it is like out there. You have to remember who's the real enemy—who has the power— who you're selling it to, who you're looking up at and trying to please. It's not other women.[37]

The sentiments of this model are echoed by many prostitutes, some of whom reveal their real need for respect. Says one prostitute: "Somehow their pity deprives me of my freedom of choice. I don't want to be saved; saved by the Christians or saved by the shrink. Whatever their rationale is, it's the same: condescending, patronizing. Something in me just resents this moralism."[38] In a wholehearted effort to obviate all such criticism, contemporary feminists are beginning to cast their discussion of prostitution in terms of determinism versus freedom. Is the prostitute the quintessential oppressed woman or the quintessential liberated woman? Or is the prostitute simply a woman who, like all women in this society, is struggling to understand and live her own sexuality?

THE PROSTITUTE AS QUINTESSENTIAL OPPRESSED WOMAN

Although they provide different reasons for their position, classical Marxist feminists, social feminists, and radical feminists agree that the prostitute is the quintessential oppressed woman.

1. *The Classical Marxist Feminist Interpretation:* With some slight variations, classical Marxist feminists adopt the Marx/Engels's analysis of prostitution: No woman under capitalism, be she a prostitute or not, can transcend the conditions that determine her and which prevent her transformation into a subject, a person who is in charge of her own destiny. Try as she might, social and economic conditions are such that she must remain an object, a plaything in the hands of those who control the contours of her existence. This is why, as Marx and Engels see it, the difference between a married woman and a prostitute—upper, middle, or lower class—is one of degree and not of kind. In the course of discussing the bourgeois family, Engels asserts that in a capitalist society who one marries is determined by the class to which one belongs. This "marriage of convenience" often turns into "the crassest prostitution"—"sometimes on both sides, but much more generally on the part of the wife who differs from the ordinary courtesan only in that she does not hire out her body, like a wage-worker, on piecework, but sells it into slavery once and for all."[39]

Nevertheless, Marx adds that it is somehow worse to be a prostitute than a wife, not only because the prostitute is reminded anew of her bondage each time she hires out her body, but also because her situation is strictly analogous to that of the proletarian worker: "Prostitution is only a *specific* expression of the *general* prostitution of the laborer, and since it is a relationship in which falls not the prostitute alone, but also the one who prostitutes—and the latter's abomination is still greater—the capitalist, etc., also comes under this head."[40] In short, the prostitute is doubly oppressed by capitalism: first as a woman, and then as a worker who must make her living by hiring out not her hands, but her genitals and orifices.

This is precisely why not only Engels and Marx, but most Marxist feminists insist that "to fight prostitution is to fight the foundations of capitalist society," especially the institution of private property and the class system it generates. According to classical Marxist analysis, the typical prostitute is a working-class female and the typical patron is an upper- or middle-class male—only these men have enough money to purchase the sexual services of women other than their wives. As long as there is a bourgeois demand for whores, and as long as working-class women are paid less than adequate wages for less than interesting work, working- class women will continue to supply their bodies to meet the bourgeois demand for female flesh. The simplest way to break this cycle is to destroy the supply of prostitutes by giving working-class women jobs that provide them with a living wage and a sense of satisfaction or accomplishment. Arguably, if women are given such jobs, they will no longer be forced to choose degrading work (prostitution).[41]

As long as the capitalist system remains intact, however, women will not be given meaningful work. Marxists maintain that capitalism requires cheap, efficient labor; it cannot "afford" to give any member of the working class either a living wage or the time to pursue less profitable but more personally-fulfilling tasks. Consequently, prostitution will persist as long as capitalism limits the work options of working-class women. Moreover, under capitalism no legal remedy can assuage the prostitute's plight, since capitalist law exists to serve the capitalist economy. Capitalists will criminalize, legalize, or decriminalize prostitution in accordance with self-interest. For example, were capitalists to legalize prostitution, they would do so not out of concern for the prostitute, but out of a desire either to fill the state's coffers with tax revenues or to line the pockets of those who would operate the legitimate "cathouses." In neither of these latter events would the condition of the prostitute herself be ameliorated.

2. *The Socialist Feminist Interpretation:* By emphasizing the economic determinants of prostitution, classical Marxism rightly points out that an individual's freedom is limited in a capitalist society, especially if that individual is a working-class woman. Nonetheless, despite the accuracy of its main contention, socialist feminists claim that the Marxist analysis is flawed, that it is too eager to prove its central thesis about women; namely, that were it not for capitalism, women would be the sexual as well as economic equals of men. As socialist feminists see it, however, women's condition is considerably more complex.

First, unless capitalism and patriarchy are inextricably intertwined, women need not be exploited under capitalism any more than men are. As a result of having achieved a measure of economic independence and legal recognition, some capitalist women no longer have to hand their bodies over to men in return for long-term financial security (marriage) or in return for short-term financial security (prostitution). Nevertheless, socialist feminists admit that it may be the case under capitalism that only upper and middle-class women can attain rough parity with men and then not with the best, brightest, and richest of men. That is, capitalism may be able to treat a few exceptional women like men, but it may not be able to treat the majority of women (working-class women) like men. But this is an empirical hypothesis and, in principle, it may be possible for capitalism to eliminate gender inequalities even if, by definition, it cannot eliminate class inequalities.

Second, *if* prostitution reflects class lines in capitalist society, these lines are considerably more complex than those traced by classical Marxists. Empirical data indicate that working-class men patronize prostitutes just as much, if not more than, middle- and upper-class men. But because working-class men do not have as much money as middle- and upper-class men, they are forced to take what they can get; namely, inexpensive hookers who have entered the life of prostitution as a way out of bleak economic circumstances. In contrast, upper- and middle-class men have the means to pay for "quality merchandise," expensive call girls who are generally drawn from "bourgeois" backgrounds.

Third, socialist feminists note the embarrassing fact that prostitution appears in noncapitalist systems as well as capitalist systems. Admittedly, it does not seem to be as prevalent in Mainland China or Russia as it is in the United States, but this may be because the People's Republic of China engages in forms of "aggressive rehabilitation"[42] directed at the patrons of prostitutes as well as the prostitutes themselves, and because the Soviets stigmatize patrons by name in a public bulletin called "Buyers of the Bodies of Women."[43] Available evidence indicates that if socialist societies were to loosen legal controls on prostitution, it would flourish there as well as in capitalist societies.

Fourth, the demand for and supply of prostitutes is not always or only a function of economics. Indeed, according to socialist feminists, the crucial error of classical Marxists feminists is to overemphasize the role the mode of production plays in women's lives without stressing enough the role other structures such as reproduction, the socialization of children, and sexuality play in women's lives.[44] Many socialist feminists agree with Lars O. Ericsson that "the classical Marxist analysis . . . is bound to fail for the simple and obvious reason that the sex drive—which constitutes a necessary condition for the demand for prostitutes—is neither an economic phenomenon nor a phenomenon less basic (in fact it is more basic) than any economic factor."[45] In other words, no matter what economic system reigns, as long as a patriarchal ideology prevails according to which women exist for-men, men will continue to demand prostitutes and women will continue to meet this demand.

3. *The Radical Feminist Interpretation:* Significantly, this previous argument is one radical feminists echo, but with some variations. As they see it, what accounts for the persistence of prostitution is not the sex drive per se, but the sex drive as it is institutionalized by society, in this case any advanced Western society, capitalist or socialist. On the one hand, radical feminists explain that men are socialized to have a certain set of sexual wants and needs and to feel entitled, as a matter of right, to these wants and needs. On the other hand, women are socialized to meet male sexual wants and needs and to feel obligated as a matter of duty to meet these wants and needs. Because male sexual requirements range from a desire to be emotionally nurtured to a desire to be erotically aroused, and because men find few

women versatile enough to meet all of their sexual requirements, men divide the world of women into two: the good, or domesticated, women (wives, mothers, aunts, lovers) and bad, or exotic, women (whores, tramps, sluts). The good women are supposed to supply men with security and the bad women are supposed to supply men with stimulation. Within this schema, prostitutes are supposed to fulfill those male sexual fantasies that would otherwise go unfulfilled. In an in-depth and extensive study of the patrons of 156 call girls, Martha Stein summarized the complex nature of the meaning of commercial sex for patrons:

> Their behavior and needs in turn determined the call girl's role on call; to the Fraternizers-a party girl; to the Promoter—a businesswoman; to the Adventurer—a playmate. The Lover sought a romantic partner; the Friend, a confidante; the Slave, a dominatrix; the Guardian, a daughter figure; the Juvenile, a mother-figure. The role playing became a kind of fantasy enactment for some of the Lovers, Friends, Slaves, Guardians, Juveniles. The part they assigned the call girl corresponded to an idealized image of woman which exerted great power over their erotic imagination, and the correspondence was a source of excitement and pleasure. The men's individual fantasies of the ideal partner can be seen as variations of female types idealized by our culture as a whole; the Sexual Superwoman; the Beloved; the Girlfriend; the Dominating Mistress; the Child-Woman; the Earth-Mother.[46]

All this sounds innocent enough, except that Stein goes on to note that prostitution affords an outlet not only for the masochistic tendencies of patrons, but for their sadistic urges: urges they are forbidden to satisfy in the "ordinary fabrics" of their lives, but which they are permitted to "act out" in the prostitute's chambers.[47]

Stripped of its clinical gloss, this piece of contemporary enlightenment simply states that men are allowed to use whores in ways that they are not allowed to use madonnas. This view is continuous with the "prostitution is society's sewer" line of reasoning, according to which the whore is the one who does the madonna's dirty work. In other words, were it not for the whore, the madonna would have to satisfy all of her man's sexual yearnings, even the kinky and cruel ones. But fortunately, for the madonnas that is, there are enough whores to go around. In the same way that society reproduces women who will be wives and mothers, it reproduces women who will be prostitutes, even if their basic economic needs are met elsewhere. According to several studies, girl-children who have been sexually abused or raped are much more likely to become prostitutes than girl-children who have not been subjected to such manhandling. In one study 65 percent of adolescent prostitutes were forced into sexual activities as children; 57 percent had been raped, and one-third of those had been raped more than once.[48] These studies also suggest that girl- children who have been rewarded for entering into sexual relations with their fathers, brothers, uncles, neighbors, and so on are even more prone than girl-children who have been forced into such relations to enter the life of prostitution.[49]

In this connection, one feminist prosecutor reported that in her district a man approached several single-parent mothers on welfare with the following proposition: In return for cash payments for them (the mothers) and gifts for their little girls (ages seven to ten), the mothers would permit him to spend time with their daughters. The mothers agreed and the daughters spent their after school hours with "Uncle Charlie," who proceeded to molest them. Curiously, a rivalry developed among the girls, each of them trying to be "Uncle Charlie's" favorite. Indeed, so attached did the girls become to "Uncle Charlie" that when one of the mothers confessed the sordid affair to the police, the little girls were depressed at the thought of not seeing him anymore. The prosecutor warned:

> Unless they get first-rate counselling, one of two things is going to happen to these girls. Either they are going to spend their lives turning men off or they are going to spend their lives turning men on. I predict most of them will turn to prostitution rather than celibacy. This is to be expected. Men need whores; they don't need nuns.[50]

Bluntly stated, prostitutes are not born. They are made by a society that teaches girls that, if all else fails, a woman can always gain attention or money by offering her body to men who both want and need it.

THE PROSTITUTE AS QUINTESSENTIAL LIBERATED WOMAN

In contrast to classical Marxist, socialist, and radical feminists, there are those feminists who paint an alternative portrait of the prostitute: one that focuses neither on the working-class woman nor on the sexually abused girl, but on the woman who insists that she has chosen to be a prostitute. According to these existentialist feminists, the prostitute is an exceptional woman who dares to challenge the sexual mores of her society. This view is rooted in several studies, especially those of ancient Greece describing the *hetairae*. In these studies, Athens is delineated as a center of prostitution, where the prostitutes were divided into at least three classes. Lowest on the status ladder were the *pornai,* who were checked over before their services were bought. Of slightly higher status were the *ayletrides,* or players, who entertained guests with their music as well as their bodies. Occupying the highest position were the *hetairae.* In some ways these intellectually gifted as well as physically endowed women were more privileged than respectable Athenian wives and mothers, who, unlike them, were largely uneducated and somewhat confined to domestic affairs. Indeed, some *hetairae* amassed great wealth and exerted considerable power in the public domain through the men they entertained—this at a time when these men's wives and mothers were without real economic and political power.[51]

Nevertheless, according to several scholars of antiquity, the *hetairae* were not necessarily the most blessed of women. Sarah B. Pomeroy, for example, notes that although the *hetaira* had access to the intellectual life of Athens, and although she had freedom to be with whomever pleased her, her life had definite shortcomings. Pomeroy observes: "That we know of some courtesans who attempted to live as respectable wives, while we know of no citizen wives who wished to be courtesans, should make us reconsider the question of which was the preferable role in Classical Athens—companion or wife."[52] In short, the price the *hetaira* paid for sexual freedom and intellectual stimulation was not only status within the Athenian community, but some of the less glamorous, though nonetheless meaningful, comforts of home. According to existentialist feminists, however, this may not have been too high a price to pay for the privilege of living in the active rather than the passive voice, thereby achieving a measure of independence from men.

In this connection, Simone de Beauvoir observes that even today's common prostitute, who lacks the wit, charm, and intelligence of "hetairahood," may nonetheless find a certain liberation in the money or other benefits that she gains from men. Provided that she is not dominated by a pimp, the money she makes need not be enslaving. It can, says de Beauvoir, have a "purifying role" to the extent that, for her, it does away with the battle of the sexes:

> If many women who are not professionals insist on extracting checks and presents from their lovers, it is not from cupidity alone, for to make the man pay . . . is to change him into an instrument. In this way the woman avoids being one. The man may perhaps think he "has" her, but his sexual possession is an illusion; it is she who has *him* . . . she will not be "taken," since she is being paid.[53]

Interestingly, de Beauvoir's thoughts are shared by members of C.O.Y.O.T.E. (Cast Off Your Old Tired Ethics), a San Francisco-based union of prostitutes. According to members of this group, their decision to enter the life was fully or nearly fully voluntary. Among the options open to them, they chose to be prostitutes. Indeed, as they see it, their choice makes better sense than that of those women who choose not to be prostitutes. If the woman who sleeps with her date because he wined and dined her is not that different from a prostitute, and if the wife who tries to be her husband's "Total Woman"—wife, mother, and lover all wrapped up in one obliging body and docile mind—is not that different from a prostitute either, then a woman may as well capitalize on her sexuality and elect to become a prostitute, especially if her decision gives her greater economic and psychological independence from men.

What C.O.Y.O.T.E., Simone de Beauvoir, and existentialist feminists may be overlooking, however, is that the only freedom women currently have is the freedom to choose that form of bondage (prostitution, marriage) that most suits them. But this type of freedom cannot be compared to the freedom to choose initially the institutions (patriarchal, matriarchal, androgynous) that will shape one's subsequent decisions. It is one thing to say that under patriarchy women may choose either a life of prostitution or a life of marriage. It is quite another to say that in the best possible world women would want to have their choices restricted to either prostitution or heterosexual-marriage. The issue is not whether a woman is free in a technical, psychological sense to choose between prostitution and marriage, but what values she chooses and why. If her values are not her own, if she simply parrots the values of her culture, then her choice is a limited one indeed.

Feminist Legal Approaches to Prostitution

From what has been said so far, it seems clear that if the prostitute is free, then she is not much more or much less free than her married counterpart. At the same time that the prostitute proclaims her freedom, she may, like her nonprostitute counterpart, also admit its fragility and limited nature. One former prostitute comments: "I'd like so much to have the illusion that I had some freedom of choice. Maybe it's just an illusion, but I need to think I had some freedom. Yet then I realize how much was determined in the way I got into prostitution."[54] But whether or not prostitutes are more or less free (determined) than other women in this society, virtually all feminists agree that prostitution should be decrimalized because present antiprostitution laws discriminate against prostitutes in at least three ways.

First, in some jurisdictions the laws against prostitution apply only to women and not to men. This means that these laws apply neither to males who prostitute themselves nor to males who patronize male or female prostitutes. Although some states have addressed these equal-protection problems by redefining a prostitute as any female *or* male who sells her *or* his sexual services and by enacting laws aimed at male patrons as well as female prostitutes, the police continue to enforce these statutes selectively against women. In 1974 in San Francisco there were 768 arrests for heterosexual prostitution, of which 756 were women.[55] And in nearby Oakland 3,663 prostitutes were arrested while only 21 clients were apprehended.[56] Indeed, in some cases there were no male clients to pick up because police decoys had masqueraded as "johns" in order to arrest women for solicitation—however, discreet. Although such police methods verge on entrapment, which is illegal, police have argued that such methods do not constitute entrapment because, *per definiens,* you cannot entrap a woman who *would* have prostituted herself to a real "john" had she not been fooled by a police decoy. In other words, she was in the process of soliciting when she was arrested.

Second, in some jurisdictions the police enforce prostitution laws in ways that invade the prostitute's privacy. Surveillance strategies are frequently excessive, as in cases where police stake out a call girl's apartment and use spying equipment to record her activities before intruding on her and her patron in the midst of sexual intercourse. Prostitution laws that make this possible are being challenged on the grounds that they violate the right to privacy. Increasingly, this right has been invoked to protect consensual sexual activities, and there seems little reason not to extend this right to the act of prostitution per se: "Prostitution, both in the preliminary solicitation and negotiations and in the act itself, is overwhelmingly a private, consensual affair between individuals who wish to make their own decisions as how to control their sexual lives and use their bodies."[57] The point is that sexual intercourse is a private affair even if it involves a preliminary business transaction on the street. The fact that money is exchanged does not necessarily bring the act of prostitution into the public domain, unless said exchange is universally offensive *and* not reasonably avoidable by unwilling spectators.

Finally, in some jurisdictions vague "antiloitering" or "repeated beckoning" laws, aimed at controlling public solicitation, have violated the due-process rights not only of prostitutes but also of nonprostitutes. In making their sweeps down the streets of New York, for example, the police have arrested "known prostitutes" who were simply taking a stroll that day. And in some instances they have even arrested women who "looked like" prostitutes but were in fact simply women visiting the "red light" districts or doing business there.[58]

One begins to appreciate just how discriminatory antiprostitution laws are when one couples these three facts with a further, even more distressing fact: Most women who are in prison are there because they are prostitutes. Significantly, the prostitutes' pimps and patrons are not likely to be incarcerated alongside them—as if the crime (*if* it is a crime) of prostitution is women's alone. Antiprostitution laws should be enforced against men as well as against women or they should not be enforced at all. One thing is certain, the prostitute does not deserve to be treated in a way stricter than her patrons or promoters.

ARGUMENTS FOR DECRIMINALIZATION WITH LICENSING (LEGALIZATION)

Even if most feminists agree that prostitution should be decriminalized, and even if they also agree that *public* solicitation for prostitution may be regulated, provided that it is universally offensive and not reasonably avoidable, they remain divided on the issue of licensing (although the majority do not favor licensing).

That only a small minority of feminists should support licensing is not surprising. Traditionally, feminists have been strident opponents of legalized or state-supervised prostitution. Nineteenth-century feminists were adamantly opposed to the state licensing of prostitutes because it imposed demoralizing and demeaning conditions on prostitutes, including public records that stigmatized them for life, intrusive medical inspections that stripped them of certain dignities, and arbitrary regulations that confined them to their brothel rooms for excessively long periods of time.[59]

Unfortunately, as a result of their attempts to help prostitutes, nineteenth-century feminists inadvertently worsened the lot of their prostitute sisters. Their campaign to end legalized prostitution resulted not in the decriminalization of prostitution, but in the criminalization of prostitution. As soon as their profession was criminalized, prostitutes were treated as lepers and exiled from their neighborhoods. Deprived of their network of community support, they were increasingly forced to rely on pimps for protection against police authorities as well as for emotional security. Says Judith Walkowitz: "Indeed, the wide prevalence of pimps in the early twentieth century meant that prostitution had shifted from a female- to a male-dominated trade, and there existed a greater number of third parties with an interest in prolonging women's stay on the street."[60] Not wanting to repeat the mistakes of the past, contemporary feminists continually remind themselves that it is up to *prostitutes* to decide whether legalization is or is not their best available option.

Those prostitutes who support legalized prostitution do so because, as they see it, state licensing would improve their health, give them protection from abusive pimps and patrons, and ensure them a steady income. Rightly conceived, state licensing could, they point out, be beneficial to prostitutes. When and where state schemes of licensing have worked against women's interests, they have been guided by the state's misguided desire to protect the male patron from venereal disease, to save him from force and fraud, and to provide him with the most pleasure possible for the least price possible. In Nevada, for example, where prostitution has been legalized, women must not only register as prostitutes, but also be fingerprinted, checked over by medical officials, and licensed. They must agree to what amounts to an informal incarceration that requires them to stay in the publicly run brothels for as long as three weeks at a time. Moreover, some Nevada locations establish strict regulations governing not only the times when prostitutes may be in town and the places where they may go (no bars, casinos, residential areas permitted), but also those with whom they may be seen (no boyfriends or husbands).[61]

Yet despite the shortcomings of Nevada-like experiments, some prostitutes continue to believe that state schemes of legalization are not necessarily pernicious. As these women see it, the state could ensure prostitutes adequate and fair protection in their business dealings "without making regulatory authorities moralistic and often sadistically retributive police."[62] It could also forge programs that would facilitate a woman's decision to exit as well as enter the "oldest profession."

ARGUMENTS FOR LAISSEZ-FAIRE DECRIMINALIZATION

It is at this point in the discussion that feminists opposed to legalization ask a pointed question: Why should prostitutes trust the state, which after all is largely male-dominated, to come up with women- centered systems of state licensing? Instead, why not simply decriminalize prostitution and leave prostitutes to control their own lives? Provided the state dispenses inexpensive, noncoercive, quality medical treatment to all victims and carriers of venereal disease, and provided that the police enforce current fraud as well as assault and battery statutes against abusive patrons and exploitative pimps, it seems likely that prostitutes can take care of themselves better than the state can. Indeed, this is the viewpoint of not only most feminists, but of C.O.Y.O.T.E., the San Francisco prostitutes who have unionized in order to bring the support of collective organizational self-protection to what has been an atomistic, each-woman-out-on-her-own profession. Should C.O.Y.O.T.E.'s efforts succeed, it may serve as a paradigm model for prostitutes elsewhere.

Yet there are reasons to oppose legalization other than the fact that the state may skew its terms in ways that favor patrons rather than prostitutes. That is, feminists who oppose legalization have ideological as well as pragmatic reasons for their point of view. Like their nineteenth-century counterparts, most twentieth-century feminists find the notion of state-operated houses of prostitution an *endorsement* of the institution of prostitution itself. Unlike their predecessors, however, contemporary feminists do not base their objections to state-endorsed prostitution on the grounds that it maintains a double standard that holds women up to higher moral norms than men. Were they to make such an objection, one could predict the following response: "Ladies, your argument is with merit. Henceforward the state, in addition to supplying men with female prostitutes, shall supply women with male prostitutes." But in the same way that andro-thanatica is not the answer to gyno- thanatica, male prostitution is not the solution to female prostitution. What feminists want is not a stable of male prostitutes, but the elimination of an ideology that teaches that women's sexuality is for-man and that there are two types of girls: good and bad. Indeed, what angers feminists most about some rationales for legalized prostitution is the suggestion that it is a good way to curb criminal rape: Supposedly if men are provided with readily accessible and reasonably priced prostitutes, they will not be tempted to rape other women.

That feminists find this rationale so irrational is not surprising. First, legalized prostitution would not necessarily serve as a rape deterrent. The behavior of the American military in Vietnam, where "officially-sanctioned" brothels for GIs were "incorporated into the base-camp recreation areas," indicates that the availability of sex for a small price is not always a deterrent to rape.[63] Many GIs adopted a both-and rather than an either-or approach to prostitution and rape. At the base they paid for Vietnamese women's sexual favors; on the front they simply took them for free. Second, and more significant, far from being a deterrent to rape, legalized prostitution may serve as a propaedeutic to rape. Comments Susan Brownmiller:

> My horror at the idea of legalized prostitution is not that it does not function as a rape deterrent, but that it institutionalizes the concept that it is a man's monetary right, if not his divine right, to gain access to the female body and that sex is a female service that should not be denied the civilized male. Perpetuation of the concept that the "powerful male impulse" must be satisfied with immediacy by a cooperative class of women, set apart and licensed for this purpose, is part and parcel of the mass psychology of rape.[64]

Finally, even if Brownmiller is wrong, even if prostitution and rape are not connected in the ways she thinks they are connected, there is something reprehensible about conceiving of prostitutes as a class of sacrificial victims. I, for one, do not like to think that somewhere a prostitute is offering up her body so that I and "my kind" can be spared from rape. I do not want to be privileged in any way that a prostitute is not, since she is no less or no more a person than I; and, therefore, I do not wish to cast my vote in favor of legalization if it promotes a state of affairs in which burdens are placed upon her that are not placed upon me.

Conclusion

When the ideological objections against legalization are coupled with the pragmatic arguments for laissez-faire decriminalization, the latter policy prevails for feminist as well as nonfeminist reasons. By decriminalizing prostitution, we do not add unnecessary burdens to those who would not be prostitutes if more attractive life-styles were available to them. And we remove unnecessary burdens from those who would still choose to be prostitutes even if other, equally attractive life-styles were available to them. But this is all we do, and it may not be enough.

It may not be enough in one sense because many women become prostitutes at an extremely young age, at a time when their knowledge is limited, and when they are especially vulnerable to coercion. Here the portrait of the runaway teenager looms large. Each year 600,000 to 1,000,000 young girls and boys, aged nine to seventeen, run away from home and a sizeable percentage of them become prostitutes. In New York City alone there are about 20,000 youngsters under sixteen fending for themselves on the streets, and girls as young as nine years old provide easy prey for pimps.[65] Decriminalization will not help these girls achieve autonomy unless it is accompanied by extralegal remedies in the form of needed social services and by laws that prohibit the sexual exploitation of minors. The former remedies will increase the adolescent's general ability to understand both the nature and consequences of prostitution and its alternatives. The latter laws will free her from the individual coercion pimps and others exert on her—a coercion that ranges from the enticement of being the best-paid and most-pampered pony in the pimp's stable to threats of beatings and worse.

Of course, this makes it sound as if young girls who enter prostitution, appraised of its nature and consequences and without any sign of individual coercion, always do so voluntarily. This may not be the case, however. In addition to *individual coercion,* the phenomenon of *institutional coercion* often plays a role in lessening the adolescent's ability to choose voluntarily the life of a prostitute. Institutional coercion is the type of pressure that flows from the structures of capitalism and patriarchy; and laissez-faire decriminalization leaves these structures untouched. Therefore, unless poor women, are given opportunities for education and employment, they will not be able to withstand the institutional pressures of capitalism. Likewise, unless sexually abused adolescents are given emotional support and psychological help, they will remain convinced that they are tainted, and they will not be able to withstand the institutional pressures of patriarchy. In short, unless one has the concrete means to transcend the institutions that work to limit one's freedom, chances are that one will submit to their constraints.

But the situation is even more complex than this. So far we have considered the institutions of capitalism and patriarchy as separate phenomena, but if we consider them as an amalgam, as capitalist-patriarchy, we will come to understand why even the woman who chooses prostitution freely is not likely to remain free for long. Says Jeffrey Bloustein: "The relation between man and woman is at present characterized by great disparities of social, economic, and political power, and the pervasive powerlessness of women often subverts sexual relations into relations of dominance and submission, regardless of the wishes and choices of the particular persons involved."[66] This suggests that the prostitute boasts idly when she insists that because she has the "goods," the buyer is in her power. In point of fact, it is not at all certain that she is ever in charge, since the buyer is probably "purchasing" something other than her sexuality. Kate Millett observes: "It is not sex the prostitute is really made to sell: it is degradation. And the buyer, the john, is not buying sexuality, but power, power over another human being, the dizzy ambition of being lord of another's will for a stated period of time."[66] If my wife or lover won't satisfy me, I'll find someone who will—a woman who will do what I say because I pay her.

Of course, Millett may be overstating her case. If distinctions can be made between degrading and nondegrading pornography, then distinctions can be made between degrading and nondegrading acts of prostitution. These distinctions probably depend on what sort of fantasies the prostitute incarnates for her patron, and whether she and her patron have mutual respect and consideration for each other. In other words, if erotic pornography is a possibility, then perhaps erotic prostitution is a possibility. After all, if it is not wrong to pay money to see sexually explicit nondegrading material, then it is probably not wrong to pay money engage in the incarnation of such material.

But in the same way that we had to wonder whether it is possible to create erotic pornography in this society without transforming it, we have to wonder whether it is possible to engage in erotic acts of prostitution here and now. In other words, we have to take very seriously Catherine MacKinnon's charge that in this society what prostitutes sell is "the unilaterality that pornography advertises."[68] If the prostitute is, by her thoughts, words, and deeds, reinforcing a conception of woman according to which *being for man* is the whole of her sexual identity, then like the rest of womankind, she must ask herself how free her choice to participate in the oldest profession is. If the prostitute can honestly say not only that her life-style is sexually liberating for herself, but that she wishes a similar sexual liberation for her daughter, then that nearly settles matters. But I doubt that any prostitute wishes to reproduce the current institution of prostitution for future generations of women: Like her nonprostitute sisters, who suffer from other, but equally confusing, sexual unfreedoms, she wishes a better life for her daughter, one in which sexual relations between persons, but especially between men and women, will be guided not by some subject-object dichotomy, but by a vision of multiplicity liberating enough to allow each person celebration of her or his own unique sexual identity.

Notes

1. Says Lars O. Ericsson in "Charges Against Prostitution: An Attempt at a Philosophical Assessment," *Ethics* 90 (April 1980):349:

No one denies that a majority of prostitutes are women, and no one denies that a majority of customers are men. But it is clear from the evidence that a large portion of the prostitutes, especially in metropolitan areas, are male homosexuals. There is also lesbian prostitution, though this is not (at least not yet) sufficiently widespread to be of any great social importance. And finally, there is male heterosexual prostitution, the prevalence of which is also rather limited. We may sum up by saying that, rather than constituting a dichotomy between the sexes, prostitution has the characteristic that a considerate portion of the prostitutes are men, and a small minority of the customers are women.

2. Simone de Beauvoir, *The Second Sex* (New York: Vintage Books, 1974), p. 618.

3. Ibid., pp. 618–19.

4. Miriam F. Hirsch, *Women and Violence* (New York: Van Nostrand Reinhold, 1981), p. 66.

5. Dorrie Klein, "Violence Against Women: Some Considerations Regarding Its Causes and Its Elimination," *Crime and Delinquency* 27 (January 1981):64–80.

6. Lord Patrick Devlin, *The Enforcement of Morals* (New York: Oxford University Press, 1965), p. 11.

7. Eugene V. Rostow, "The Enforcement of Morals," *Cambridge Law Journal* 174 (November 1960):197.

8. Devlin, *The Enforcement of Morals*, pp. 22–23.

9. David A. J. Richards, Commmercial Sex and the Rights of the Person: A Moral Argument for the Decriminalization of Prostitution," *University of Pennsylvania Law Review* 127 (May 1979):1233.

10. For a full explication of these pseudoreasons, see Ronald Dworkin, *Taking Rights Seriously* (Cambridge, Mass.: Harvard University Press, 1977), pp. 249–250.

11. Richards, "Commercial Sex and the Rights of the Person," p. 1238.

12. One could imagine, for example, a patron who always asks for the same prostitute. Over a long period of time this relationship could easily assume many of the features of romantic love.

13. Richards, "Commercial Sex and the Rights of the Person," pp. 1240–44.

14. Ibid., pp. 1250–55.

15. Ibid., p. 1254.

16. Ibid., p. 1256.

17. Ibid., pp. 1257–59.

18. Ibid., p. 1259.

19. One is reminded of Nietzsche's complaints here.

20. Supposedly, red-blooded American boys get their women for free.

21. President's Commission on Law Enforcement and Administration of Justice, *The Challenge of Crime in a Free Society: A Report* (Washington, D.C.: U.S. Government Printing Office, 1967), p. 189.

22. It is significant that standard, nonfeminist arguments that invoke the harm principle do not consider the harm done to wives by unfaithful husbands who patronize prostitutes. But unless one wishes to argue that adultery should, once again, be restricted by law, then it is wise not to base one's argument for the legal restriction of prostitution on the grounds that it facilitates adultery.

23. M. Anne Jennings, "The Victim as Criminal: A Consideration of California's Prostitution Law," *California Law Review* 64 (July 1976):1248.

24. John Stuart Mill, *On Liberty* (New York: Liberal Arts Press, 1956), p. 117.

25. Joel Feinberg, *Social Philosophy* (Englewood Cliffs, N. J.: Prentice-Hall, 1973), p. 47.

26. Ibid., p. 48.

27. Joel Feinberg, *Rights, Justice and the Bounds of Liberty: Essays in Social Philosophy* (Princeton, N.J.: Princeton University Press, 1980), p. 88.

28. Ibid., p. 89.

29. Richards, "Commercial Sex and the Rights of the Person," p. 1282.

30. Charles Winick and Paul M. Kinsie, *The Lively Commerce* (New York: Quadrangle Books, 1971), p. 3.

31. Richards, "Commercial Sex and the Rights of the Person," p. 1285.

32. It is important to keep in mind that at least some feminists accept the idea of, if not "happy," then "colorful" hookers.

33. Richards, "Commercial Sex and the Rights of the Person," p. 1212.

34. David J. Pivar, *Purity Crusade: Sexual Morality and Social Control, 1868–1900* (Westport, Conn.: Greenwood Press, 1973), pp. 51–52.

35. Judith R. Walkowitz, *Prostitution and Victorian Society: Women, Class and the State* (Cambridge: Cambridge University Press, 1980).

36. Marina Warner, "The Chastity Lobby," *Times Literary Supplement,* (July 14, 1978, p. 793.

37. Laura Lederer, "Then and Now: An Interview with a Former Pornography Model," in *Take Back the Night,* Laura Lederer, ed.(New York: William Morrow, 1980), p. 69.

38. Voice "J" in Kate Millett, "A Quartet for Female Voices," in *Women in Sexist Society,* Vivian Gornick and Barbara K. Moran, eds. (New York: Basic Books, 1971), p. 69.

39. Ericsson, "Charges Against Prostitution," p. 344.

40. Karl Marx, *Economic and Philosophical Manuscripts of 1844,* translated by M. Mulligan (New York: International Publishers, 1964), p. 133 n.

41. Ericsson, "Charges Against Prostitution," p. 345.

42. Ruth Sidel, *Women and Child Care in China* (New York: Hill & Wang, 1972), pp. 50–51.

43. Leo Kanowitz, *Women and the Law* (Albuquerque: University of New Mexico Press, 1969), pp. 17–18.

44. Juliet Mitchell, *Women's Estate* (New York: Pantheon Books, 1971), pp. 144–51.

45. Ericsson, "Charges Against Prostitution," p. 347.

46. Martha L. Stein, *Lovers, Friends, Slaves: The Nine Male Sexual Types: Their Psycho-Sexual Transactions with Call Girls* (New York: Berkley, 1974), pp. 313–14.

47. Ibid., p. 52.

48. Jennifer James and Jane Myerding, "Early Sexual Experiences and Prostitution," *American Journal of Psychiatry* 134 (December 1977):1383.

49. Ibid.

50. Lee Flourney, an assistant district attorney with the Berkshire County Office, Pittsfield, Massachusetts, recounted this case to me. The name of the defendant and some details of the case were altered.

51. Will Durant, *The Life of Greece* (New York: Simon & Schuster, 1939).

52. Sarah B. Pomeroy, *Goddesses, Whores, Wives, and Slaves* (New York: Schocken, 1975), p. 92.

53. Simone de Beauvoir, *The Second Sex* (New York: Vintage Books, l974), p. 632.

54. Voice "J" in Millett, "A Quartet for Female Voices," p. 69.

55. Jennings, "The Victim as Criminal," p. 1278.

56. M. Shiels et al., "Flatfoot Floozies," *Newsweek,* June 28, 1976, pp. 27–28.

57. Charles Rosenbleet and Barbara J. Puriente, "The Prostitution of the Criminal Law," *American Criminal Law Review* 11 (Winter 1973):373.

58. Jennings, The Victim as Criminal, p. 1278.

59. Judith R. Walkowitz, "The Politics of Prostitution," *Signs : Journal of Women in Culture and Society* 6, no. 1 (Autumn 1980): 128.

60. Ibid.

61. Richards, "Commercial Sex and the Rights of the Person," p. 1284, n. 440.

62. Ibid., p. 1281.

63. Susan Brownmiller, *Against Our Will: Men, Women and Rape* (New York: Bantam, 1976), p. 440.

64. Ibid.

65. "Youth for Sale on the Streets," *Time,* November 28, 1977, p. 23.

66. In an unpublished paper by Jeffrey Bloustein, Department of Philosophy, Barnard College, New York City.

67. Millett, "A Quartet for Female Voices," p. 42.

68. Catherine MacKinnon, "Feminism, Marxism, Method, and the State," *Signs: Journal of Women in Culture and Society* 7, no. 3 (Spring 1982):532.

CHAPTER 3

SEXUAL HARASSMENT

A March 1980 article in *Newsweek* begins:

> It may be as subtle as a leer and a series of off-color jokes, or as direct as grabbing a woman's breast. It can be found in typing pools and factories, Army barracks and legislature suites, city rooms and college lecture halls. It is fundamentally a man's problem, an exercise of power almost analogous to rape, for which women pay with their jobs, and sometimes their health. It's as traditional as underpaying women—and now appears to be just as illegal. Sexual harassment, the boss's dirty little fringe benefit, has been dragged out of the closet.[1]

Indeed, sexual harassment has been brought out into the open and, unlike pornography and prostitution which have been perceived as feminist issues, sexual harassment has been labeled a woman's issue: an issue that can directly affect any women in this country. It is surely odd to distinguish between feminist and women's issues, as if the two were mutually exclusive.

But this is the way the public tends to think.[2] Nonetheless, had it not been for feminists, the problem of sexual harassment would never have been named, let alone confronted.

Before the 1970s women largely accepted as an unpleasant fact of life what some of them called the "little rapes." With the emergence of consciousness-raising groups, many women (especially working women and students) began to feel that they need not and should not have to submit to these nagging violations of their persons. Speaking to women, Andrea Medea and Kathleen Thompson observed:

> If you are subjected . . . to this kind of violation every day, a gradual erosion begins—an erosion of your self-respect and privacy. You lose a little when you are shaken out of your daydreams by the whistles and comments of the construction workers you have to pass. You lose a little when a junior executive looks down your blouse or gives you a familiar pat at work. You lose a little to the obnoxious drunk at the next table, to that man on the subway, to the guys in the drive-in.[3]

As a result of people realizing that such abuses are common, the problem of sexual harassment was named in 1975. No sooner was the problem named than its seriousness as well as pervasiveness became apparent. For example, a 1976 issue of *Redbook* (by no means a feminist publication) reported that out of a sample of 9,000 readers, 88 percent had experienced some form of sexual harassment, and 92 percent considered the problem of sexual harassment serious.[4] Most women find that their job or academic performance degenerates as they are forced to take time and energy away from work or school to deal with sexual harassers. Indeed, fending off offensive sexual advances, especially if they are sustained over several weeks, months, or years, causes women tension, anxiety, frustration, and above all anger. Unfortunately, many women turn this anger not against their harassers, but against themselves. Gradually, they transform their initial feelings of righteous indignation into feelings of shame or guilt. Shame is experienced when a woman feels that she has not lived up to a self-imposed ideal image of herself as a person who can control men's reactions to her body. In contrast, guilt is experienced when a woman feels that she has not lived up to society's standards for female behavior, one of which instructs women to meet men's sexual wants and needs with grace, generosity, and good humor. Plagued by intense feelings of shame (failure) or guilt (transgression), an increasing number of women workers and students suffer from what has been termed "sexual harassment syndrome." Victims of this syndrome can experience psychological depression, if not also physical ailments, such as "stomachaches, headaches, nausea, involuntary muscular spasms, insomnia, hypertension, and other medical illnesses."[5]

Unfortunately, victims of sexual harassment syndrome are sometimes scoffed at. When five women students and a male assistant professor filed a class-action suit at Yale, contending that male faculty members had engaged in sexually offensive behavior, resulting in a multitude of harms, university officials responded in a defensive manner. As one spokesman for Yale said, "It's not a new thing, but it is also not a major problem." Another university official added, "There is a stronger argument that if women students aren't smart enough to outwit some obnoxious professor, they shouldn't be here in the first place. Like every other institution, Yale has its share of twisted souls."[6]

Given such varied reactions to sexual harassment and its deleterious consequences, it poses problems of definition analogous to those posed by pornography and prostitution. This chapter will discuss recent attempts to define sexual harassment and to distinguish it clearly from sexual attraction. Standard as well as preferred feminist legal responses to sexual harassment will be evaluated, noting that the former tend to invoke versions of both the offense principle and the harm principle, whereas the latter tend to invoke only the harm principle. Finally, the discussion will focus on when the appropriate response to an incident of sexual harassment is a legal remedy and when it is an extralegal remedy, arguing that the law is best invoked when the price one must pay for her sexual integrity is an education or occupational opportunity/position.

The Ubiquitous Phenomenon

Although definitions of sexual harassment are by no means uniform, many feminist antiharassers agree that sexual harassment involves four conditions: (1) an annoying or unwelcome sexual advance or imposition; (2) a negative response to this sexual advance/imposition; (3) the presence of intimidation or coercion when the sexual harasser holds more power than the person sexually harassed and, frequently, (4) the suggestion that institutionally inappropriate rewards or penalties will result from compliance or refusal to comply.

This preliminary definition, critics point out, leaves much to be desired. First, it fails to illuminate the connection between the sexual advance/imposition, the negative response, and the institutional consequences. For instance, how forceful must the response be? How serious must the consequences be? Second, the definition fails to make clear who this society's power-holders are. Must one be an employer or a professor in order to have power over a woman employee or a woman student? Or does the mere fact that a person is male give him an automatic power over a female's fate? Third, it fails to distinguish between the kind of coercion that consists of a threatened penalty and the kind that consists of a promised reward. Properly speaking, is not the latter form of coercion more aptly described as a pressure tactic or an incentive technique? Fourth, and most important, the definition fails to indicate which of the four conditions are necessary for sexual harassment and which are sufficient.

In response to these criticisms, but especially the last one, feminists have refined their definition of sexual harassment. As they see it, there are two types of sexual harassment: coercive and noncoercive. Coercive sexual harassment includes (1) sexual misconduct that offers a benefit or reward to the person to whom it is directed, as well as (2) sexual misconduct that threatens some harm to the person to whom it is directed. An example of the first instance would be offering someone a promotion only if she provides a sexual favor. An example of the second instance would be stating that one will assign a student a failing grade unless she performs a sexual favor. In contrast, noncoercive sexual harassment denotes sexual misconduct that merely annoys or offends the person to whom it is directed. Examples of noncoercive sexual misconduct are repeatedly using a lewd nickname ("Boobs") to refer to an attractive co-worker, or prowling around the women's dormitory after midnight. What coercive and noncoercive modes of sexual harassment have in common, of course, is that they are unsolicited, unwelcome, and generally unwanted by the women to whom they are directed.[7]

COERCIVE SEXUAL HARASSMENT

According to feminists, a coercive act is "one where the person coerced is made to feel compelled to do something he or she would not normally do."[8] This compulsion is accomplished by the coercer's "adversely changing the options available for the victim's choosing."[9] The paradigm case of coercion is, of course, the use of physical or psychological restraint, but *threats* of physical or psychological restraint/reprisal are also coercive to a lesser degree. Although it is difficult to determine whether a sexual harasser has in fact narrowed for the worse the options available for a woman's choosing, John Hughes and Larry May provide two tests to facilitate such determinations: would the woman have "freely chosen" to change her situation before the alleged threat was made for her situation after the broaching of the alleged threat; and, would the woman be made "worse off" than she otherwise would be by not complying with the offer?[10]

Relying on Hughes and May's twofold test, feminists maintain that sexual advances/impositions that threaten some harm to the person to whom they are directed are clearly coercive. "If you don't go to bed with me, Suzy, I'll fail you in this course." Assuming that Suzy has not been secretly longing to sleep with her professor or to flunk her course, she would not freely choose to change her situation to one in which the only way she can attain a passing grade is by sleeping with him. Therefore, because Suzy's professor has adversely altered her options, he has coerced her into a very tight corner; and since a coercive sexual advance is by definition an instance of sexual harassment, Suzy's professor is guilty of sexual harassment.

In contrast to sexual advances backed by threats, feminists admit that sexual advances backed by offers do not constitute clear cases of sexual harassment. Nonetheless, like sexual threats, sexual offers are coercive. It is just that the bitter pill of coercion is coated with a sugary promise: "If you go to bed with me, Suzy, I'll give you an 'A' in this course." According to critics, however, feminists confuse seduction with sexual harassment when they conflate sexual offers with sexual threats—when they insist that every time a man pressures a woman for a sexual favor by promising her a reward, he coerces her into saying an unwilling yes to his request. In this connection, Michael Bayles asks feminists to ponder the following hypothetical case:

> Assume there is a mediocre woman graduate student who would not receive an assistantship. Suppose the department chairman offers her one if she goes to bed with him, and she does so. In what sense has the graduate student acted against her will? She apparently preferred having the assistantship and sleeping with the chairman to not sleeping with the chairman

and not having the assistantship . . . the fact that choice has undesirable consequences does not make it against one's will. One may prefer having clean teeth without having to brush them; nonetheless, one is not acting against one's will when one brushes them.[11]

As Bayles sees it, the department chairman has not coerced the graduate student to sleep with him. Rather he has seduced her to sleep with him. Consequently, whatever the chairman is guilty of, it is not sexual harassment. Bayles's reasons for insisting that the graduate student has not been coerced are two. First, she would have freely chosen to move from the preoffer stage (no chance of an assistantship) to the postoffer stage (a chance of an assistantship). Second, her options after the sexual offer are not worse than before. If she refuses the sexual offer, she will not lose a chance for an assistantship because she was never in the running; and if she accepts the sexual offer, she will have not only a chance for an assistantship, but an assistantship. Despite the superficial plausibility of Bayles's analysis, feminists (once again following Hughes and May) insist that a deeper reading of the graduate student's dilemma indicates that she has in fact been coerced by her department chairman. In the first place, assuming the graduate student has not been dying to go to bed with her chairman, and that she is not a calculating mercenary who has been hoping for a sexual offer to bail her out of a dead-end career trajectory, it is not clear that she would have freely chosen to move from the preoffer stage to the postoffer stage. The best reason for her not wishing to move to the postoffer stage is that it places her in a "damned if you do, damned if you don't" predicament.

On the one hand, if the graduate student refuses to sleep with her chairman, she will of course *not* receive an undeserved assistantship. In addition, she will place herself at considerable risk. Perhaps the chairman is talking sweetly today only because he thinks the graduate student will be in his bed tomorrow. Should she disappoint him, he may turn against her. This is a real possibility, given the unpredictable character of sexual feelings and the history of reprisals against women who turn down sexual offers. On the other hand, if the graduate student agrees to sleep with the chairman—either because she wants an assistantship or because she fears angering him (a possibility that Bayles overlooks)—she increases her vulnerability to other professors as well as to the chairman. Other professors might imitate their chairman's behavior—after all, he got away with it—adding a degree of instability and potential for arbitrary treatment not only to this particular student's future, but to all female graduate students' futures. Once such considerations are factored in, feminists observe that the chairman has in fact boxed his graduate student into a corner from which she cannot emerge unscathed. Consequently, whatever else the chairman is guilty of (such as depriving a worthy candidate of an assistantship), he is also guilty of sexual harassment.[12]

NONCOERCIVE SEXUAL HARASSMENT

Clear cases of coercive sexual harassment affect a woman's options so adversely that she gives in to her harasser's threats or offers simply because her other options seem so much worse. Unlike the sexual seducer who showers a woman with gifts so that she will at long last *willingly* leap into his arms, the coercive sexual harasser waves his stick or carrot in front of a woman, not caring how *unwilling* she is when she jumps into his bed. Significantly, what distinguishes the noncoercive sexual harasser from both the sexual seducer and the coercive sexual harasser is that his primary aim is not to get a woman to perform sexually for him, but simply to annoy or offend her.

Although it is possible to argue that the ogler's, pincher's, or squeezer's sexual misconduct is coercive, it is difficult. Many women fear calling attention not only to the sexual misconduct of their employers and professors, who can cost them their jobs or academic standing, but also to the sexual misconduct of strangers—strangers who have no long-term economic or intellectual power over them, but who nonetheless have the short-term power of physical strength over them. For example, in a recent *New York Times* article, Victoria Balfour reported that although women are frequently sexually harassed at movie theaters, they very rarely complain to theater managers. One highly educated woman who had been afraid to report an incident of sexual harassment to the theater manager commented: "He might think that somehow I had done something that made the man want to bother me, that I had provoked him. To me, harassment has its implications, like rape."[13] Two other women silently endured a harasser for the duration of another film. Although their harasser's behavior was extremely offensive, they did not report the incident: "He was staring heavily, breathing heavily and making strange noises. We didn't move because we were afraid if we got somebody to deal with him, he'd be waiting outside afterward with a knife."[14] All three of these women kept silent because they feared provoking their harassers to some heinous deed.

To claim that these theatergoers were *coerced* into silence is, according to feminists, to accomplish some good at the risk of effecting considerable harm. On the one hand, the public ought to realize that, for women, being bothered at the movies, in the subways, and on the streets by youthful girl-watchers, middle-aged creeps, and dirty old men is a routine occurrence. On the other hand, women ought not to think of themselves as helpless victims who dare not confront their harassers for fear of retaliatory violence. Therefore, on balance, feminists are of the opinion that it is best to reserve the term *coercive* for cases of sexual harassment that involve specific threats or offers, especially if these threats or offers are made in the context of the workplace or academy. This is not to suggest, however, that feminists think that cases of noncoercive sexual harassment are always less serious than cases of coercive sexual harassment. No woman wants to be coerced into a man's bed; but neither does a woman want to be hounded by a man who takes delight in insulting, belittling, or demeaning her, and who may even find satisfaction in driving her to distraction. This being the case, feminists insist that the law attend to cases of unwanted *noncoercive* as well as unwanted *coercive* sexual harassment. But this is no light request to make of a law that, like some Freudians, is still wondering what women really want.

Standard Legal Responses

Although the law is better suited to deal with cases of coercive sexual harassment than with cases of noncoercive sexual harassment, it has attempted to provide remedies for both types of misconduct. Traditionally, the two major legal avenues open to victims of sexual harassment have been criminal proceedings and civil suits, which invoke tort law. The rationale behind the criminal-proceedings approach depends straightforwardly on the harm principle, whereas the rationale behind civil suits relies on a mixture of the harm and offense principles. The fact that these two rationales differ is not without consequence. The civil law (=tort law) tends to take sexual harassment even less seriously than the criminal law does.

CRIMINAL PROCEEDINGS: INVOKING THE HARM PRINCIPLE

Criminal proceedings are now, as in the past, less frequently employed than civil suits. This is not surprising given that the criminal sanction is appropriate only if the sexually harassed woman is a victim of rape, indecent assault, common assault, assault causing bodily harm, threats, intimidation, or solicitation. That is, unless a woman is *seriously* harmed by her harasser, a prosecutor is not likely to press criminal charges, and if she is seriously harmed, the prosecutor is not likely to charge her harasser with sexual harassment but with rape, indecent assault, and so on.

The prosecutor's course of action is prima facie rational. If a woman's "harasser" is in no way connected with her place of education or employment, it is confusing and trivializing to describe his rape of her as an extreme incident of sexual harassment. But if a woman is coerced to submit to sexual intercourse as a condition of successful employment or education, then her rape is technically best described as aggravated sexual harassment. If the prosecutor wishes to be precise about the whole affair, then he should work toward an aggravated sexual harassment conviction rather than a rape conviction. But be this as it may, a victim of sexual harassment who seeks the aegis of the criminal law is not likely to get very far. Should an adult working woman or an adult student complain of indecent assault, the police are not likely either to lay charges for her or to pursue her case absent of witnesses, other than herself, to the episode. Says one police officer:

> If a girl came to us and told us her boss had called her into the office, put his arm around her, and grabbed her breast, we would first investigate to see if there was some additional evidence. No judge would convict without further evidence. Our practice is that we will not deal with complaints of this kind without some corroborating evidence. It's just too easy for her employer, an upstanding man in the community, to testify that she had asked him for a raise, that he had turned her down, and that this false cry of assault was her ploy to get even.[15]

If a victim of sexual harassment encounters such a police officer, she may, in absence of his support, lay criminal charges herself. Should she pursue this course of action, however, the district attorney would probably not argue her case. She would be forced to hire a private prosecutor to do her arguing and "it is common knowledge that the judges who hear private prosecutors treat them with much less concern than they do police-laid charges."[16] Realizing this, victims of sexual harassment have tended to bypass the criminal sanction unless they are able to find other women who have been similarly harassed by the particular man involved. The sole victim of *even* extreme forms of sexual harassment is unlikely to be taken seriously. Oftentimes police officers and prosecutors are unable to recognize the special coercion, the extra harm, inherent in extreme forms of sexual harassment that occur in the workplace or the academy. They are apt to think that such cases are episodes of mutually agreeable sexual relations gone awry: "A guy and a gal are together—she's prepared to go along for a few months—after that she wants to cut it off and he doesn't."[17] In short, male members of the criminal justice system are quite reluctant to invoke the harm principle against sexual harassers because they remain unconvinced, on some level, that sexual harassment can indeed constitute a serious harm to a woman's physical or psychological integrity.

CIVIL TORTS: INVOKING THE HARM AND OFFENSE PRINCIPLES

Given the criminal law's limitations, victims of sexual harassment have turned instead to the civil law, which seems better suited to succor the individual woman who has been sexually harassed. Whereas criminal liability exists to exact a penalty from a wrongdoer in order to protect society as a whole, tort liability exists primarily to compensate the injured person by requiring the wrongdoer to pay for the damage he or she has done. Like criminal law, tort law designates that liability is progressively greater as the defendant's actions range from mere inadvertence, to negligence of likely consequences, to intentional invasion of another's rights under the mistaken notion that no harm is being committed, to instances where the motive is a "malevolent desire to do harm."[18] Because tort law is oriented to victim compensation in a way that the criminal law is not, and because guilty tort-feasors are punished less severely than guilty criminal offenders, in many more instances than the criminal law, tort law will take a strict liability approach, often requiring even the person who merely acted inadvertently or negligently to compensate the individual(s) harmed by his or her thoughtless or careless action(s). Likewise, tort law will, in many more instances than the criminal law, address what I have termed "offenses" (behavior that embarrasses, shames, disgusts, or annoys someone), sometimes requiring the merely offensive person to compensate his or her victim.

1. *Types of Torts:* While new torts are emerging all the time, there are several existing torts that may be particularly applicable to cases of sexual harassment: battery, assault, and the intentional infliction of mental or emotional disturbance.

a. *The Battery Tort:* Battery is defined as "an intentional and unpermitted contact, other than that permitted by social usage."[19] While contact must be intentional, intent to cause all the damages that resulted from the contact is not necessary to establish liability. In other words, a harasser may be guilty of battery simply because he intended to touch a woman without her consent, even though he meant her no harm or offense. So, for example, battery includes instances in which a compliment is intended. Absent her consent, it is tortious, for example, to kiss an "unappreciative woman" under the mistletoe. Because the battery tort considers contact with the body or anything already in contact with the body (such as clothing), it is a useful tort for victims to use against harassers who go beyond verbal abuse. Usually physical contact is not tortious unless it represents socially unacceptable behavior ("breast squeezing" or "fanny-pinching"). Nonetheless, in some cases, socially acceptable behavior ("cheek kissing" or "hand pressing") may be tortious if it is known by the harassers that the receiver of such contacts objects to and does not permit them.[20] In either event, the victim of battery may win her suit, especially since she need not prove—as the victim of rape has had to prove until recently—her lack of consent through some show of resistance.

b. *The Assault Tort:* Where physical contact has not occurred, the tort of assault may be actionable. Assault is "an intentional act, short of contact, which produces *apprehension* of a battery."[21] As Catherine MacKinnon notes, the tort of assault applies to the person placed in fear of an immediately harmful and minimally offensive "touching of the mind, if not of the body." Since the invasion is mental, the defendant must have intended at least to arouse psychic apprehension in his victim. Although the fear-producing event must consist of "more than words alone," without words the intentions of the harasser may remain equivocal.[22]

Because the lines between psychic and physical battery are easily crossed, battery and assault doctrines are frequently combined in practice. Catherine MacKinnon provides several examples of successful torts brought under this combined doctrine in the early 1900s. In an age of heightened sexual sensibilities, it was not unusual for cases to be brought forward such as the one in which "a railroad was found responsible for the embarrasssment and humiliation of a woman passenger caused when a drunken man, of whose boisterous conduct and inebriated condition the railroad was aware, fell down on top of her and kissed her on the cheek."[23] In another case, "a woman recovered damages for assault and battery against a man who squeezed her breast and laid his hand on her face."[24]

THE INTENTIONAL INFLICTION OF MENTAL OR EMOTIONAL DISTURBANCE TORT

Contemporary sexual mores make it difficult to take altogether seriously the cases MacKinnon describes in today's courts. Unlike her early twentieth-century counterpart, today's woman does not take umbrage at every peck on the cheek or laying on of hands. This does not mean, however, that today's woman either *does* or *should* take in stride every obnoxious ogle, every offensive touch, and every suggestive gesture. As in the past, unwanted or annoying sexual advances/impositions can affect a woman adversely. For this reason, the tort of intentional infliction, in words or acts, of mental or emotional disturbance is gaining currency. Although this tort may be the most difficult to use against sexual harassers, because it includes only those offenses that cause "purely emotional disturbance,[25] it is also the most promising in that it probably covers those forms of sexual harassment calculated to wear down a woman's resistance.

Consider, for example, the specific tort of intentional infliction of nervous shock. In order for this tort to apply, the sexual harasser must have either purposely, knowingly, or recklessly desired to cause alarm or fright in his victim. Moreover, his conduct must have been serious enough to cause nervous shock in a normal person (unless he was aware of his victim's peculiar susceptibility to emotional shock);[26] and the victim's nervous shock must have physical or psychopathological consequences. Given that sexual harassers often badger their victims systematically over a long period of time, some women do suffer from nervous shock, or sexual harassment syndrome. An example may clarify matters. Over an eight-month period, David Eccles had "persistently telephoned" Marcia Samms at all hours of the night or day, begging her to have sexual intercourse with him. Although Mrs. Samms repeatedly told Eccles to stop bothering her, he kept on soliciting her. Eventually, Mrs. Samms became so emotionally distressed that she brought suit against Eccles for three thousand dollars in damages. The Supreme Court of

Utah in *Samms* v. *Eccles* (1961) found that Mrs. Samms had grounds for suit (cause of action).[27] The court decision reads:

> We quite agree with the idea that under usual circumstances, the solicitation to sexual intercourse would not be actionable even though it may be offensive to the offeree. It seems to be a custom of longstanding and one which in all likelihood will continue. The assumption is usually indulged that most solicitations occur under such conditions as to fall within the well known phrase of Chief Judge Magruder that "there is no harm in asking." The Supreme Court of Kentucky has observed that an action will not lie in favor of a woman against a man who, without trespass or assault, makes such a request; and that the reverse is also true: that a man would have no right of action against a woman for such a solicitation. But the situation just described, where tolerance for the conduct referred to is indulged, is clearly distinguishable from the aggravated circumstances the plaintiff claims existed here.[28]

1. *Problems with the Tort Approach:* This case is important in that it offers recourse to women who are subjected to both aggravated and severely disturbing sexual harassment. Nonetheless, for at least three reasons the tort approach is problematic not only in this form, but in its battery and assault forms.

a. *The Issue of Consent:* At least in battery cases, the harasser may claim that the woman consented to his sexual advances. This objection is significant because the harasser is not liable for his actions if the woman agreed to submit to them. Unfortunately, it is no easy matter to determine if a woman consented to a sexual advance. For this reason, in cases of sexual harassment, as in cases of rape and woman-battering, the law has straddled between two approaches: One focuses on whether the sexual misconduct was clearly consented to; the other focuses on the consequences of the sexual misconduct without emphasizing issues of consent. Where the law has favored the consent strategy, it has adopted methods similar to those it uses in rape cases. That is, it has sought to establish consent (a mental state) by looking to the victim's resistance or lack thereof (a behavioral manifestation).

In some sense the victim who fails to resist the man who paws her does consent to his pawing. But given that women are still socialized to be "nice" to men, it will take a strong woman to say a loud "No, thank you" to a man who has more arms than an octopus has tentacles. Andrea Medea and Kathleen Thompson report that one woman went so far as to follow her eventual rapist into a dark alley because she feared "offending" him by implying that he might rape her. Rather than berating the woman for her naivete, Medea and Thompson ask their female readers to recall all those times and places in which they paid attention to a man for fear of hurting his feelings.[29]

Realizing that many women are currently unable to express forcefully their nonconsent to an unwanted sexual advance/imposition, the law has recently experimented with the so-called consequences approach. This approach assumes that it is easier to measure the effect that unwanted sexual propositions have on female victims than it is to determine whether a female victim's lack of overt resistance to them is a sign of her tacit consent to them. If Jane experiences depression, anxiety, frustration, and even nausea or vomiting as a result of being repeatedly manhandled by Dick, she has been sexually harassed whether or not she was able to communicate her nonconsent to Dick by telling him to "shove off" or by splashing a glass of ice water on his face.

The consequences approach is an *effective* way to handle sexual harassment cases. But critics wonder whether it is a *fair* way to handle such cases, since Dick, for example, may have sincerely believed that Jane was enjoying his pawings and pattings. Under such circumstances, it does not seem unambiguously just to penalize Dick, since much of Anglo-American law teaches that unless a man knowingly or recklessly harms someone, he is not to be sanctioned for the harm he effects, unless, of course, a standard of negligence is employed.[30] This being the case, even when the consequences approach is employed and the harassed woman does not have to prove her lack of consent, her case is strengthened where she has made her dissent quite clear through words and actions.

b. *The Issue of Hypersensitivity:* Where consent is not an issue, the harasser may claim that he had no reason to believe that the woman whom he touched or threatened to touch would be offended or frightened. That is , he had no reason to believe that his target was a hypersensitive individual. In such cases, the harasser will be liable only if his conduct would have been offensive to a person of ordinary sensibilities. So, for example, Dick is liable for the battery of Jane, whom he patted on the posterior, if, but only if, a person of ordinary sensibilities would have been offended by such physical contact. But since this person of ordinary sensibilities is generally termed "the ordinary *man*," problems could arise for the female victim of sexual harassment. As Catherine MacKinnon notes:

> Ordinary women probably find offensive sexual contact and proposals that ordinary men find trivial or sexual stimulating coming from women. Sex is peculiarly an area where a presumption of gender sameness, or judgments by men of women, are not illuminating as standards for equal treatment, since to remind a man of his sexuality is to build his sense of potency, while for a man to remind a woman of hers is often experienced as intrusive, denigrating, and depotentiating.[31]

To summarize, although a typical man in this culture may like it when a strange woman squeezes muscles, a typical woman will probably not like it when a strange man squeezes her breasts or buttocks. And there will be times when a man will not be able to understand, say, why a woman does not always (or usually) appreciate wolf whistles. Of course, these differences of perspective could be remedied by a supplemental ordinary *woman* test, but this would require the law to confront squarely its male-biases—a major review for which it may not be ready.

2. *The Issue of Harm:* Where neither consent nor hypersensitivity is an issue, the harasser may argue that his victim did not suffer the harm she claims to have suffered. Such a defense is likely to set off a battle between *his* medical experts and *her* medical experts, the former arguing that Jane is of sound body and mind, the latter insisting that Jane is the shell of her former self. Unless such battles can be avoided, it may not be worth the victim's time, energy, and reputation to sue her harasser.

Feminist Legal Responses: Antidiscrimination Law

Even if it can be shown that a woman has not consented to her harasser's sexual advances, that she is not a hypersensitive individual, and that she has indeed suffered harm as a result of her harasser's sexual misconduct, it is not clear that the tort approach best serves sexually harassed women's interests. Catherine MacKinnon notes that the "aura of the pedestal," more properly viewed as a "cage," distorts cases such as the one in which a judge preached, "every woman has the right to assume that a passenger car is not a brothel and that when she travels in it, she will meet nothing, see nothing, hear nothing, to wound her delicacy or insult her womanhood."[32] But to construe resistance to sexual harassment as a return to prudery is, according to feminists, to miss the point: Sexual harassment is not so much an issue of offensive behavior as an issue of abusive power.

But if sexual harassment is more an issue of power than an issue of offense, the tort approach, which emphasizes unseemly sexual conduct, must, in the estimation of feminists, be supplemented by a legal approach stressing that women often submit to unwanted sexual advances simply because their position in society is inferior relative to men. Not only are most men physically more powerful than most women, but it is men and not women who hold the balance of power in the political, economic, and social institutions that govern us all. Because antidiscrimination law is sensitive to these power dynamics, it can accomplish more for sexually harassed women than tort law. Whereas tort law views sexual harassment as an outrage to an individual woman's sensibilities and to a society's purported values, antidiscrimination law casts the same act either as one of *economic* coercion, in which the material survival of women in general is threatened, or as one of *intellectual* coercion, in which the spiritual survival of women in general is similarly jeopardized. If a woman wishes to argue that she has been sexually harassed not because she is vulnerable Sally Jones, but because she is a woman, a member of a gender that suffers from institutionalized inferiority and relative powerlessness, then the antidiscrimination approach obviously suits her purposes best.[33]

DISCRIMINATORY SEXUAL HARASSMENT: A HISTORICAL SURVEY

Despite the cogency of this line of reasoning, feminists were *initially* unable to convince the courts that sexual harassment could in fact constitute sex-based discrimination in the workplace and in the academy. The workplace decisions, resting on Title VII, which prohibits sex-based discrimination in employment, represent an upward struggle from the first case brought under it, *Corne* v. *Bausch and Lomb, Inc.*,[34] through several subsequent cases (*Miller* v. *Bank of America*[35] and *Tomkins* v. *Public Service Electric and Gas Co.*,[36] to the landmark case *Barnes* v. *Costle*).[37] To a greater or lesser extent all these cases reveal two attitudes the courts had to overcome on the way to recognizing discriminatory sexual harassment: (1) sexual attraction between a man and a woman is a personal matter in which the courts should not intervene; and (2) the practice of sexual harassment is so prevalent that if courts became involved they would be flooded with complaints, many of which might be false or trivial.

In *Corne* v. *Bausch and Lomb, Inc.*, two female clerical workers sued for a violation of their civil rights based on sex discrimination. As a result of the offensive and unwelcome sexual liberties their male supervisor had taken with them, these two women were forced to resign their positions. In dismissing their complaint, the court gave several reasons, the chief of which was that sexual harassment is a "personal proclivity, peculiarity, or mannerism," which employers can not be expected to extirpate in their employees.[38] Said the court, "The only sure way an employer could avoid such charges would be to have employees who were asexual."[39] Incidentally, the trial judge found unimaginable precisely what Margaret Mead has encouraged; namely, that society establish a sexual taboo in the workplace (and by parity of reasoning, in the academy.) Flatly stated, Mead's incest taboo asserts that "You don't make passes at or sleep with the people you work with."[40]

Although many feminists think Mead's asexual approach is too drastic, it gains strength in view of *Miller* v. *Bank of America*. In this case the court dismissed the complaint of a female bank worker who was fired when she refused to be "sexually cooperative" with her male supervisor. The court concluded that "The attraction of males to females and females to males is a natural sex phenomenon and it is probable that this attraction plays at least a subtle part in most personnel decisions. Such being the case, it would seem wise for the courts to refrain from delving into these matters."[41] This decision is particularly distressing not only because it conflates sexual attraction (a desirable social phenomenon) with sexual harassment (an undesirable social phenomenon), but because it suggests that unwanted manhandling is something that "big girls" must accept unless the company that employs their harassers *explicitly* endorses such hanky panky as a matter of policy (or some sort of fringe benefit for male employees).

That the courts have had trouble taking sexual harassment seriously as well as distinguishing between sexual attraction and sexual harassment is even more apparent in a case that followed *Miller*. In *Tomkins* v. *Public Service Electric and Gas Co.*, the court dismissed Tomkins's complaint, commenting that a sexually motivated assault that takes place in a "corporate corridor" is no more the concern of Title VII than a sexually motivated assault that takes place in a "back alley."[42] Title VII does not address the labyrinthine issue of sexual desires, and were the courts to encourage women to sue male co-workers and employees whose sexual attentions they had tired of, "an invitation to dinner could become an invitation to a federal lawsuit, if some harmonious relationship turned sour at a later time."[43] This court decision supposes that vindictive women would sue their male subordinates on trumped-up charges; similarly, hysterical or hypersensitive women would sue their male superordinates for the most trivial of reasons.

Fortunately, not all courts are as benighted as those that ruled in *Corne, Miller,* and *Tomkins*. In *Barnes* v. *Train (Costle)*, the Washington, D.C., District Court originally found against the plaintiff, a woman who was first denied promotion and then fired for having refused the sexual advances of her supervisor. Ironically, the woman's supervisor was none other than the director of the Environmental Protection Agency's Equal Employment Opportunities Division. The suit was initially rejected on the grounds that sexual harassment does not constitute sex discrimination. The court contended that the woman plaintiff had been denied promotion not because of her sex,[44] but because of her refusal to accede to the director's sexual demands. Conceding that the supervisor's behavior may have been inexcusable, the court nonetheless insisted that the behavior did not constitute an "arbitrary barrier to continued employment based on plaintiff's sex."[45] On appeal, the D.C. circuit court reversed, declaring that discrimination *was* involved, since the declined invitation had been issued only because the plaintiff was a woman. Said Judge Robinson for the court:

> But for her womanhood, from aught that appears, her participation in sexual activity would never have been solicited. To say, then, that she was victimized in her employment simply because she declined the invitation is to ignore the asserted fact that she was invited only because she was a woman subordinate to the inviter in the hierarchy of agency personnel. Put another way, she became the target of her superior's sexual desires because she was a woman, and was asked to bow to his demands as the price for holding her job.[46]

As a result of this decision, the courts now seem prepared to find sex based discrimination in the workplace.

In the same way that Title VII is an available remedy for sexually harassed working women, Title IX (1972 Education Amendments) is an available remedy for sexually harassed students. With the exception of the still-pending *Alexander* v. *Yale* case, in which five women students and a male assistant professor filed a class-action suit, contending that male faculty members had engaged in sexually offensive conversations and behavior resulting in a multitude of harms, the courts have not, as yet, handled Title IX cases.[47] However, should such cases be generated and processed, they will probably follow Title VII precedents. Such litigations explicitly promise to reveal the limits of antidiscrimination law as it has developed so far. In handling the grievances of working women and also of female students (who are sexually harassed more frequently by their fellow students than by their male professors), the courts will have to confront squarely the problem of peer-on-peer sexual harassment, a type of harassment that they have already encountered in *Continental Can Co.* v. *Minnesota*.[48] In this case, the Minnesota Supreme Court extended employer liability beyond the actions of supervisory personnel to those of co-workers. To the degree that *Continental Can Co.* sets a precedent for other jurisdictions, it requires the courts to rethink the three major conditions for discriminatory sexual harassment outlined in *Barnes.* There the court ruled that sex-based discrimination may be found only (1) when the victims of sexual harassment are of only one sex; (2) when the harasser is in a position to affect the terms or conditions of the victim's employment; and (3) when the harassment has a verifiably adverse impact on the victim (that is, it is not trivial).

DISCRIMINATORY SEXUAL HARASSMENT: A DOCTRINAL ANALYSIS

The first major condition for discriminatory sexual harassment is that it does not exist unless *only women* or *only men* are being harassed by a particular supervisor or professor. Arguably, neither Title VII nor Title IX prohibits a bisexual male supervisor/professor from sexually harassing his employees/students—provided that he harasses men as well as women.

1. *The Disparate Treatment Approach:* Regarding on Title VII, sexual harassment is discriminatory when a male supervisor, for example, sexually pursues a woman simply because she is a woman, pawing and patting her when there is nothing except her sexuality to separate her from similarly situated male employees. Likewise, it is discriminatory when a female supervisor sexually pursues a man simply because he is a man, coming on to him when there is nothing except his sexuality to separate him from similarly situated female employees. Much the same could be said about male homosexual or lesbian supervisors with the necessary adjustments.

The problem with the "disparate-treatment" approach is that only a fraction of women/men present in an employment situation is likely to be victimized by any particular incident of sexual harassment.[49] As a result, there will be a tendency to detach the incident from the group referent necessary to establish a case under Title VII. This is precisely what happened in the cases preceding *Barnes* v. *Costle*. In these cases the courts suggested that the female employees had been singled out for sexual attention not so much because they were members of the gender group women, but either because of their unique personal characteristics, such as red hair, or because of their sex-specific characteristics, such as large breasts. (A sex-specific characteristic is one that is not shared by both genders and which is possessed by only a subset of the gender class in question.) Since there is no sex discrimination unless a plaintiff can show that her personal injury contains a sufficient gender referent, a red headed, large-breasted, sexually harassed woman employee must be able to explain why her employer has not harassed similarly situated blond, flat-chested women, if all he was interested in was *a woman* and not a specific kind of woman with red hair and large breasts. Supposedly, if she cannot explain this, she does not have cause to invoke Title VII, although she may have grounds for an assault or battery tort action.[50]

But all this seems rather ludicrous. The sexually harassed red-haired or large-breasted woman does have an explanation for her employer's conduct: He would not be sexually harassing her were she a man or were she her employer's boss. In other words, when a woman invokes Title VII rather than slapping her harasser with an assault or battery suit, she wants to stress that had she not been a female employee in a subordinate position she would not have been sexually harassed.

Implicit in this argument is the suggestion that harassment is not an expression of sexual lust, but a show of power. Contrary to the *Tomkins* court, there is a difference, at least of degree, between an incident of sexual harassment that occurs in a "corporate corridor" and one that occurs in a "back alley." An employer has control over one's life in a way that a stranger does not. And when a company tolerates the sexual harassment of one female employee, it makes an implicit statement to all female employees, telling them that their merits are to be measured not in terms of their skills or job performance, but in terms of their sexual attractiveness and compliance. In short, when a heterosexual male employer harasses only one female employee, he not only treats her disparately but also affects her reference group disparately.

2. *The Disparate-Impact Approach:* According to the "disparate-impact" approach to discriminatory sexual harassment, the motivating impetus for harassment is indeed sexuality (whether male or female), which results in discrimination "only when conjoined with social traditions of male heterosexual predominance in academic and employment hierarchies."[51] Therefore,

this approach suggests that when an individual male employee is sexually harassed by a female employer, the discrimination he experiences is of the disparate-treatment rather than the disparate-impact variety. Given the way society is still structured, men are less likely than women to become fearful as a group when one of their number is sexually harassed by an employer of the opposite sex.

3. *Comparing the Disparate-Treatment and Disparate-Impact Approaches:* Regarding women, the disparate-impact approach to discriminatory sexual harassment seems more serviceable and promising than the disparate-treatment approach. Because the disparate-impact approach focuses on structural considerations (women's general position in society), it reminds the courts that women have yet to achieve parity with men either in the workplace or in the academy. In the past, the courts were either not served this reminder or they chose to ignore it. More recently, the courts have taken off their blinders. Increasingly, they are realizing that sexual harassment is a serious problem for many working and learning women. For example, the female worker may find herself at the mercy of her male supervisor, who, in an attempt to avoid liability and follow the letter of his company's official antiharassment policy, may not discharge or demote her, but may instead make working conditions so intolerable for her that she will "voluntarily" resign. Fortunately, the courts have come to see these "voluntary" resignations for what they are: "constructive discharges."

As a result of such realizations, the courts are taking a stronger line with respect to those institutions that fail to protect their employees from even the more subtle forms of adverse consequences attendant upon discriminatory sexual harassment: the assignment of undesirable work, close surveillance of performance, failure to enlist co-worker cooperation where necessary, unwillingness to provide adequate training, and failure to release recommendations for promotion. Despite a history of vacillation, the courts now seem prepared to hold employers liable for all acts of sexual harassment perpetrated by their employees, "regardless of whether the employer knew or should have known of their occurrence" except sexual harassment by co-workers.[52] In other words, if Tilly is sexually harassed by her foreman, then the foreman's employer is liable for his actions. It matters not that the employer did not know, or should not have been expected to know, what his foreman was doing. The employer is strictly liable. In contrast, if Tilly is harassed by her co-worker Joe, then the employer must have *actual* or constructive knowledge of Joe's misbehavior in order to be liable for it.

This last point is worth developing because most sexual harassment occurs between peers. There is no reason to view such sexual harassment as discriminatory, however offensive it may be, unless an employer (such as a corporation or a university) is understood to tolerate, endorse, or condone it. By failing to sanction the sexually-harassing conduct of its nonmanagerial and nonsupervisory employees, the employer lets them poison the work atmosphere. If the men on the assembly line are making passes at Rosy the Riveter and Betty the Bolter, and the employer, Cast Iron Works, does nothing to stop them, even though its managers and supervisors either know or should know what is going on, then Cast Iron Works is liable for their misbehavior where the other tests of liability under Title VII are met. Similarly, if the fraternity boys are sexually harassing members of the Feminist Alliance and the university does nothing to stop them, even though its deans and professors either know or should know what is going on, then the university is liable for their misbehavior when the other tests of liability under Title IX are met.

Extralegal Remedies

The current trend of the courts is to hold employers (corporations or universities) responsible for what goes on in the workplace or in the academy. In fact, Title IX already requires universities to adopt and publish grievance procedures providing for prompt and equitable resolution of student complaints of sexual harassment.[53] Because sexual harassment has been kept in the closets of colleges and universities for many years, most grievance procedures are not capable of providing prompt and equitable resolution of student complaints. In the past, students have complained about members of the faculty or school staff who have harassed them, and some of this harassment has been explicitly sexual; however, quite a bit of it has been so-called gender harassment.

Gender harassment is related to sexual harassment as genus is to species: Sexual harassment is a form of gender harassment. Catherine MacKinnon comments "Gender *is* a power division and sexuality is one sphere of its expression. One thing wrong with sexual harassment . . . is that it eroticizes women's subordination. It acts out and deepens the powerlessness of women as a gender, *as women*."[54] Whereas gender harassment is a relatively abstract way to remind women that their gender role is one of subordination, sexual harassment is an extremely concrete way to remind women that their subordination as a gender is intimately tied to their sexuality, in particular to their reproductive capacities and in general to their bodily contours.

Examples of verbal sexual harassment include those comments (in this case, written comments) to which female coal miners were subjected at the Shoemaker Mine in the late 1970s. Because women had never worked in the mine before, they were, from the moment they appeared on the scene, scrutinized by male eyes. Although the tension between the female and male coal miners was considerable, it was bearable until a rash of graffiti appeared on the mine walls. The graffiti focused on the women's physical characteristics. For example, one woman who had small breasts was called "inverted nipples," and another woman who supposedly had protruding lower vaginal lips was called the "low-lip express."[55] Subjected to such offensive social commentary on this and other occasions, the female miners found it increasingly difficult to maintain their sense of self-respect, and their personal and professional lives began to deteriorate.[56]

In contrast to these examples of verbal sexual harassment stand more sanitized but not necessarily less devastating examples of verbal gender harassment. Unlike instances of verbal sexual harassment that focus on women's bodies, these latter comments, illustrations, and jokes call attention to women's gender traits and roles. It is interesting that a gender harasser may describe female gender traits and roles either in negative terms (women are irrational, hysterical, defective) or in seemingly positive terms (women are nurturing, self-sacrificing, closer to nature). In both cases, however, the gender harasser will add credence to the *"kinder, kirche, kuche"* theory of womanhood, according to which women's biology and psychology naturally suit them for bearing and raising children, praying in church, and cooking.[57]

Although women are routinely subjected to gender harassment, society as a whole remains unconvinced that female students, for example, should take umbrage when their professors gender harass them. Nonetheless, given the educational mission of academic institutions, and the fact that women students may be more vulnerable to their professors' sexist remarks ("Women can't do math") than their professors' sexual innuendos ("It's a joy having your body—oops! your *person*—in this class, Miss Jones"), Title IX should, and probably does, cover cases of gender harassment.

In this connection, it is important to note that Title VII has already covered several gender-harassment cases. Recently, for example, a woman named Ms. Bay, who was employed by EFCS (Executive Financial Counselling Service) in Philadelphia, won a successful sex-discrimination suit against her boss, Gordon Campbell. Although Mr. Campbell never sexually harassed Ms. Bay by calling attention to or touching her body in any way, he did gender-harass her. On one occasion Mr. Campbell asked Ms. Bay whether her husband would "suffer for food and clean clothes while she was away on business trips." On other occasions he contacted clients, on his own initiative, to inquire whether they objected to dealing with a woman and to see what they thought of Ms. Bay, "although such evaluations had never been requested for a male member of the EFCS staff." On still another occasion he arranged a seminar training program for a male employee while providing no such training program for Ms. Bay, despite her requests and despite Mr. Campbell's private comments to his superiors that her seminar performance was weak and in need of improvement. After listening to the recounting of these and other incidents, the judge ruled that, although Ms.

Bay quit, she was really fired because "any reasonable person would have reacted to the situation at EFCS much as she did."[58]

Realizing that liability for sexual harassment and gender harassment belong to them as well as to authorities in the workplace, academic deans and other college personnel have tried to handle student harassment complaints informally. Their attempts have not always been successful. Not wanting to make mountains out of molehills, and arguing that young women frequently "imagine" things, some college officials have downplayed student reports of gender and sexual harassment. Even where they have taken such reports seriously and acted upon them, they have tended to keep them quiet in the name of discretion, preferring to let things "cool off" or "work themselves out." As a result of the students' rights movement, students have pressed their respective colleges and universities to handle such matters in a more formal and public manner. Students have also become much more concerned about student-on-student sexual harassment, which is a very pervasive fact of campus life. Understandably, deans and professors, who have by and large abandoned their *in loco parentis* roles, fear to invade their students' privacy. Realizing that students who come from diverse backgrounds will, as a matter of course, experience some difficulty in adjusting to one another's sexual mores, they fear making an issue out of what may be nothing more than normal social adjustment. And even when college officials discern a problem on campus, they resist setting up quasi- legal procedures to handle it. Predictably, deans and professors tend to argue that the way to handle sensitive problems such as sexual harassment is through educational forums rather than litigation.

Indeed, education is needed. Despite the breakdown of many sexual stereotypes, the macho ideal of the strong man lives on, as does the ideal of the vulnerable female. In large measure, this fact explains the growing incidence of "date-rape" on campuses. Crossed signals and mixed messages characterize many student sexual relations. Says one man:

> I get told "no," . . . and I keep going. I guess if someone said, "Look, sorry, I thought I wanted to, but I changed my mind, no way!" I'd listen, but if we're lying on the bed and she puts her little hands up in front of her chest and says, "Oh, please, no, I'm not sure about this," I ignore it. Nobody complains afterward."[59]

Women have to learn to say no, and men have to learn to take a *no* at face value. Moreover, women have to stop blaming themselves when men sexually harass them. This may be particularly difficult for a young woman to do. She may not have met enough different types of men to realize that it's not always something about her or her body that turns a man on, but something about his need to assert himself. Arguably, the more secure a man is about his masculinity, the less need he will have to harass women sexually or otherwise. Failing to understand this, a young woman may berate herself for her harasser's conduct. She may punish herself for being sexed by starving or neglecting her body. The epidemic of anorexia on many campuses is not unrelated to young women's fear of their own sexuality; and the unkempt appearance of some young women is often evidence of their attempt to kill the "temptress" in themselves.

Not surprisingly, educators want to help students escape these destructive prisons. But, as always, education is a long-term process. In the interim, college officials must set up and enforce internal grievance procedures to handle both faculty-on-student and student-on-student sexual harassment. Such quasi-legal remedies are not in opposition to a college's educational mission. On the contrary, they serve to remind the college community that it is susceptible to the same human foibles and power plays that characterize society in general.

Internal grievance procedures have been set up in many workplaces as well as at many academic institutions even though Title VII does not require employers to *maintain* grievance procedures. Since agreement has arisen in Title VII sexual harassment cases that there is no cause for judicial action *if* the employer takes prompt and remedial action upon acquiring knowledge of an incident, prudent employers have decided to set up mechanisms that can facilitate quick and corrective action. Unfortunately, these internal grievance procedures can be subverted. Company officials can convince all but the most determined of women that it is in her best interest to keep things quiet. One government official, who was interviewed by Constance Backhouse and Leah Cohen, opined that women should avoid both internal grievance procedures and complaints made directly to a personnel manager or management:

> The personnel director will most likely go to the sexual harasser and have a quiet little chat and a good laugh and express any number of the following statements:
>
> She brought it on herself.
> She can take care of herself.
> She was obviously willing.
> She is vindictive, as a result of a love affair gone sour.
> In fact, this is an isolated incident, not a serious problem.
> She is a troublemaker.[60]

This official went on to add that, if at all possible, the sexually harassed woman should either start looking for another job—"A woman is in real jeopardy if she can't get along in government. Who will hire you in private industry, if you are fired by the government?"—or if this is not a viable option, she should start looking for a "tough feminist lawyer" who will take the case as a "personal challenge."[61]

Conclusion

Sexual harassment is a phenomenon deeply rooted in the sexist assumptions that women can turn men "on" or "off" at will, and that sexual harassment is nothing more serious than old-fashioned flirtation. As such, it clearly must be approached on social and cultural as well as legal levels. However, because of its intangible or blurry-edged nature, sexual harassment often seems to be a problem with which the law, in its insistence on clear definitions and consistent guidelines, does not seem best suited to deal. The broad concept of institutional liability, which encourages the development of internal grievance procedures and internal education programs, may thus be the ideal way of confronting and remedying cases of sexual harassment. But the ideal is not always realized, and women—especially women workers and students —find themselves without effective remedies, short of quitting their jobs or leaving school. As Catherine MacKinnon has noted, the sexual subordination of women interacts with other forms of social power that men have over women. To be precise: "Economic power is to sexual harassment as physical force is to rape."[62] And regarding Title IX, intellectual power is to gender harassment on the campus as economic power is to gender or sexual harassment in the workplace as physical force is to rape anywhere. Rape and harassment are abuses of power as well as expressions of male sexuality. The power that makes rape or harassment effective derives from the superior position that the rapist or harasser holds by virtue of his social position.

As in the past, men remain powerful today. Their power is currently derived not so much from their brawn or their brains as from the fact that the major institutions of society—law, education, medicine, government, business, and science—are still largely controlled by them. Only when these institutions, for whatever reasons, begin to evolve in ways that allow women full access to them will the balance of power between men and women equalize. Fortunately, this institutional evolution is already in process.

In particular, the law is being tailored to fit women's as well as men's needs. Avenues of legal action against sexual harassers are both a powerful educational tool and an important means for women to assert and protect their rights to personal respect and self-determination, especially in the workplace and in the academy, while they wait for those rights to be accepted into the canon of cultural assumptions.

Faced with the possibility of legal consequences, men may be forced to reconsider their assumptions about women, employers may be forced to recognize their workers as workers rather than sexually exploitable conveniences, and institutes of higher education may be forced to extend their promise of an environment supportive rather than inhibitive of intellectual growth to female students. Once this happens, the incidences of gender harassment, especially its sexual forms, are likely to decrease. Where neither men nor women have superior power as a group, there is no need to use "sexuality" as a cruel weapon, reminding the powerless just how limited their options are.

Notes

1. A. Press et al., "Abusing Sex at the Office," *Newsweek,* March 10, 1980, p. 81.

2. It is not only the general public that thinks this way. Members of the academic community, for example, are contiually making it clear that Women's Studies is not to be confused with Feminist Studies.

3. Andrea Medea and Kathleen Thompson, *Against Rape* (New York: Farrar, Straus and Giroux, 1974), p. 50.

4. Constance Backhouse and Leah Cohen, *Sexual Harassment on the Job* (Englewood Cliffs, N. J.: Prentice-Hall, 1982), p. 34.

5. Ibid., pp. 38–39.

6. Ibid., pp. 39–40.

7. John C. Hughes and Larry May, "Sexual Harassment," *Social Theory and Practice* 6 (Fall 1980):251.

8. Ibid., p. 252.

9. Ibid.

10. Ibid.

11. Ibid., p. 249; cf. Michael Bayles, "Coercive Offers and Public Benefits," *The Personalist* 55 (Spring 1974): 142–43.

12. For a detailed version of this argument, see Hughes and May, "Sexual Harassment," pp. 255–56.

13. Victoria Balfour, "Harassment at Movies: Complaints Rare," *New York Times,* November 17, 1982, p. C24.

14. Ibid.

15. Backhouse and Cohen, *Sexual Harassment on the Job,* p. 101.

16. Ibid.

17. Ibid., p. 103.

18. Frank J. Till, *Sexual Harassment: A Report on the Sexual Harassment of Students* (Washington, D.C.: National Advisory Council on Women's Educational Programs, 1980), pt. II, p. 13.

19. Ibid.

20. Ibid., p. 14.

21. Ibid.

22. Catherine MacKinnon, *Sexual Harassment of Working Women* (New Haven, Conn.: Yale University Press, 1979), pp. 165–66.

23. Ibid., p. 166.

24. Ibid.

25. Ibid., p. 167.

26. This qualification is analogous to one in criminal law. If I want to scare someone, I may wear a Halloween mask. If my target dies of fright, I will not be held liable for manslaughter or murder unless I knew that my target was extremely sensitive to the mildest of pranks.

27. *Samms* v. *Eccles* (1961), in Wright I. Linden, *Canadian Tort Law,* 6th ed. (Toronto: Butterworths, 1975), pp. 52–54.

28. Ibid.

29. Medea and Thompson, *Against Rape,* p. 52.

30. In the latter event, Dick is liable for his sexual misconduct provided that a "reasonable man" would have known better than repeatedly to paw and pat Jane.

31. MacKinnon, *Sexual Harassment of Working Women,* p. 171.

32. Ibid., p. 172.

33. Ibid., p. 173.

34. 390 F. Supp. 161 (1975), U.S. Dist. Ct., D. Arizona.

35. 418 F. Supp. 233 (1976), U.S. Dist. Ct., N.D. California.

36. 422 F. Supp. 553 (1976), U.S. Dist. Ct., New Jersey.

37. 561 F. 2nd. 983 (1977), U.S. Ct. of Appeals, D.C. Circuit.

38. Backhouse and Cohen, *Sexual Harassment on the Job,* p. 119.

39. Ibid.

40. Margaret Mead, "A Proposal: We Need Taboos on Sex at Work," *Redbook,* April 1978, p. 31.

41. *Miller* v. *Bank of America,* 418 F. Supp. 233 (1976), U.S. Dist. Ct., N.D. California.

42. Backhouse and Cohen, Sexual Harassment on the Job, p. 121.

43. Ibid., p. 122.

44. Here the courts employ the term *sex* to refer to what most term *gender.*

45. *Barnes* v. *Train* (Costle), 13 FEP Cases 123, 124 (D.D.C. 1974).

46. *Barnes* v. *Costle,* 561 F. 2d at 992, n. 68 (D.C. Cir. 1977).

47. *Alexander et al.* v. *Yale University,* 459 F. Supp. 1 (D. Conn. 1977).

48. *Continental Can Co.* v. *Minnesota* (Minn. S.C. 1980).

49. Hughes and May, "Sexual Harassment," pp. 260–61.

50. Ibid., pp. 262–63.

51. Ibid., pp. 260–61.

52. Till, *Sexual Harassment,* pt. II, p. 9.

53. Phyllis Franklin et al., *Sexual and Gender Harassment in the Academy* (New York: The Modern Languages Association of Women, 1981), p. 5.

54. MacKinnon, *Sexual Harassment of Working Women,* pp. 220–21.

55. Raymond M. Lane, "A Man's World: An Update on Sexual Harassment," *The Village Voice,* December 16, 1981, p. 20.

56. As in the case with many women who are sexually harassed, these women coal miners suffered physical and psychological problems, such as loss of appetite, insomnia, and a feeling of guilt and self-loathing. See ibid.

57. Women as well as men may of course be guilty of gender, or even sexual, harassment of women. For example, some female opponents of the Equal Rights Amendment gender-harassed their feminist sisters, arguing that woman's role was to defer to man. And conceivably, a lesbian could sexually harass a female employee or student whom she found attractive, a particularly awkward and distressing situation in the event that the latter woman proves to be heterosexual. Likewise, women as well as men may also be guilty of gender and sexual harassment of men. A female English professor may repeatedly remind her male students that "Men are incapable of understanding poetry," or she may sexually harass one of her less able but more handsome male students. In practice, however, the harassment of men is not likely to be effective in a society such as ours, where men are socialized not to take abuse. Consequently, gender harassment will remain largely a woman's problem for some time, whether or not it manifests itself as sexual harassment.

58. *Philadelphia Inquirer,* September 9, 1982, p. 1A.

59. Karen Barrett, "Sex on a Saturday Night," *Ms.,* September 1982, p. 50.

60. Backhouse and Cohen, *Sexual Harassment on the Job,* p. 72.

61. Ibid.

62. MacKinnon, *Sexual Harassment of Working Women,* pp. 217–18.

CHAPTER 4
RAPE

In the last decade feminists have seized on the issue of rape as a symbol of woman's plight in sexist society. Not only have they aroused greater sympathy for victims of rape, they have also convincingly argued that until recently rape law has been more a means of protecting the inviolability of a man's property rights than the integrity of a woman's body. In her incisive article on rape, Susan Griffin quotes a 1952–53 *Yale Law Journal* tract on rape law:

> The consent standard in our society does more than protect a significant item of social currency for women; it fosters, and is in turn bolstered by, a masculine pride in the exclusive possession of a sexual object. The consent of a woman to sexual intercourse awards the man a privilege of bodily access, a personal "prize" whose value is enhanced by sole ownership. An additional reason for the man's condemnation of rape may be found in the threat of his status from a decrease in the value of his sexual possession which would result from forcible violation.[1]

According to this view, rape is an offense one male commits upon another; and if no father or husband or lover intercedes on her behalf, the victim of rape must go unavenged: a "defiled blossom." Should she seek to avenge herself, the rape victim must be prepared to face indignities at the hands of criminal justice personnel and, in some instances, the scorn of her family and friends. Under such unsupportive circumstances, it is difficult for a woman to maintain her sense of integrity—her certainty that she does the right thing in reporting and prosecuting a sexual assault. Society's twofold goal must be not only to secure the conviction of rapists, but to minimize the trauma of rape victims. Unless the relatively unsympathetic attitude of the entire criminal justice system toward rape victims is transformed, unless police officers, prosecutors and judges balance their concern for the rapist with an equal concern for his victim, the new rape laws will be feebly enforced and the rate of rape is not likely to diminish.

Contemporary legal thought on the subject of rape, like traditional legal thought, continues to be tainted by two misogynistic images of woman:

woman as temptress and woman as liar. As these interrelated images of woman begin to disappear, rape law is being reformed in three ways: The first sort of reform attempts to alter those rules of evidence which have in the past made it extremely difficult (if not altogether impossible) for the state to prosecute successfully cases of rape; the second reform redefines rape in terms of the perpetrator's conduct rather than the victim's consent; and the third redefines rape as a crime of violence, as either sexual assault or as assault pure and simple.

Thus, rape law is being reformed, guided in large part by the work of concerned feminists. Yet there are still myriad questions to be raised. Could it be that reforms are benefiting rape victims without justly punishing rape defendants, and are some of them simply putting rape victims on trial? Are the reforms promoting or impeding such feminist goals as equality between the sexes and the right of a woman to control her own body? This chapter will confront these and related questions.

Traditional and Contemporary Definitions

In English common law, rape was the "illicit carnal knowledge of a female by force and against her will."[2] According to this definition, rape has four necessary conditions: (1) it must be sex-specific (men rape women, women do not rape men); (2) it must include penetration of the vagina by the penis; (3) it must be extramarital (husbands cannot rape their wives); and (4) it must be forcible. Each of these conditions warrants separate treatment, and each has been challenged by feminists.

THE REQUIREMENT OF SEX-SPECIFICITY

Traditionally, only a female could be raped and only a male could be charged with rape. Eventually, however, a woman who assisted a male in raping another woman could also be charged with rape. According to current beliefs, this way of conceptualizing rape no longer meshes with reality. Not only can and do men rape other men (homosexual rape), women also can and do rape other women (lesbian rape); moreover, some social commentators insist that women can and do rape men. As a result of such criticism, several states have made rape a sex-neutral crime, incorporating into their statutes the *supposed* rhetoric of the sexual revolution—"anything he can do, she can do better." What represents progress in rape legislation for some feminists, however, may pose an ideological problem for other feminists, especially for radical feminists who wish to stress male sexual violence against women. That is, broadening the definition of rape to include not only homosexual and lesbian rape but also female on male rape deflates the notion that rape is a crime perpetrated by men against women, a crime through which *men* maintain women in a state of powerlessness or fear. This could, according to radical feminists, lead people to believe either that rape is no more a problem for women than it is for men or that rape is "no big thing." Although this is a possibility to consider, feminists outside the radical community observe that if rape is understood as a crime of the powerful against the less powerful or the powerless, then the public need not adopt such mistaken beliefs. Exceptions to the male on female rape rule will run in the direction of the rape of young boys by adult men rather than in the direction of the rape of men by women. So long as women remain relatively less powerful than men, where power is translated by psychological and social as well as physical terms, then female on male rape will be rare, and rape will continue to have a disparate impact on women. Therefore, it does no harm to female victims of rape and some good to male victims of rape when the state defines rape in sex-neutral terms; like the female victim of heterosexual rape, the male victim of homosexual rape sustains considerable physical and psychological harm.[3]

THE REQUIREMENT OF VAGINAL PENETRATION

The second condition for rape as traditionally defined is "carnal knowledge," that is, vaginal penetration, however slight, by a penis. According to standard feminist analysis, the law's customary preoccupation with penetration is a reflection of man's persistent desire to maintain exclusive control over woman's vagina so that his need to be "sole physical instrument governing impregnation, progeny and inheritance rights" is met.[4] The rapist either robs the father of his daughter's virginity before this valuable "commodity" reaches the matrimonial market, or he robs the husband of certitude with respect to the fatherhood of his progeny, in addition to damaging or stigmatizing his prized possession.

Although this way of analyzing rape seems archaic, vestiges of it persist today. For example, traditional responses to rape surfaced during the conflict between the Bengalis and the Pakistanis in the 1970s. Approximately 300,000 to 400,000 Bengali women were raped by Pakistani soldiers, and about 25,000 of these women became pregnant. Some Bengalis speculated that these rapes were so systematic and so pervasive that they had to be conscious Pakistani policy, a deliberate effort to create a new race or to dilute Bengali nationalism. In any event, no matter what the official Pakistani policy was, it had the effect of creating a class of female Bengali outcasts who, once raped by the Pakistanis, were no longer acceptable to Bengali men.[5] In this connection, recent American studies on mates and families of rape victims indicate that some male mates continue to express anger over the fact that the victim has "allowed herself" to become "devalued" or "damaged merchandise." One boyfriend, for instance, wondered whether he would ever be able to escape the thought that his girlfriend was "tainted" by her experience. Another felt that his lover would bear a permanent stigma, "like a Scarlet R on her forehead." A husband described feeling physically disgusted when approaching his "unclean" wife sexually, following her rape.[6]

Comments such as these suggest that like their precedessors some contemporary men have difficulty overcoming emotional reactions to rape. Nevertheless, as traditional ideas about paternity, female virginity, and female chastity give way to contemporary interpretations, society is slowly changing the way it *intellectualizes* about rape. First, the issue of *paternity* is more easily resolvable today than in the past. There are blood tests for purported fathers, and the availability of "morning-after" pills and other abortifacients makes it possible for a woman to terminate a pregnancy if she is bothered by the question of the father's identity. Second, largely because there are these scientific ways to establish and even to prevent paternity (no child, no father), the importance of *female virginity* is declining. In addition, its value as a social virtue may be waning for the same reason it has waned in the past; namely, that men are fundamentally ambivalent about virginal brides:

> The male's hesitation between fear and desire, between the fear of being in the power of uncontrollable forces and the wish to win them over, is strikingly reflected in the myth of Virginity. Now feared by the male, now desired or even demanded, the virgin would seem to represent the most consummate form of the feminine mystery; she is therefore its most fascinating aspect. According to whether man feels himself overwhelmed by encircling forces or proudly believes himself capable of taking control of them, he declines or demands to have his wife delivered to him a virgin.[7]

In any event, whether today's men feel overwhelmed by the forces of female sexual liberation or whether they believe they can control them, they seem to care less about female virginity than they did a generation ago.[8] In fact, many men profess a distinct preference for women who are not virgins. Because intercourse with a sexually experienced woman is likely to be more pleasurable and less anxiety-producing than intercourse with a neophyte, many a man is willing to pay the price of not being able to boast that it was he, despite many obstacles, who finally laid claim to a virginal vagina.

Finally, and relatedly, contemporary society cares less about *female chastity*. Today, the woman who has an extramarital affair before, during, or after marriage is less likely either to be ostracized from the community or to be sactioned severely by it. Female chastity is not the value it was in the past eras for at least two reasons. First, men can keep tabs on their future progeny without buckling their wives into chastity belts or keeping them sequestered behind closed doors. Second, society is no longer convinced that the primary or only purpose of sexual intercourse is the reproduction of future generations. If nothing else, the combined pressure of the population explosion and the so-called sexual revolution has discredited this narrow, functionalist interpretation of human sexual intercourse. Increasingly, people are linking sex with pleasure rather than with procreation. But if society is no longer focusing on sex-for- procreation but instead on sex-for-pleasure, there is, according to feminist antirapists, no need for it to think of sex as something that happens when a man's penis penetrates a woman's vagina. Therefore, *all* jurisdictions should follow the lead of those states that have ruled that rape can be oral or anal as well as vaginal, and that penetration need not be by a penis, but can be accomplished by tongue, fingers, toes, or artificial instruments.[9]

THE REQUIREMENT OF EXTRAMARITAL INTERCOURSE

The traditional definition of rape stresses the qualifier "illicit." All sexual intercourse between a man and a woman is illicit unless the man and woman are married to each other. The notion of rape as illicit sexual activity has caused many women considerable anguish. If a woman who is not married to her rapist takes him to court, chances are that she will set into motion her own trial as well as his. That is, if he is proven innocent of rape, she will *ipso facto* be proven guilty of either fornication or adultery. Either he's a rapist or she's a fornicator/adulteress. The plight of the married woman is even more dramatic. Should she accuse her husband of rape, chances are that she will be laughed out of court, for what is forbidden outside of marriage is not only licit (permitted), but supposedly required in marriage. Comments one unhappily married woman:

> After we had been married nine months I no longer had any feeling for him, yet I felt that I couldn't refuse to have intercourse with him. He expected it, even though we were completely alienated by this time. I finally got to the point where there was no feeling in my body when we had relations, yet he insisted on his "marital" rights. This is a part of the marriage contract, that a wife must be ready to have sex on demand, no matter what her feelings are. Withholding it is grounds for divorce, yet the reverse is not true. The husband does not have to provide sex for his wife.[10]

The source of this unfortunate common law doctrine is Sir Matthew Hale who proclaimed (circa 1678) that "the husband cannot be guilty of rape committed by himself upon his lawful wife, for by their mutual matrimonial consent and contract the wife hath given up her self in this kind unto her husband which she cannot retract."[11] On the basis of this *single* statement, many Anglo-American courts adopted the so-called marital exception rule for forcible rape, according to which a husband cannot rape his wife for the same reason that he cannot burglarize his own house and land; namely, that a man cannot steal that to which he has a right.

Several policy considerations have been advanced in favor of the marital-exception rule. First, were this rule not adopted, wives would make false complaints against their husbands out of spite or in an attempt to obtain a better divorce or property settlement. Second, rape laws are designed to protect women from the grave physical, mental, and social dangers of sexual attacks by *malign* strangers; they are not designed to protect headachy wives from the discomfort of having to have sex with their basically *benign* husbands. Third, allowing women to charge their husbands with rape will prevent their reconciliation.[12]

According to feminists, not only are these policy considerations flimsy, but the notion upon which the marital-exception rule is founded—the notion of an unconditional intercourse contract—is bogus. Professors of contract law teach that a contract contains only those items to which two parties have agreed. Feminists point out that most women certainly do not believe when they marry that they are agreeing to sexual intercourse with their husbands on demand: "It is unreasonable to infer that a wife intends to make her body accessible to her husband whenever he wants her. By marrying she indicates that usually she will consent to intercourse, but she also probably believes that she can expressly decline the act at any given time."[13] Moreover, feminists continue, even if unilateral, unconditional consent to intercourse were implied in the marriage contract, the legal remedy for abridgement would not be self-enforcement by the offended party (the husband) against the breaching party (the wife).

Citizens are not allowed to enforce their contracts without legal intervention; and under prevailing contract law a husband could not obtain such intervention unless his wife's supposed intercourse contract was (1) explicitly stated, (2) enforced in a way not resulting in undue hardship, and (3) enforced in a strictly equitable and just manner. According to feminists, however, none of these three conditions is met. First, at no point in the marriage ceremony does a woman vow herself into sexual slavery, agreeing unconditionally to surrender her body to her husband without daring to ask the same irrational behavior of him. Second, were a woman to make such an explicit contract, its enforcement would constitute a real hardship to police officers, who would have to spend much time and energy supervising her and other recalcitrant wives as they undressed and begrudgingly submitted to their husbands. Third, were police officers asked to enforce such unpleasant sexual exchanges, chances are that they would go about their onerous duty in an inequitable or unjust manner. Fearing possible repercussions, police officers would probably shy away from the homes of the rich and powerful, concentrating their energies on the homes of the poor and vulnerable. Therefore, feminists conclude, even if unconditional intercourse contracts exist, they cannot be enforced; and an unenforceable contract is, for all practical purposes, null and void.[14]

Feminists also make short shrift of the policy reasons advanced in favor of the marital-exception rule. First, it is not in the best interest of a woman falsely to accuse her husband of rape, when the law already provides her with the ability to charge her husband with many other crimes (assault, battery, larceny, fraud), all of which are more easy to prove than rape.[15] Second, it is false to assume that all husbands are jolly good fellows who would never dream of hurting their wives. As the reports of battered wives indicate, a husband who would force his wife into sexual intercourse is not likely to be less dangerous than a stranger rapist. Third, "reconciliation after a forcible sexual attack by the husband cannot be regarded as a strong possibility," and wives who have no interest in opening deep wounds should be allowed to initiate rape charges against their husbands.[16] Largely as a result of these feminist challenges, states are beginning to question the cogency of the marital-exception rule, especially in cases where at least one spouse has filed for separate maintenance or divorce.[17] Like feminists, many legal authorities are increasingly convinced that what makes rape wrong is not that it takes place outside the marital chamber, but simply that it is a blatant instance of *nonconsensual* sexual intercourse.

THE REQUIREMENT OF NONCONSENT PROVEN THROUGH A SHOW OF RESISTANCE

Even though interspousal rapes are just as nonconsensual as extramarital rapes, society is reluctant to admit this. People want to believe that at least married couples respect each other's sensibilities, interests, and rights as sexual beings. In fact, people want to believe this about everyone, married or not. For this reason, the law has traditionally operated on the assumption that all sexual intercourse is consensual unless proven otherwise—preferably by a show of strenuous resistance on the alleged victim's part. This point is complex and merits some elaboration.

Traditional Anglo-American legal theory teaches that rape consists in the concurrence of a criminal act (the unconsented-to sexual intercourse) with a criminal intent (the intention or knowledge of having the intercourse without the consent of the victim). In other words, there is no rape unless the victim fails to consent to sexual intercourse *and* the perpetrator both knows and disregards this fact. Therefore, or so the argument goes, it is important for the victim to manifest her lack of interior consent by engaging in exterior acts of resistance (kicking, biting, screaming, protesting, pleading, crying), so that courts can determine whether it is the alleged victim who is telling the truth when she claims that she did not consent to sexual intercourse or whether it is instead her alleged rapist who is telling the truth when he claims that she did consent to sexual intercourse. After all, she failed to resist him "tooth and nail." Significantly, major discrepancies between the alleged victim's version of the truth and that of her alleged rapist routinely emerge in at least three types of cases: (1) in a few instances there will be criminal intent where there is no criminal act; (2) in more typical cases there will be no criminal intent where there is a criminal act; and (3) finally, there will be instances in which there may or may not be criminal intent, and in which there may or may not be a criminal act.[18]

The first type of situation is relatively rare, yet one can imagine a man determined to rape a woman who *wants* to have sexual intercourse with him. Despite the woman's show of readiness and willingness, the would-be rapist obdurately interprets her strong signals of acceptance as subtle signs of nonconsent and proceeds to "rape" her, or so he erroneously thinks. Should such a "rapist" turn himself in to the authorities, they will quickly release him upon hearing the "victim's" version of the episode.

The second type of situation (no criminal intent, but a criminal act) generally occurs when a "macho" man meets a woman who is selective about when, how, and with whom she has sexual intercourse. What El Macho may term the "art of seduction"—plying a woman with drugs and alcohol or wearing her down with coaxing and cajoling–she is likely to term "strong-arm tactics" aimed at weakening her resolve not to have sexual intercourse with him. When pressed by El Macho for sexual intercourse, this woman will clearly and distinctly say a simple "No, thank you," but El Macho will interpret her nay-saying as ladylike baiting or female coyness. Any resistance short of kicking, biting, or clawing is unlikely to dissuade El Macho, and even such behavior may be interpreted by him as a come-on. Worse yet, if El Macho goes ahead and foists himself upon his nay-saying, kicking, biting, and clawing victim, a court of law may agree with him that she did not resist his advances forcefully enough; and this because the perceptions of many judges and jurors are guided by the still-prevailing cultural assumption that it is the natural masculine role to proceed aggressively toward the stated goal, while the natural feminine role is first resistance and then submission.

Similar notions about male aggression and female submission are behind the third and most frequent set of contested rapes: those in which the criminality of both the intent and the act are in question. Susan Brownmiller provides a telling example:

> This was on an arranged date, my mother had arranged it with his aunt. He was an intern at NYU Med School and he asked me if I wanted to see where he lived, where the interns lived, before we had dinner. We got to his room and he threw me on the bed and raped me, just like that. Afterwards he got up as if nothing had happened. I thought to myself, I wonder what happens now. I kept thinking about my mother, she'd never believe it. I'll tell you what happened next. We went out to have dinner. We proceeded along with the date as if nothing had happened. I was in such a state of shock I just went along with the rest of the date.[19]

In such a case, if the man were to be honest with himself and others, he might see that he had crossed the line between consensual intercourse and forcible rape. And were the woman to be honest with herself and others, she might see that she is her own victim as well as the victim of the man who forced himself upon her. But because the woman, as well as the man, is unable to escape the snares of certain deeply ingrained sexist beliefs, they go out to dinner together—an event that can only cause skeptical courts to wonder whether the woman was merely exaggerating when she previously cried "Rape!"

Indeed, confusion over whether or not a man intended to rape a woman, and whether a woman consented to or resisted sexual intercourse, is clearly the primary reason for contemporary law's inability to modify the fourth condition of the traditional definition of rape. But according to feminists, other factors are inhibiting this needed modification, the most salient of which are certain misogynistic images that have affected the theory and practice of Anglo-American law. Because women are traditionally viewed as wily temptresses and incorrigible liars, skeptical police officers, prosecutors, and judges prefer it when the *alleged* rape victim resists her *alleged* rapist until she can resist him no more. To expect or demand this much in the way of resistance, however, may be to ask women for too much. Resistance is not always the best strategy for dealing with a rapist who may, on the one hand, flee in search of a more passive woman, but who may, on the other hand, turn his rape attempt into a savage assault and battery or even a homicide.[20] Therefore, feminists conclude, the law must exorcise from its corpus those misogynistic images that tempt it to put unfair burdens upon women in general and upon female victims of rape in particular.

The Effect of Misogynistic Images on Legal Theory and Practice

For centuries there were two systems of justice in England: one secular, the other ecclesiastical. Around the thirteenth century the two systems of justice began to intermingle in interesting ways. Prior to this time, the secular courts had been exclusively conduct- or harm-oriented. What mattered was that a person had been maimed or killed, and not that he or she who had effected the harm had done so intentionally or unintentionally, voluntarily or involuntarily. It is not surprising that the ecclesiastical courts viewed this behavioristic system of criminal justice unfavorably. What mattered to the priests who officiated in the courts was not so much that a person had been harmed, but that someone had done so purposely, knowingly, recklessly, or negligently. As Christianity took root in England, the influence of the ecclesiastical courts increased, and English law, from which American law is derived, experienced the following shifts: It progressed from a system of strict liability to a system of liability based on personal blameworthiness;

from a tendency "not to penetrate beyond the external visible fact, the *damnum corpore, corpari datum,*" to a mandatory inquiry "into the internal condition of the defendant, his culpability or innocence";[21] and from a means merely of crime prevention and punishment to a means of protecting and preserving individual rights.

This progressive development of Anglo-American criminal law is summarized in the maxim *Actus non facit reum, nisi mens sit rea*—the act alone does not amount to guilt, it must be accompanied by a guilty mind.[22] Unfortunately, the ecclesiastical courts' contributions to the secular courts were not all so glorious. Church law may have given Anglo Saxon law *mens rea,* but as feminists point out, it also infused it with the interrelated images of woman as temptress and as liar, two poisonous images that continue to pervade certain streams of Western thought.

THE IMAGE OF WOMAN AS LYING TEMPTRESS

According to many feminists, a malignant image of the male-female relationship and of the nature of woman was, beginning with Eve in the Garden of Eden myth, projected into Western religious thought. Woman is the temptress, the seductress who destroys man's innocence. Her body is the instrument of evil, and for this she must be punished. In a letter to his wife, Tertullian blatantly and unabashedly states:

> In pain shall you bring forth children, woman, and you shall turn to your husband and he shall rule over you. And do you not know that you are Eve? God's sentence hangs still over all your sex and his punishment weighs down upon you. You are the Devil's gateway; you are she who first violated the forbidden tree and broke the law of God.[23]

Compared to Augustine, however, Tertullian's vituperations are mild. According to the eminent Bishop of Hippo, the original Adam was unitary in person but compounded in nature, consisting of male spirit and female bodiliness. When Eve was taken from the side of Adam, she stood not only for the bodily side of Adam in particular, but for the bodily side of humankind in general. Since she is essentially only body, woman is a radically incomplete being—a half-person. This being the case, woman is constitutionally unsuited for any type of intellectual or spiritual endeavor, so much so that when blood is diverted from her womb to her brain she is rendered infertile.[24] Being body, woman has but one role: to serve as a vehicle for procreation; and it is through the pain of childbirth that she can ordinarily expect to find wholeness or salvation.[25]

Having shown woman her place, Augustine elaborates his teachings on human sexuality. In the original creation, he assures us, there would have been "virginal intercourse";[26] that is to say, bisexual but nonsensuous reproduction. Therefore, in this fallen world, those who are trying to redeem themselves should engage in sex with as little feeling as possible. It is a duty and no more. To take pleasure in sex is to give way to one's carnality and to the disorder of sin. Indeed, "nothing so casts down the manly mind from its heights as the fondling of woman and those bodily contacts which belong to the married state."[27] Although a man may love his wife's spiritual nature, he should despise all her bodily functions as wife and mother: "A good Christian is found toward one and the same woman, to love the creature of God whom he desires to be transformed and renewed, but to hate in her the corruptible and mortal conjugal connection, sexual intercourse and all that pertains to her as a wife."[28] Yet, Augustine opines, there is hope for woman. At the resurrection her body will be cleansed. So that she may be "suited to glory rather than to shame," woman will be resurrected minus those organs having to do with intercourse and childbearing.[29]

Augustine's misogynistic analysis of woman was echoed throughout the ages by many Church Fathers, most of whom claimed that because of her sexual being and reproductive function, woman was less rational and less spiritual than man; that is, less able to distinguish between truth and falsity and less able to discern between good and evil. If a woman wishes to be rational and spiritual—if she too wishes to be a person—then she must, they speculated, deny her femaleness, her sexuality, her life-giving powers, and remain a virgin: "Happy virgin! . . . . She does not weigh down sluggish limbs with an imprisoned embryo; she is not depressed and worn out by its awkward weight."[30] Some theologians went so far as to suggest that if a woman is to be saved she must become a man:

> Peter said: "Let Miraham go away from us, for women are not worthy of this life." Jesus said: "Lo, I will draw her, so that I will make her a man, so that she too may become a living spirit which is like you men; for every woman who makes herself a man will enter into the kingdom of heaven."[31]

Thus virginity became the paradigm for sanctity. And much of the Western world came to think that all sexuality, but especially female sexuality, was wicked and destructive; that had it not been for Eve's sexual charms, Adam would never have eaten of the forbidden fruit.

THE EFFECT OF THE LYING TEMPTRESS IMAGE ON RAPE LAW

1. *Woman as Liar:* Given such tales and teachings, it is no wonder that the image of woman as lying temptress has skewed rape law in directions that fail to serve the legitimate interests of rape victims. Feminists believe that the image of woman as liar largely explains why the rules of evidence governing rape have been and to some degree still are so stringent and irregular. Supposedly, great pains must be taken to determine whether an alleged victim of rape is a real victim of rape, because women are only too eager to lie about

what men have or have not done to them. This exaggerated fear of women's mendacity, especially when it comes to matters that bear on sexuality, is reflected in the words of John H. Wigmore, the leading expert on evidence:

> Modern psychiatrists have amply studied the behavior of errant young girls and women coming before the court in all sorts of cases. Their psychic complexes are multifarious, distorted partly by inherent defects, partly by diseased derangements, partly by bad social environment, partly by temporary psychological or emotional conditions. One form taken by these complexes is that of contriving false charges of sexual offenses by men. The unchaste (let us call it) mentality finds incidental but direct expression in the narration of imaginary sex incidents of which the narrator is the heroine or the victim. On the surface the narration is straightforward and convincing. The real victim, however, too often in such cases is the innocent man; for the respect and sympathy naturally felt by any tribunal for a wronged female helps to give easy credit to such a plausible tale.[32]

Despite this abnormal fear of the false complainant, feminists observe that all available evidence contradicts it. First, there are not a disproportionate number of false rape complaints. To be sure, some criminologists cite standard studies according to which anywhere from 15 to 20 percent of rapes are unfounded, that is, exposed as false by police questioning. Recent studies indicate, however, that when police *women* or trained rape investigators take rape reports, the unfounded rape has a tendency to drop to 2 or 3 percent, a rate that resembles that for all other violent crimes.[33] Second, the few complaints that are false are readily screened out before trial. Prosecutors are especially cautious, even overzealous, about rape complaints. Realizing how difficult it is to win a rape case, they rarely go to trial unless their case is airtight. Third, jury attitudes favor the defendant and not the victim. *Female* as well as male jurors are generally biased against the raped woman, for as Susan Brownmiller points out:

> The feeling persists that a virtuous woman either cannot get raped or does not get into situations that leave her open to assault. Thus the questions in the jury room become "Was she or wasn't she asking for it?" "If she had been a decent woman, wouldn't she have fought to the death to defend her treasure?" and "Is this bimbo worth the ruination of a man's career and reputation?"[34]

Finally, there is little reason to think that men are falsely convicted of rape more often than they are falsely convicted of any other crime. Those who imply that men are frequently falsely convicted of rape fail to back up their claim with compelling statistics. Wigmore, for example, relies on five case histories of mentally ill girls who made false sexual accusations against men, without advising his readers that none of these men was convicted of the sexual crimes falsely charged against them.[35] Another authority who claims men are often falsely convicted of rape cites an unfortunate 1931 case in which nine black men (the "Scottsboro Boys") were indeed falsely convicted of raping two white women.[36] In that case, however, the conviction seems to have stemmed not so much or only from the mendacity of the alleged victims as from the racial prejudices of the presiding judge and jury.[37]

2. *Woman as Temptress:* The image of woman as temptress also skews rape law in ways that disfavor women. Feminists believe that this image is behind the theory of "victim precipitated forcible rape."[38] According to this theory, whether or not a woman is aware of it, her body is continually speaking to men and especially to potential rapists. Says Professor Menachim Amir:

> In the sexual sphere, a man can interpret verbal and non-verbal behavior on the part of a woman in such a way as being contrary to the expectations of appropriate female behavior or, even as conflicting with the whole image of a woman's propriety. She will be placed, then, in the category of a sexually available female. Thus, wrongly or rightly, a woman's behavior, if passive, may be seen as worthy to suit action, and if active it may be taken as an actual promise of her access for one's sexual intentions. The offender then will react as seems appropriate toward such a woman.[39]

Despite its cautious wording, the effect of this theory is to make the victim partially if not entirely responsible for the rape having occurred, thereby lessening the responsibility of the rapist. By voluntarily entering into a dangerous situation, a woman supposedly precipitates her own rape. So, for example, if a woman has a drink or two with a man, her accusation of rape is weakened, "since by drinking she took a chance, made herself vulnerable, and also introduced an element of stimulation for the male."[40] Or if a woman allows a man to come to her apartment, or if she goes to his, she is either signaling a willingness to engage in sexual intercourse or indicating her readiness to assume the risk of rape.[41] Or if a woman allows a man to hug, kiss, or pet her, she is playing with fire, "posing as a possible 'bad' girl who in the end turns out to be a 'good' girl."[42] In any event, the woman is partly to blame for her rape—after all, she led the man on—thereby unleashing his sexual passions only to refuse his ultimate advances.

Although feminists concede that there may be situations in which a woman does indeed lead a man on, they point out that Amir and his disciples suggest that all a woman has to do to precipitate her own rape is to spend more than five minutes alone with a man, especially if that man is acquainted with her. Indeed, they continue, it is theories like Amir's that have affected the problematic way in which the criminal justice system classifies rapes. Until recently, police officers were trained to distinguish between good (un-precipitated) rapes and bad (precipitated) rapes. A good rape involves a clear lack of consent on the part of the victim: significant resistance, injuries to the victim, the presence of a weapon, breaking and entering, or an abduction off the street. The paradigm instance of a good rape is the so-called blitz, or stranger-on-stranger, rape. Here the victim is proceeding with her business as usual when, for no apparent reason, she is pounced upon by a rapist. He appears out of the blue, does his "thing," and disappears.[43] In contrast to a good rape, a bad rape is one in which the issue of consent is ambiguous. The paradigm instance of a bad rape is the so-called confidence, or acquaintance-on acquaintance, rape. In this sort of rape, the victim knows her assailant casually or intimately; in some instances she may even have had previous sexual relations with him.[44] Because criminal justice personnel tend to believe that women are predisposed to have sexual intercourse with acquaintances (date, neighbor, relative, spouse, friend, lover), they also tend to take all acquaintance-on-acquaintance rapes with a grain of salt.

Although feminists concede that stranger-on-stranger rapes are less ambiguous than acquaintance-on-acquaintance rapes, and although they admit that a woman may not always know whether she wants or does not want sex with an acquaintance, they insist that if a woman claims she has been raped, then her word must be taken seriously no matter what the circumstances of her rape are. It is a mistake either to trivialize or to scoff at acquaintance- on-acquaintance rapes. First, it is a mistake to trivialize such rapes because acquaintances, no less than strangers, are capable of raping women.In the typical confidence rape, the assailant gains access to his victim under false pretenses by using deceit, then betrayal, and often violence.[45] For example, an estranged husband comes to see his wife supposedly about a monetary matter, gains entry to her apartment, and proceeds not only to rape her, but to batter her. Since such rapes are frequently motivated by hatred and an urge to humiliate, they are sometimes psychologically, if not also physically, more hurtful than blitz rapes.[46] Second, it is a mistake to scoff at acquaintance-on-acquaintance rapes because such skepticism can have, among other effects, the effect of casting a chilling spell on women's sexual experimentation. On the one hand, today's woman may think that she has a right to initiate sexual activity; on the other hand, she may still be worried about being a temptress. When a sexual situation gets out of her control or suddenly assumes ugly, violent contours, she may see her assailant's determination to have sex with her as a punishment for her boldness, carelessness, or fantasies. In other words, by suggesting that acquaintance-on-acquaintance rapes are not *real* rapes, criminal justice personnel can contribute to many women's tendency to view themselves as bad girls who deserve whatever sexual abuse they get.

From what has been said so far, it is clear that both the image of woman as liar and the image of woman as temptress have skewed Anglo-American law in ways that disfavor the victim of rape. This is why feminists have fought to exorcise these misogynistic images from legal thought. As a result, rape laws are being reformed in three ways. Although feminists maintain that all these reforms have ameliorated the situation of rape victims, in their estimation none of them is without problems. In any event, each of the present reforms merits separate treatment, and together they suggest ways in which future rape law may be developed.

Recent Reforms in Rape Law

REFORM I: EVIDENTIARY RULES

The first reform in rape law has focused on any rule of evidence in which the source seems to be the image of woman as shameless liar. Among these rules are those governing corroboration requirements, cautionary instructions, and references to the victim's prior sexual history. Although these rules have been and are continuing to be modified as the image of the lying woman loses its hold over Anglo-American law, feminists are of the opinion that more progress needs to be made before only rapists and not also their victims are put on trial.

1. *Corroboration Rules:* If women are not the liars they have been made out to be, then no state should still *require* that rape charges be corroborated with some evidence other than the victim's testimony. Although only a handful of states continue to require corroboration in rape cases, until relatively recently many jurisdictions asked for some corroborative evidence, and a few jurisdictions insisted on independent corroborative proof for each element of the crime of rape (identification, penetration, and lack of consent)—if not in all cases then in cases such as when the victim is under a certain age, where a late complaint is made, or where the victim's story is not likely.[47] In order to take a case to trial in some states, the prosecution had to produce evidence such as an eyewitness to some phase of the rape, evidence of the defendant's opportunity to commit the crime, or the victim's verifiable recollection of the identifying details of the defendant's possessions.

Similarly, in order to prove penetration, the prosecution had to provide evidence such as vaginal tears, sperm, or pregnancy. Finally, in order to prove lack of consent, it had to produce evidence such as body bruises, a weapon, torn clothing, victim hysteria, or victim flight.

Because it was nearly impossible to obtain independent corroborative proof of each element of the crime of rape, and because, other than perjury, rape was the only crime in which corroboration of the victim's testimony was required to go to trial, feminists petitioned jurisdictions with stringent corroboration rules to abandon them. They argued that the major reason behind these rules seemed to be an excessive fear of mendacious females, and that, when strictly enforced, stringent corroboration rules made it nearly impossible to convict a rapist. (For example, in New York 2,415 rape complaints yielded 1,085 arrests, 100 grand-jury hearings, 34 indictments, and 18 convictions.) Persuaded by these arguments, most states either abandoned all corroboration requirements or modified them significantly.[48]

Of course, it is one thing to eliminate corroboration rules as a *sine qua non* for taking a rape case to trial and quite another to insist that corroboration is not at all necessary in a rape trial. Ideally, the truth or falsity of the victim's testimony will become apparent as the trial progresses. When a jury has only the word of the complainant against the defendant that a rape even occurred, the jury will experience considerable discomfort. That is, in a judicial system that systematically favors defendants, juries are going to have difficulty with uncorroborated rape cases. No matter how enlightened and favorably disposed to rape victims a jury is, it is going to hope that the victim of rape can corroborate her testimony, thereby shifting its judgment in her favor. This suggests that an unenlightened jury, unfavorably disposed to rape victims, will not change its bias in the direction of the defendant unless the complainant can produce some fairly dramatic evidence to confirm her rape. Although unenlightened juries are by no means rarities, feminists admit that their obtuseness cannot be neutralized without jeopardizing or violating the rights of defendants (by ruling, for example, that in rape cases the victim's version of the facts is gospel truth). Therefore, feminists conclude, until society as a whole overcomes its negative reactions to rape victims, rapists are likely to receive a "fairer" trial than perpetrators of other felonious crimes.

2. *Cautionary Instructions:* Not only have corroboration rules made it difficult for the prosecution to secure rape convictions, so, too, have cautionary instructions. The effect of these instructions, which continue to apply at the discretion of a judge in approximately thirteen states, is to advise the jury to take special care in evaluating a rape victim's testimony.[49] A standard version of this instruction reads:

> A charge such as that made against the defendant in this case, is one which is easily made and, once made, difficult to defend against, even if the person accused is innocent. Therefore, the law requires that you examine the testimony of the female person named in the information with caution.[50]

Unable to provide any real reasons for mistrusting female testimony more than male testimony, most states have banned the mandatory and even discretional reading of these instructions. After all, if there is no *factual* basis for the instruction, it serves only to encourage acquittals irrespective of the defendant's guilt; and it is anything but a court's role to give such encouragement. But even when apparently enlightened jurisdictions decide to eliminate cautionary instructions, they may do so half-heartedly. Spurred on by a number of writers, including Wigmore, who suggested that "No judge should ever let a sex-offense charge go to the jury unless the female com-

plainant's social history and mental makeup have been examined and testified to by a qualified physician"),[51] an ambivalent jurisdiction may discard
its cautionary instructions only to introduce something that strikes feminists
as more pernicious; namely, psychiatric examinations and even lie detector
tests for rape victims.

Although some jurisdictions have forbidden psychiatric examinations either on the grounds that they facilitate victim harassment by the defense[52]
or on the grounds that "it has not been demonstrated that the art of psychiatry has yet developed into a science so exact as to warrant such a basic
intrusion into the jury process,"[53] other jurisdictions (such as California) are
inclined toward psychiatric examinations, which, in their opinion, may constitute a minimum protection for a defendant charged with a sex offense,
particularly if the charge involves child molestation.[54] Although a survey of
states indicates that defense requests for psychiatric exams are "generally
denied," feminists are nonetheless concerned that these requests are being
made with "some frequency."[55]

3. *Prior Sexual History:* In the same way that corroboration requirements and
cautionary instructions have been used and still are used, although to a lesser
extent, to summon forth the specter of woman as liar, so too has the rape
victim's prior sexual history been used against her. Although approximately
twenty-two states have recently enacted laws that control to some extent the
admissibility of evidence of the rape victim's past sexual conduct,[56] feminists
observe that even in these jurisdictions a victim's past will at least obliquely
affect not only the issue of her consent to sexual intercourse but also her
credibility as a witness.

a. *Prior Sexual History and Consent:* Although feminists largely disagree with
the argument that a victim's prior sexual history helps to establish whether
she did or did not consent to sexual intercourse, its logic is straightforward:
A propensity to consent to sexual intercourse, established by prior acts,
indicates a likelihood that a woman will consent on any given occasion. This
propensity can be of two sorts, specific or general. The defense can point to
specific prior acts of the rape victim that suggest that she has a propensity to
consent to sexual intercourse under certain conditions. So, for example, if the
defense can show that on March 18, 1984, Sally did willingly prostitute
herself to patrons x, y, and z, then the defense can suggest that these past
indiscretions indicate that Sally probably engaged in consensual sexual intercourse with Sam, who claims that Sally screamed "Rape!" only after he
refused to pay her $100 for a rather disappointing "trick." Where the defense
is unable to produce a specific list of past indiscretions, it can instead show
that the alleged victim of rape has a *general* reputation in the community for
promiscuity. That is, the defense can simply argue that if Suzy likes to have
sex with all sorts of men (at least that's what the neighbors say), then it is

not likely that she would be adamant about not having sex on any particular occasion.

Feminists find both the specific and the general version of the above argument deficient. First, just because a woman sells her sexual services for a living does not mean that she is willing to accept any patron, no matter how kinky his sexual tastes are. Query M. D. Schwartz and T. P. Clear: "If a musician were forcibly kidnapped and made to play at a private party under threats of death, would it be a valid defense to a charge of kidnapping that the musician had previously accepted pay to entertain at a party?"[57] If such a defense would be overruled as invalid, then, ask feminists, why is it a valid defense to a charge of rape that the alleged victim, a prostitute, had previously accepted pay to engage in sexual intercourse? Second, just because a woman has a general reputation for being promiscuous does not mean that this reputation is deserved, or that it is an accurate indicator of a tendency to consent to sexual relations with anyone, anywhere, and at anytime. In the same way that there are distinctions to be made between the gourmand (the indiscriminate eater) and the gourmet (the discriminating eater), there are distinctions to be drawn between the sexually voracious woman (the indiscriminate "sexer") and the sexually promiscuous woman (the discriminating "sexer"). Although the promiscuous woman is just as focused on sex as the voracious woman, the former orders her sexual experiences in ways that the latter does not.

b. *Prior Sexual History and Credibility:* In the same way that some courts claim that a woman's past sexual history helps to establish present consent or nonconsent to an act of sexual intercourse, other courts insist that this same history helps to establish whether or not an alleged rape victim is a credible witness. Some courts still operate, either explicitly or implicitly, on the dubious assumption that an unchaste woman is more likely to lie than a chaste woman. Like the argument that preceded it, this argument has two versions, one specific and the other general. The *specific* form of the argument maintains that in contrast to chaste women, unchaste women are more prone to lie about their sexual conduct. If caught, for example, in the act of adultery or fornication, the unchaste woman is supposedly more likely than the chaste woman to cry "Rape!" hoping thereby to preserve a veneer of social respectability. The *general* form of the argument maintains that in contrast to chaste women, unchaste women are more prone to lie not only about their sexual conduct, but about anything and everything. In this connection, one Georgia court opined:

> [No] evil habitude of humanity so depraves the nature, so deadens the moral sense, and obliterates the distinctions between right and wrong, as common, licentious indulgence. Particularly is this true of women, the

citadel whose character is virtue; when that is lost, all is gone; her love of justice, sense of character, and regard for truth.[58]

In sum, unless a woman possesses the virtue of chastity, she can possess no other virtue.

It is no surprise that feminists find both the specific and the general version of the credibility argument deficient. First, today's unchaste woman is probably no more likely and perhaps less likely to deny consent to sexual intercourse than the chaste woman who may regret her sexual indiscretions. Since extramarital intercourse per se is no longer automatically classified as an immoral act, the unchaste woman is no longer automatically classified as a fallen person, tramp, or slut. On the contrary, in many circles the unchaste woman is admired for her freewheeling and swinging life-style. Therefore, an unchaste woman has more to lose by falsely accusing a man of rape than by truthfully admitting her act of fornication or adultery. Although society is not likely to sanction the latter behavior, it is sure to condemn the former. Second, there is no established empirical or logical link between being unchaste and being mendacious. Comments Noreen Connell: "The assumption that if the rape victim is unchaste she could not possibly be telling the truth is founded on the medieval logic that anyone who cannot walk across a bed of coals must indeed be a heretic."[59] If courts are nonetheless intuitively convinced that such a relationship exists, then the question of female chastity should logically be raised in all cases where a woman is a witness and not only in rape cases.

Because there are not strongly established empirical links between a woman's prior sexual history and some specific or general tendency on her part either to consent to sexual intercourse or to tell lies about her sexual exchanges, feminists have urged the courts to outlaw all questions about a rape victim's past sexual history. But it is not clear that such a ban is constitutional under the Sixth Amendment which gives defendants the right to cross-examine and confront the witnesses against them. Although defendants have never had the right to introduce evidence that is irrelevant or unnecessarily harmful to other people, they have always had the right to introduce evidence crucial to their defense. Arguably, there are situations where evidence about the alleged victim's previous sexual history would be *crucial* to the alleged rapist's defense. For example, suppose the prosecutor introduces evidence of semen in Jane's vagina to support the claim that Peter raped Jane. Defense counsel brings forth witnesses to establish that Jane had sexual intercourse with Paul one hour before the alleged rape occurred. This would explain the presence of the semen, but in a way that would exonerate Peter, who maintains that he is an innocent virgin.[60]

Although feminists do not wish to railroad the defendant in a case like this or in a case where the complainant has an axe to grind with the defendant, feminists nevertheless believe that exceptions to a no-prior-sexual-history rule, especially ones made in cases of acquaintance-on- acquaintance rapes, serve to bolster the position of those who think that rape is not really rape when it involves persons who have previously been sexual partners.[61] Several states have responded to this challenge by providing for closed or *in camera* hearings to determine whether evidence of the victim's prior sexual history is *crucial* for the defendant's defense.[62] Although feminists welcome this compromise, they are generally of the opinion that unless reforms in evidentiary rules are accompanied by other reforms, the court's attention will continue to focus on the rape victim rather than on the rapist.

REFORM II: THE CRIMINAL-CIRCUMSTANCES APPROACH

The second reform in rape law builds on the first. In an attempt to free rape victims from the court's scrutiny, some feminists have sought to focus the court's attention on those circumstances that characterize unambiguous rapes. Given certain circumstances, one can simply assume, indeed *conclude,* that a rape has occurred, that consent to sexual intercourse has not been given. Such circumstances include sexual intercourse accomplished by means of a weapon; sexual intercourse accomplished with a victim under a certain age or in a certain blood or authority relationship with the perpetrator; sexual intercourse accomplished with a victim who is unconscious or drugged; sexual intercourse accomplished during a kidnapping or burglary; and, more ambiguously, "sexual intercourse accomplished under circumstances reasonably calculated to coerce the victim into submission."[63] According to feminists who favor this reform, where any one or more of these circumstances are present, there is no need for courts to corroborate the elements of rape, to issue cautionary instructions to juries, or to inquire into the prior sexual history of victims. The circumstances speak for themselves as coercive, and any act of sexual intercourse performed under them is *per definiens* rape.

1. *Problems with Institutional Coercion:* Although feminists think that Reform II, like Reform I, is a step in the right direction, they are well aware of its limitations. First, it is an approach meant to accommodate cases of individual coercion and not cases of what radical[64] and also Marxist[65] feminists term institutional coercion. Insofar as rape is concerned, individual coercion involves a particular man's deliberate effort to pressure a particular woman into an act of sexual intercourse. Coercive efforts range from overt threats (as in when a man puts a knife to a woman's throat and says, "Pull up your dress and don't scream, or I'll kill you") to relatively less obvious means (as in when a man plies a woman with drugs or alcohol). Institutional coercion flows from the structure of economic and social relations between men and women in general—a type of structure that discourages women from assert-

ing themselves physically, emotionally, socially, or financially, and that encourages women to submit to men's demands:

> Women, constantly propositioned by men and even manhandled (the phrase is no accident), are trained to feel that they must be gentle and inoffensive in their rejections. This conditioning, which makes many women afraid or incapable of opposing men (the woman's marriage vow runs, significantly, "love, honor, and obey"), also reduces the verbal and physical forcefulness of their resistance, and it is thus easy for men to ignore or mistake their meaning, with disastrous consequences to the woman.[66]

Although virtually all feminists agree that many men think women are saying yes when in fact they are saying no, at least some feminists (especially liberal and existentialist feminists)[67] deny that the forces of institutional coercion make it impossible for individual men and women ever to get their signals straight. It is one thing to claim that patriarchal institutions narrow, limit, impede, constrain, and constrict women's choices as sexual beings and quite another to insist that patriarchal institutions *determine* women's choices as sexual beings. Likewise, it is one thing to claim that this society "*encourages* women to be perennial victims, men to be continual predators, and sexual relations to be fundamentally aggressive"[68] and quite another to insist that in this society all sexual intercourse is *per definiens* rape. Finally, it is one thing to claim that women's sexual wants and needs are shaped by their culture and quite another to insist that no individual woman can ever break the mold culture initially imposes upon her sexual wants and needs.

In this connection Judith Butler comments:

> If our desires and fantasies are informed by surrounding culture, does that mean that we are thoroughly subject to the political realities responsible for this "construction?" What sense can we make of sexual choice if our sexuality is itself a product of external forces? It feels to me that if we are all determined by the existing social and political order, then we are all in a sense the dominant culture's masochists. And I'm not sure I want to play that role.[69]

In other words, if the notion of institutional coercion is overemphasized, all real choice is impossible—including the choice of women to change the structures of society in ways that *discourage* women from being perennial victims, men from being continual predators, and sexual relations from being fundamentally coercive. Therefore, according to Butler and like-minded feminists, it is in the best interests of women to admit that the forces of institutional coercion are not as limiting as the forces of individual coercion. If this means that any list of criminal circumstances can include only types of individual coercion, in which individual men deliberately tamper with individual women's ability to give informed consent to sexual intercourse, then so be it. Any other alternative—for example, listing the institution of compulsory heterosexuality (see Chapter 3) as a circumstance conclusive of rape—not only jeopardizes the alleged rapist's chance for a fair trial but also deprives every man and woman of the self respect that comes from knowing that however limited and limiting one's environment is, one can always transcend it—if only partially and provisionally. Although this conclusion is not one that pleases radical and Marxist feminists, who generally maintain that institutions can be just as coercive if not more coercive than individuals, it is a conclusion that meshes well with the principles of Anglo-American law, informed as they are by a liberal ethos.

2. *Individual Coercion:* The second problem with the criminal circumstances approach has to do with the notion of individual coercion itself. Can it simply be assumed that if certain circumstances are present, then rape has been committed no matter what the alleged rapist or the alleged victim of rape says? Or do certain circumstances simply constitute a prima facie case for rape rebuttable by some appeal to consent? In connection with these queries, critics ask feminists who favor Reform II to consider a 1978 bill to reform Virginia's rape law. Among other things, this bill specifies that a person who uses a position of authority to accomplish sexual penetration/ contact is guilty of sexual assault (rape) in one degree or another. The bill defines "position of authority" as:

> Any relationship in which the actor appears to the victim to have a status which implies the right of the actor to expect or demand obedience, acquiescence or submission on the part of the victim. Authority or appearance of authority may be established by, but is not limited to, evidence of the relative ages, maturity, or occupations of the victim and actor; the blood or household relationship of the actor to the victim; or the actor's position of trust relative to the victim such as that involved in the support, care, comfort, discipline, custody, education or counseling of the victim.[70]

On the one hand, if the courts have before them a doctor who has had sexual intercourse with his mentally retarded patient, then his "position of authority" seems to constitute an unambiguous criminal circumstance. On the other hand, if the courts have before them a professor who has had sexual intercourse with one of his students, then his "position of authority" seems to constitute an ambiguous criminal circumstance. Although appeals to consent seem outrageous in the former case, they seem warranted in the latter case. In sum, observe the critics, unambiguous criminal circumstances are few and far between. Reform II, like Reform I, will not be able to deflate issues of consent unless the coercion applied to the alleged victim of rape by the alleged rapist assumes a very standard form, such as sexual intercourse at gunpoint.

REFORM III: THE ASSIMILATION OF RAPE LAW TO ASSAULT LAW

Conceding that the critics have a point, feminists who initially favored Reform II have joined with those feminists who have been working on other reforms in rape law. Significantly, this coalition brings together radical, Marxist, liberal, and existentialist feminists, all of whom are coming to agree that the best way to deflate issues of victim consent is by convincing the courts in particular and society in general that rape is more a crime of violence than of sexual passion:

> It is a vain delusion that rape is the expression of uncontrollable desire or some kind of compulsive response to overwhelming attraction. Any girl who has been bashed and raped can tell you how ludicrous it is when she pleads for a reason and her assailant replies "Because I love you" or "Because you're so beautiful" or some such rubbish. The act is one of murderous aggression, spawned in self-loathing and enacted upon the hated other.[71]

If this line of reasoning is correct—*if* it is not primarily sex but domination, revenge, and other similar motives that are behind most rapes, and if rape represents loss of control less over one's sexual passions than over one's aggressive drives—then feminists are right to subsume rape under assault laws.

1. *The Advantages of an Assimilation of Rape Law to Assault Law:* As feminists currently see it, a redefinition of rape either as sexual assault or as assault *sans phrase* would have several advantages. To better understand what these advantages are, it may be useful to include a schematized version of how the crime or rape would be analyzed under assault law. The following outline is one that Schwartz and Clear have devised, but it is duplicated by many feminists in essential detail.

> *Harrassment:* sexual contact, including the touching of intimate parts of the body or the clothing covering such parts for the purpose of sexual arousal or gratification, and against the will of the person being touched. Misdemeanor, punishable by a sentence of up to two months' imprisonment.

> *Assault in the fourth degree:* attempted physical assault that does not result in physical injury, but for which *mens rea* to cause injury can be proven; sexual contact with another person accomplished by force or coercion . . . ; or consensual penetration, with one partner under fourteen and the other at least seven years older. Misdemeanor, punishable by a term of up to six months' imprisonment.

> *Assault in the third degree:* assault with some physical injury or assault with sexual penetration. Felony, punishable by a term of up to two years' imprisonment.

Assault in the second degree: assault with serious physical injury or assault with sexual penetration and physical injury. Felony, punishable by a term of up to five years' imprisonment.

Assault in the first degree: assault with grievous bodily harm or assault with sexual penetration and serious physical injury. Felony, punishable by a term of up to ten years' imprisonment.

Aggravated assault: assault with sexual penetration and grievous bodily harm. Felony, punishable by a term of up to fifteen years' imprisonment.[72]

Schwartz and Clear note that for all the above degrees of assault, the law would explain that the offender and the victim may be of either sex, and that sexual penetration can be accomplished vaginally, orally, or anally with any natural or artificial object.[73]

In the opinion of many feminists, the major advantages of such a redefinition of rape are: (1) it eliminates residual corrobation rules; (2) it lowers the overly high age of consent for sexual intercourse; (3) it eliminates as admissible evidence the victim's past sexual history; (4) it eliminates the marital-exception rule; and (5) it reduces the penalties for rape. Each of these advantages is significant.

a. *It eliminates residual corroboration rules.* Currently, if two men get into a fight, one of them can go to the police and say, "He beat me up, unprovoked, and he was using a knife." On that man's word alone he can take the witness stand and testify as to what happened; he need not corroborate his word with further evidence. Certainly, he need not corroborate his lack of consent. "Imagine," say Schwartz and Clear, "a trial for a stabbing, 'What did you do to convey to the defendant that you did not wish to be stabbed?' the prosecutor asks the victim. 'Did you take any steps to parry his knife thrust?'"[74] By redefining rape as assault, the victim of rape would be spared equally silly questions, even in that handful of states that currently clings to its rape corroboration rules. "What did you do to convey to the defendant that you did not wish to be violated? Did you take any steps to parry his penis thrust?" In the same way one assumes that the victim of assault on the head has not consented to his assault, it should be assumed that the victim of assault in the vagina has not consented to her assault.

b. *It lowers the overly high age of consent for sexual intercourse.* Recently feminists have begun to express serious reservations about prevailing statutory rape provisions. On the surface these statutes seem in accord with feminist goals. Because immature girls lack the ability to give informed consent, they should be protected from men who would prey on their vulnerability. Unfortunately, most statutory rape provisions rely too heavily on the chronological age of the female victim (sixteen to twenty-one years of age depending on the jurisdiction) and overlook her psychic and physical maturity. A woman of sixteen or twenty may be capable of consensual sex with a man, especially if he is only slightly her senior. But no matter how much Juliet (age eighteen) protests that she knew what she was doing when she had sexual intercourse with Romeo (age eighteen), in some jurisdictions Romeo will be charged with statutory rape. Not only does this not seem fair to Romeo, it poses a threat to the sexual autonomy of Juliet. In this connection, Lilia Melani and Linda Fodaski comment:

> Boys who satisfy their sexual desire with similarly motivated girls are legally declared rapists and fall into the same category as assaultive offenders. The only real connection between statutory rape and assaultive rape is that both deny the female the right to *choose* the sexual experience; on the one hand, the law restricts the female minor from having sex, on the other, the rapist forces her to submit to it.[75]

If this line of reasoning is correct, as many feminists think it is, then it makes sense for the law not only to lower the age of consent (twelve to fourteen years of age) but also to make distinctions between a fifteen year-old girl who goes "all the way" with her boyfriend after the junior prom and a fifteen-year-old girl who is enticed into bed with a fifty-four year-old "talent scout."

c. *It eliminates as admissible evidence the victim's past sexual history.* Once rape is incorporated into assault law, the victim's prior sexual history becomes just as irrelevant to the court's proceedings as her prior work history or her prior academic history. Feminists are especially pleased by this feature of the reform under discusion because in some jurisdictions, where rape law has not been subsumed under assault law or otherwise reformed, the defense can question the victim on any previous sexual experience during any part of her life. Although all women find this badgering degrading, it is particularly distressing for the shy woman who wishes to keep her sexual secrets to herself, for the hurt woman who does not want to open old sexual wounds, and for the repentant woman who does not want to confess her past sexual indiscretions in public. Nonetheless, it is unlikely that the victim's prior sexual relationship to the *defendant* can be kept back from the jury in those cases where, in the estimation of the judge, that evidence is crucial for the alleged rapist's defense.

d. *It eliminates the marital-exception rule.* Since husbands are not permitted by law to assault and batter their wives (at least not anymore), once rape is subsumed under assault law, husbands will not be permitted to invoke a defunct marital-exception rule. Whether it is perpetrated by a stranger or an acquaintance, an assault is an assault.

e. *It reduces the penalties for rape.* Although this may not seem like an advantage of placing rape into assault law, it probably is. Because they feel that the punishment is disproportional to the crime (twenty-five years, life imprisonment, death), juries frequently refrain from convicting rapists. In many jurisdictions, for example, sticking a knife deeply into the stomach of a person, causing a bullet to pass through his or her thigh, or beating him or her senseless with a bat is a less serious crime than a rape accomplished without a physical injury. Originally, feminists were inclined to argue that harsh penalties were not disproportional to the crime of rape, even when it involved no physical injury or permanent psychological damage. On reflection, however, they conceded that in the same way that not all murders are equally cold-blooded, not all rapes are equally violent. Therefore, it is better to reserve the more stringent penalties for felonious rapes, meting out less stringent penalties for misdemeanor rapes. Not only is this a more fair penalty system, it is a more effective penalty system in that it inclines juries to convict more rapists—if only for a lesser degree of assaultive rape. Even though some rapists will be getting away with a lower penalty than they should, fewer rapists will be getting away with no penalty at all. This higher conviction rate will convince society that the courts do not condone rape, and it may also convince men that in the same way that they cannot get away with murder easily, they cannot get away with rape easily. In summary, when it comes to rape, certainty of slight punishment may be more a deterrent to rapists than uncertainty of severe punishment.[76]

2. *The Disadvantages of an Assimilation of Rape Law to Assault Law.* Despite all the advantages of this third reform, it is plagued by pragmatic deficiencies as well as theoretical dilemmas. Of these disadvantages, however, the latter are the more crucial to resolve.

a. *Pragmatic Deficiencies.* Although feminists continue to favor rape's definition as assault, they admit that the ideal statute has yet to be written. Under existing assault statutes, including the model assault statute presented above, rape would rarely be punished at all—at least not severely—unless it involved substantial *physical* trauma. In other words, since many victims of rape are not subjected to beatings and bruisings, and since current assault law is written in ways that respond primarily to beatings and bruisings, a redefinition of rape as assault may have the effect of further trivializing it: "Listen, lady, he may have stuck his penis in your vagina, but he didn't hurt you. So what's the big beef?" Although many victims of rape sustain at least some physical injuries, few victims of rape sustain serious physical injuries. In fact, some victims of rape sustain no discernible physical injury at all. This is not surprising given that the harm peculiar to rape is not so much physical harm as a type of psychological harm, consisting of fear of death and feelings of degradation and humiliation sustained during the rape as well as after it. This psychological harm is no less devastating in its effects on a person's life, however, than the effects of some physical harms. One woman speaks at length about a movie that highlighted the tragic consequences rape had on one victim's life:

It [the movie] was about a high school girl coming home from school on a train with a boy and girl holding hands; they were obviously a couple . . . romantic love, arms around each other. The girl was walking home, and she was thinking all these pleasant thoughts about love and romance, the way it was going to be when she fell in love. She was walking through the park in broad daylight. She was raped. The next scene is when she wakes up. She goes home and the whole process is to destroy all her clothes; she burns everything, she takes a bath, she scrubs herself clean. Then she leaves home and wanders around the city . . . . She had been studying for a career, and she took menial jobs after that, wound up in a menial sort of job and considered herself a skunk.[77]

In sum, it is sometimes easier to go on living one's life after a serious physical injury (a gunshot wound) than after a serious psychological injury. Therefore, if rape law is to be subsumed under assault law, assault law has to be altered in ways that accommodate psychological as well as physical injuries.

Interestingly, even though feminists agree that assault law has to be altered if it is to serve rape victims, they wonder whether it is always in the best interest of rape victims to stress the fact that they have been *psychologically* harmed. Some of the law's major problems come from its overreliance on psychiatric testimony (such as in the insanity defense), and the opening of another controversial area does not bode well. Feminist antirapists predict with Schwartz and Clear messy arguments between the psychiatrist for the prosecution and that for the defense over the cause of the rape victim's distraught mental condition, with the defendant's freedom in the balance and with the victim's image and livelihood at stake. The more unstable, overwrought, and unbalanced the woman seems, the greater the chances not only of her rapist's conviction, but of her being stigmatized.

This is not to suggest that psychological harm should be ignored in rape cases. However, if the sexual-assault approach were to be at all successful, then certain degrees of rape would have to be treated as if they did in fact always cause a certain kind of psychological harm, with the question of actual psychic injury ignored in any individual case. That is, assault law would have to treat all cases of rape at gunpoint as always causing severe trauma, even though one or more actual victims reported no such trauma under these circumstances. Similarly, assault law would have to treat all cases of rape by unarmed, sweet-talking, small-boned men as always causing minimum fright, even though one or more actual victims reported maximum fright under these circumstances. By determining the amount of psychological harm certain types of rape cause in advance, the focus of the court's proceedings would correctly shift from the victim's psychic condition back to the defendant's conduct; and the rapist's sentence would in no way depend on his "blind luck," whether, for example, he raped a psychologically strong person or an emotional cripple.[78]

b. *Theoretical Dilemmas.* Although it is relatively easy to adjust assault law so that it can address psychological harms, it is considerably more difficult to resolve the theoretical dilemmas that have been generated by attempts to assimilate rape law into assault law.

Recently, feminists have begun to argue among themselves over what may seem a trivial point, although it is not. The point at issue is whether rape should be defined as *sexual assault* or whether it should be defined as *assault sans phrase.*

1. *Rape as Sexual Assault—The Argument.* Feminists who favor the rape-as-*sexual*-assault approach wish to stress rape's violent character without denying its sexual overtones or undercurrents. Like many psychiatrists, these feminists are convinced that the aggression of so- called anger rapists and power rapists (clinical categories into which most, though not all, rapists fit) is directed against *female sexuality.*[79] That is, the anger rapist is not simply a man who, hating people in general, lashes out at a vulnerable and easily accessible subset of people, namely, women. Rather he is also a man who at some unconscious or conscious level hates women in particular. For him, the act of rape is an attempt to make up for what he perceives as the many hurtful acts that women in his life have committed against him, and so he seeks to hurt those parts of woman's body that distinguish her as a woman. Similarly, the power rapist is not simply a man who, desiring to control human beings in general, chooses to dominate a vulnerable and easily accessible subset of human beings, namely, women. Rather he is also a man who at some unconscious or conscious level has a need to control women in particular. For him, the act of rape is an opportunity to assert his domination over all the women who have ever dominated him—such as his mother, wife, aunts, teachers, girlfriends.

For the power rapist as well as the anger rapist, the choice of the vagina or anus as the object of aggression is not accidental, but essential. The fact that he so frequently chooses to penetrate a woman's vagina with his penis rather than to hit her on the head with a baseball bat indicates that he is interested not so much in inflicting damage on her, but in inflicting a *certain kind* of damage on her. In the same way that a vindictive person may smash a pianist's fingers, break a figure skater's leg, or gouge out an artist's eyes, the rapist seeks to spoil, corrupt, or even destroy those aspects of a woman's person that should be a source of pride, joy, and power for her rather than a source of shame, depression, and humiliation. Therefore, feminists who favor the rape-as-*sexual*- assault approach argue that rape is not just like any other assault; it has a cruel edge that should not be blunted in the name of legal efficiency.

2. *Rape as Assault Sans Phrase—The Argument.* Feminists who favor the rape-as-assault approach insist that rape is an assault like any other assault. According to this second group, the rapist's choice of the vagina or anus as

the target of his aggression is no more significant than the barroom brawler's choice of a man's arm or leg as the target of his aggression. Therefore, there is no logical reason to have a separate category for assaults on the vagina or anus than there is to have a separate category for assaults on the arm or leg.

Significantly, feminists who favor the rape-as-assault approach have pragmatic as well as logical reasons for their position. As they see it, special sexual-assault laws would reinforce the "special" (unequal and lesser) status of women and their sexuality. Schwartz and Clear comment:

> There is no reason to separate the state's concern for protecting women's sexual integrity from the law's concern for protecting the general physical integrity of all citizens. This is not to say the state cannot legally make such distinctions, but that to make them is counterproductive to ultimate goals for women's equality. It is our contention that the perceived need for a special set of laws to protect a woman's genitals is one of the barriers that prevent women from being the equals of men under the law, just as do female labor laws or combat restrictions.[80]

The argument continues that in addition to supporting the "special protection" status of women, special sexual-assault laws should cater to a myth of rape according to which the invasion of sexual integrity is so traumatic that the victim's psychic wounds never heal. Therefore, concludes this second group of feminists, women should conceive of rape as they conceive of any assault—a frightening and possibly physically painful experience, but nothing to be ashamed of.

3. *Rape as Sexual Assault or as Assault Sans Phrase—The Argument Tentatively Resolved.* What is of special interest about the above debate is that it is a version of a debate encountered several times in this book: whether or not it is in women's best interest to think of themselves as victims.

Feminists who favor the rape-as-assault approach wish to downplay the woman-as-victim theme. As they see it, *special* sexual assault laws serve primarily to remind women that their open orifices are handy targets for assailants' jabs and pricks, thereby exacerbating women's sense of vulnerability. Because they fear the omnipresent rapist, some women put themselves under house arrest. (My sixteen-year-old babysitter, for example, locks all the doors and windows, pulls down all the shades, turns on all the lights, sits close to the phone, and jumps every time the heat goes on.) According to the proponents of the rape-as-assault (*sans phrase*) approach, such self-imposed incarceration imposes limits on feminist gains: "Since the object of rape is . . . a statement of male domination, to fight back by admitting defeat may in the short run produce victory (no physical rape), but is certainly counterproductive in the long run (women's place as an equal in law and in society)."[81] In summary, by obsessing about rape, by staying where they belong (that is, at home), and especially by thinking of themselves as damsels in distress, women delay their entrance into "man's world." Although feminists who favor the rape-as-*sexual*-assault approach agree that it is not good to encourage women to think and act like victims, they disagree that the best way to make women strong is for the law to adopt a policy according to which rape is no "big deal," provided that the woman is not beaten or mutilated. They note, for example, that in a recent case Inez García was convicted of second-degree murder after shooting and killing the man she claimed had helped another man rape her.[82] When asked whether a woman could ever argue self-defense if she killed her rapist *during* an attack, a juror responded: "No, because the guy's not trying to kill her. He's just trying to screw her and give her a good time. To get off the guy will have to do her bodily harm and giving a girl a screw isn't giving her bodily harm."[83] If the law adopts a rape-like-any- other-assault position too quickly, it may inadvertently contribute to such a mentality. Although victims of rape should be encouraged to pick up the pieces of their lives, it is because they should feel no shame or guilt about what happened to them, and not because rape is a trivial, "nothing to get upset about" ordeal.

Although the debate between feminists who favor the rape-as-*sexual*- assault approach and feminists who advocate the rape-as-assault approach is not likely to end tomorrow, there is no more reason to deny that rape constitutes *sexual* assault (a specific type of assault directed against women on account of their sexuality) than there is to deny that repeatedly calling attention to a woman's body when she would prefer it to go unnoticed constitutes *sexual* harassment (a specific type of harassment directed against women on account of their sexuality). Those who wish to stress the assaultive, nonerotic nature of rape and sexual harassment are correct to the degree that rape and sexual harassment are power plays. Nevertheless, rape is also very much related to this culture's view of women as persons who exist to serve male sexual desires and interests no matter the cost to their own female sexual desires and interests. This being the case, rape is a type of assault that would occur less frequently if (1) women were not viewed and treated as social, economic, and political inferiors of men, and (2) were they not viewed and treated as persons whose own sexual desires and interests must always play second fiddle to those of men. Therefore, until such time as women are the sexual as well as the social, economic, and political equals of men, it is best to define rape as *sexual* assault rather than as assault *sans phrase*.

Conclusion

Reforms may be able to alleviate the ways in which the victims of rape have been put on trial alongside their rapists. But until the time when the rape victim is no longer looked upon with suspicion and distrust, most rapists are likely to escape punishment. Although it comes as a shock to many people, the bias against the rape victim is enormous. Recent books, articles, and pamphlets note that not only police officers, prosecutors, and judges, but also families, friends, psychiatrists, doctors, and even nurses tend to treat the victim of rape callously and cruelly.[84] If the plight of raped women is finally to be ameliorated, people must become convinced of the quandary in which the rape victim is placed by a society that tends to adopt a male perspective. In particular, the personnel of the criminal justice system must overcome their propensity to see things from the alleged rapist's point of view. Indeed, this is precisely what the National Institute of Law Enforcement and Criminal Justice concluded in its study of forcible rape:

> Ultimately, the attitudes and commitments of police and prosecutors may determine the impact of legislation. Unless these enforcement personnel believe victims and aggressively pursue cases, the more refined legal issues will never be raised. The job of legislative reform is a first step toward effective enforcement of rape laws. The implementation of these reforms, however, requires that the criminal justice system embrace their assumptions. To the extent that the criminal justice system only reflects the values of the general society, the job of implementation has only begun.[85]

This is a sobering message, but at least it tells us where to begin: in our schools, in our churches, and in our homes. If our children can transcend the patterns of male sexual aggression and female sexual submission that have held us captive for so long, then rape need no longer be the pervasive problem that it is today.

Notes

1. Susan Griffin, "Rape: The All-American Crime," *Ramparts,* September 1971, p. 30.
2. H. C. Black, *Black's Law Dictionary,* 4th ed. rev. (St. Paul: West Publishing Co., 1968), p. 1427.
3. Male homosexual rapes are on the increase. Frequently, such rapes take place in prisons or other institutions, where the victim of rape is literally at his rapist's mercy.
4. Susan Brownmiller, *Against Our Will: Men, Women and Rape* (New York: Bantam Books, 1975), p. 422.
5. Ibid., pp. 80–81.
6. Daniel Silverman and Sharon L. McCombie, "Counseling the Mates and Families of Rape Victims," in the *Rape Crisis Intervention Handbook,* Sharon L. McCombie, ed. (New York: Plenum Press, 1980), p. 175.
7. Simone de Beauvoir, *The Second Sex* (New York: Vintage Books, 1974), p. 172.
8. Women also care less about female virginity today than twenty-five years ago. It is estimated that more than half of all women have intercourse before the age of twenty, and only a quarter of these women are married. Battelle Law and Justice Study Center, *Forcible Rape: An Analysis of Legal Issues* (Washington, D.C.: National Institute of Law Enforcement and Criminal Justice Law Enforcement Assistance Administration, U.S. Department of Justice, U.S. Government Printing Office, 1978), p. 24.

9. Several states have already expanded their rape statutes to include penetrations other than vaginal. For a listing of these jurisdictions, see ibid., pp. 5–20.

10. Noreen Connell and Cassandra Wilson, "Personal Testimony," in *Rape: The First Sourcebook for Women,* Noreen Connell and Cassandra Wilson, eds. (New York: New American Library, Plenum, 1974), pp. 34–35.

11. Sir Matthew Hale, *Pleas of the Crown* (London: 1678; Emelyn ed., 1847), pp. 628–29.

12. Comment, "The Common Law Does Not Support a Marital Exclusion for Forcible Rape," *Womens' Rights Law Reporter* 5 (Spring 1979):183, 185.

13. Comment, "Rape and Battery Between Husband and Wife," *Stanford Law Review* 6 (July 1954):722–23.

14. Comment, "The Common Law Does Not Support a Marital Exclusion for Forcible Rape," p. 184.

15. *State* v. *Smith,* 148 New Jersey Superior Court, 225–26; 372 A. 2d 389 (Essex County Court, 1977).

16. Comment "The Common Law Does Not Support a Marital Exclusion for Forcible Rape," p. 185.

17. Battelle, *Forcible Rape,* pp. 6–7.

18. Ibid., p. 18.

19. Brownmiller, *Against Our Will,* p. 402.

20. John Leo, "Deadly Dilemma for Women," *Time,* September 21, 1981, p. 75.

21. Oliver W. Holmes, *The Common Law* (1881; reprint, Boston: Little, Brown, 1963), p. 7.

22. *Rex* v. *Banks,* I Esq. 145 (1974); *Fowler* v. *Padget,* 7 T.R. 509, 514 (1798).

23. Tertullian, *Treatises on Marriage and Remarriage: To His Wife,* translated by William P. Le Saint, S.J., S.T.D. (Westminster, Md.: The Newman Press, 1951), p. 1.

24. Rosemary R. Ruether, *Liberation Theology* (New York: Paulist Press, 1972), p. 99.

25. Timothy, *The New Oxford Annotated Bible with the Apocrypha,* Revised Standard Edition, Herbert G. May and Bruce M. Metzgy, eds. (New York: Oxford University Press, 1973).

26. Ruether, *Liberation Theology,* p. 103.

27. Ibid.

28. Ibid.

29. Ibid.

30. Ibid.

31. George H. Tavard, *Women in Christian Tradition* (Notre Dame, Ind.: Notre Dame Press, 1973), p. 48.

32. John H. Wigmore, *Evidence* (Boston: Little, Brown, 1934), p. 379.

33. Brownmiller, *Against Our Will,* p. 435.

34. Ibid., p. 433.

35. Note, "Corroborating Charges of Rape," *Columbia Law Review* 67 (June 1967):1137, 1139.

36. Stanley Rosenblatt, *Justice Denied* (Los Angeles, Cal.: Nash Publishers, 1971), p. 36.

37. Ibid.

38. Menachim Amir, "Victim Precipitated Forcible Rape," *Journal of Criminal Law, Criminology, and Police Studies* 58 (1967):493, 498.

39. Ibid., p. 494.

40. Menachim Amir, *Patterns in Forcible Rape* (Chicago: University of Chicago Press, 1971), p. 22.

41. Amir, "Victim Precipitated Forcible Rape," p. 497.

42. Amir, *Patterns in Forcible Rape,* p. 252.

43. Ann Wolbert Burgess and Lynda Little Holmstrom, "Rape Typology and the Coping Behavior of Rape Victims," in McCombie, ed., *Rape Crisis Intervention Handbook*, pp. 28–29.

44. Ibid., p. 29.

45. Ibid.

46. Battelle, *Forcible Rape*, p. 15.

47. Ibid., p. 28.

48. Ibid.

49. Ibid., p. 30.

50. Cautionary instructions are rooted in Sir Matthew Hale's seventeenth-century observation that rape is "an accusation easily to be made and hard to be proved, and harder to be defended by the party accused, though ever so innocent." Hale, *Pleas of the Crown*, p. 635.

51. Wigmore, *Evidence*, p. 379.

52. Battelle, *Forcible Rape*, p. 32.

53. *State* v. *Walgraeve*, 243 Oregon 328 (1966).

54. Battelle, *Forcible Rape*, p. 32.

55. Ibid.

56. Ibid., p. 25.

57. Martin D. Schwartz and Todd R. Clear, "Toward a New Law on Rape," *Crime and Delinquency* 27 (April 1980):148.

58. *Camp* v. *State*, 3 Ga. (1847), pp. 417, 422.

59. Noreen Connell, "Introduction," in *Rape: The First Sourcebook for Women*, Connell and Wilson, eds., pp. 129–30.

60. Schwartz and Clear, "Toward a New Law on Rape," pp. 148–49.

61. Vicki McNickle Rose, "Rape as a Social Problem: A Byproduct of the Feminist Movement," *Social Problems* 25 (October 1977):80 n.

62. Battelle, *Forcible Rape*, p. 27.

63. Ibid., p. 8.

64. A radical feminist believes that sexual inequality is the byproduct of female biology. Once technology frees women of their reproductive responsibilities, women will be equal with men.

65. A Marxist feminist believes that sexual inequality is the byproduct of capitalism.

66. Lilia Melani and Linda Fodaski, "The Psychology of the Rapist and His Victim," in Connell and Wilson, eds., *Rape: The First Sourcebook*, p. 89.

67. A liberal feminist believes that individual women can overcome certain handicaps and make it in "man's world" provided that educational and legal institutions do not actively discriminate against women; an existentialist feminist is generally opposed to any form of determinism. As she sees it, individual women are always free to shape their futures.

68. Melani and Fodaski, "The Psychology of the Rapist," p. 49.

69. Judith Butler, review of *Diary of a Conference on Sexuality*, *Gay Community News* 9 (December 1981):6.

70. Senate Bill No. 291, LD1312, Offered to Virginia State Legislature January 30, 1978; Patrons were Walker, Gatlan, and Edmunds et al.

71. Pamela Lakes Wood, "The Victim in a Forcible Rape Case: A Feminist View," in Connell and Wilson, eds., *Rape: The First Sourcebook*, p. 158, n. 28.

72. Schwartz and Clear, "Toward a New Law on Rape," pp. 141–42.

73. Ibid., p. 142.

74. Ibid., pp. 145–46.

75. Melani and Fodaski, "The Psychology of the Rapist and His Victim," p. 82.

76. It is generally agreed by criminologists that certainty of punishment is a more effective deterrent than severity of punishment. Charles E. Silberman, *Criminal Violence, Criminal Justice* (New York: Random House, 1978), pp. 169–99.

77. "Conscious-Raising on Rape" (From the NYRF Rape Conference Workshop on the Psychology of the Rapist, His Victim and Rape Fantasies), in Connell and Wilson, eds., *Rape: The First Sourcebook*, p. 17.

78. Schwartz and Clear, "Toward a New Law on Rape," pp. 139–40.

79. Nicholas A. Groth and Ann Wolbert Burgess, "Rape: A Sexual Deviation," *American Journal of Orthopsychiatry* 47 (July 1970):400.

80. Schwartz and Clear, "Rape Law Reform and Women's Equality," *USA Today* 108 (November 1979):37.

81. Schwartz and Clear, "Toward a New Law on Rape," p. 135.

82. Said García in response to her act: "I'm not sorry I did it. I am only sorry I missed Luis Castillo (the alleged rapist). I meant to kill him, too. That's the only thing I'm sorry about." David Ben-Horin, "Is Rape a Sex Crime?" *Nation,* August 1975, p. 114.

83. Quoted in García's supplemental opening brief. *People* v. *García* 1 Crim. 14104, in the Court of Appeals of the State of California, First Appellate Division 55 (1976).

84. Barbara Schuler Gilmore and Janet Weeks Evans, "The Nursing Care of Rape Victims," in McCombie, ed., *Rape Crisis Intervention Handbook*, p. 53.

85. Battelle, *Forcible Rape,* p. 50.

CHAPTER 5

WOMAN-BATTERING

One-third to one-half of all women who live with male companions experience degradation in the form of brutality or threatened brutality.[1] Statistics also indicate that 41 percent of all women killed in the United States are killed by their husbands.[2] Clearly, both the women's movement and the legal network must come to terms with woman-battering as a serious social and legal problem.

Like rape and sexual harassment, woman-battering has been perceived as a trivial or a largely imagined phenomenon, as a woman's deserved treatment rather than the criminal violation of her rights. The battered woman, like the rape victim, has been ignored, insulted, disbelieved, and blamed for her own victimization. The dominant image of woman in battery cases persists as that of the shrew who needs to be tamed or the hag who needs to be silenced. Like the victim of sexual harassment, the abused wife's or girlfriend's attempts to improve her situation have met with society's denial that her pain is real. Our society in general and our legal system in particular prefer to believe that the woman with the black eye and the broken ribs fell down the stairs, and not that her husband hit her.

Recently, there have been increasing efforts to develop both legal and extralegal responses to the battered woman's pain and the battering man's anger. This chapter will examine the legal doctrines which govern woman battering and feminist responses to them. Next it will describe standard civil and criminal law remedies for woman-battering, detailing the feminist community's debate over whether the civil or criminal law is more appropriate in cases of woman-battering. Finally, the ways feminists have attempted to make police officers, prosecutors, and judges more sensitive to battered women will be noted, suggesting that the phenomenon of woman battering will probably not diminish unless battering men and battered women learn to change certain aspects of their behavior, most especially a predisposition in the men toward either victimizing or violence and a predisposition in the women toward either victimization or submission.

Definition and Causes

Whether woman-battering is called wife beating, marital violence, domestic violence, or spouse abuse, it denotes violence. The various ways to define woman-battering are based either on (1) the harmful effects sustained by the victim or on (2) the intention of the assailant. In an effort to avoid, at least for now, the question of whose perception (victim's or assailant's) should determine whether an act of battery (and all that it implies) has occurred, woman-battering may be tentatively defined as "assaultive behavior between adults in an intimate, sexual, theoretically peer, and usually cohabitating relationship."[3] Assaultive behavior ordinarily assumes one or more of the following forms: (1) physical battering, (2) sexual battering, (3) psychological battering, and (4) the destruction of property and pets.[4] Not only the destruction of property and pets but also sexual battering has been overlooked as part of the battering syndrome. This oversight is unfortunate because it has hindered attempts to link ideologically sexual harassment and rape to woman-battering.

Of the four forms of battering, physical battering is the most conspicuous. It includes pushing, shoving, kicking, hitting, punching, choking, burning, stabbing, clubbing, knifing, and shooting.

Sexual battering includes physical attacks on the victim's breasts/genitals or forced sexual activity accompanied by either physical violence or the threat of physical violence. For example, one wife relates the following predicament. Her husband brings home pornographic magazines. If she refuses to imitate the sexual activity in the magazines, he will beat her, reviling her for being a "prude." If she complies, he will beat her for engaging in "dirty sex" with him and castigate her for being a "slut."[5] When feminists observe that husbands can and do rape their wives, they do not necessarily have such scenes of extreme violence in mind. Nonetheless, the scenes they do envisage are usually characterized by some show of violence. This suggests that if feminists wish to assimilate rape law to assault law, they must forsake any clear distinction between spousal rape and spousal sexual battery. The two crimes become identical for all practical purposes.

In contrast to both physical and sexual battering, psychological battering does not involve infliction of bodily harm on the victim. It refers to control of the victim's daily activities and encompasses a variety of behaviors, such as constantly attacking a mate's self-esteem and intentionally frightening and threatening one's spouse. Psychological battery is distinguished from simple emotional abuse by the atmosphere of intimidation in which it takes place. Although an emotionally abused woman may have the psychic strength to tell her husband to cut it out, the psychologically battered woman will remain silent. As a result of past incidents of physical or sexual violence, she is frightened because she knows that her man is capable of backing his psychological battering with physical battering. She will feel helpless when he calls her names or forbids her to have friends of her own or makes fun of her attempts to improve her body or mind. In many ways the situation of some battered women is analogous to that of prisoners of war, who lose individual control over where they go, who they see, and even their eating/ sleeping habits. Feminists have observed, however, that the psychologically battered woman is probably more confused, bewildered, and otherwise disoriented than the brainwashed POW, who lives in constant fear of torture. Unlike the POW, who is being brainwashed by individuals who are clearly understood to be enemies, the battered woman is being abused by an intimate, by a person who is supposed to love her.[6]

The final form of woman-battering involves the destruction of property and pets. Although the batterer does not directly assault the victim herself, he breaks something that means a lot to her or kills a favorite pet. Such actions are symbolic: the batterer serves notice to his victim that she, like her china, is breakable and, like her cat, expendable.

All four modes of battering have several features in common: (1) all result in physical and/or psychic harm to the victim; (2) all are manifestations of control and domination; and (3) all occur in a context of intimacy. Not only is it this third feature that distinguishes woman battering from most cases of sexual harassment and some cases of rape, but it is that which dissuades the criminal justice system from interfering with woman batterers.

Traditionally, Anglo-American law is reluctant to intrude upon the privacy of family life.[7] Clearly, the law's predisposition results from a belief that the family stands secure as a peaceful retreat within a violent world. In the opinion of many, the family provides a salutary buffer between the unsocialized individual and the socializing state, which exerts its control through education and the law.[8] In absence of the private realm, there would exist a world "without the possibility of concealment, a world . . . with no hiding places, nor refuge, nor solace, nor alternate to the force of the public sphere."[9] Feminists are rightfully wary of state intervention when it comes to the private issues of sexual relations and family planning (issues of contraception and abortion, for instance). Yet they are becoming aware that the family unit is not always a peaceful unit. When a family exists not as a salutary refuge but as a homefront of brutality, feminists endorse state intervention in the interest of abused or neglected children and battered wives. When family members have neither the psychic energy nor the economic strength to escape a harmful situation, feminists are claiming that the state must serve as a check on those family members who do not treat their "loved ones" with consideration and respect. Clearly, the fact that a woman is someone's wife does not negate the existence of her rights, rights that the state must protect, even when it means protecting her from those who describe themselves as her intimates.

Traditional Legal Doctrine

The state has not always served the best interests of women. From time to time it has operated on the assumption that women's rights, within as well as outside the family, are fewer or less full-bodied than men's rights. As a result, traditional Anglo-American law treated a husband's assault upon his wife as an "acceptable practice."[10] In early nineteenth-century America, for example, a man was legally permitted to chastise his wife "without subjecting himself to vexatious prosecutions for assault and battery, resulting in the mutual discredit and shame of all parties concerned."[11] This rule was derived from English common law, which not only permitted husbands to beat their wayward wives, but instructed wives to "kiss the rod that beat them."[12]

In sharp contrast, husband killing historically, has, been viewed as a crime against the state—a form of treason. Blackstone explained that since a husband was the lord of his wife, a wife's murder of her husband constituted treachery analogous to murdering the king.[13] Indeed, husband killing struck at the root of all civil government:

> Husband and wife, in the language of the law, are styled baron and feme. The word baron, or lord, attributes to the husband not a very courteous superiority. But we might be inclined to think this merely an unmeaning technical phrase, if we did not recollect that if the baron kills his feme it is the same as if he had killed a stranger, or any other person; but if the feme kills her baron, it is regarded by the laws as a much more atrocious crime, as she not only breaks through the restraints of humanity and conjugal affection, but throws off all subjection to the authority of her husband. And therefore the law denominates her crime a species of treason, and condemns her to the same punishment as if she had killed the king. And for every species of treason . . . the sentence of woman was to be drawn and burnt alive.[14]

To the extent that the exercise of *merely defensive* force by women challenged traditional views of appropriate female conduct, to an even greater degree the use of *deadly* force by a woman against her husband must not only have contradicted social stereotypes of the dependent, passive, and submissive female but also threatened traditional society's conviction that the family is an institution of love, nourishment, and protection. Because the myth of the ideal family did not always conform to reality, suffragists and others began to protest against family violence during the second half of the nineteenth century. Reform progressed slowly. It was not until the 1860s that reformers persuaded several jurisdictions to abandon the so-called chastisement rule, according to which husbands had been entrusted with the right and power to restrain their wives in any manner they saw fit. In 1864, for example, a North Carolina court ruled that the state could interfere with a husband's domestic chastisement of his wife, but only in those cases where some permanent injury resulted from a husband's violence.[15] In the absence of permanent injury or excessive violence, most courts (including North Carolina courts) continued to invoke the "curtain rule," according to which the law would "not invade the domestic forum or go beyond the curtain."[16] The courts' disposition was to "leave the parties to themselves, as the best mode of inducing them to make the matter up and live together as man and wife should."[17]

Not until 1871 was this policy of nonintervention overturned in favor of a policy that afforded wives the possibility of real protection against the blows of their husbands. In that year an Alabama court declared that "the moral sense of the community revolts at the idea that the husband may inflict chastisement upon his wife, even for the most outrageous conduct."[18] Following Alabama's lead, court after court waxed eloquently about how civilized modern husbands and wives had become. In 1871 a Massachusetts court decision stated: "Blackstone published his commentaries when society was much more rude . . . . Since then, however, learning, with its humanizing influences, has made great progress. Therefore, a rod which may be drawn through the wedding ring is not now deemed necessary to teach the wife her duty and subjection to the husband."[19] Nevertheless, although husbands were advised to throw away the rod, wife-beating did not cease in part because (1) police officers, prosecutors, and judges failed to adopt aggressive policies against woman batterers; (2) battered women were not yet convinced that they could or should complain about their marital woes, which, they seem to have believed, were largely of their own doing; and (3) husbands were still socialized to believe that their acts of wife beating were not outright wrong.

Civil and Criminal Remedies

Although the situation of battered women has improved since the nineteenth century, neither civil justice personnel nor criminal justice personnel take the rights of this century's battered women seriously enough, largely because they, like the general public, are not entirely convinced that woman-battering is either a crime or a tort. However, a brief survey of tort and criminal law establishes in no uncertain terms that woman battering is indeed both a crime and a tort.

The aim of the criminal law is to protect the public against harm by punishing those whose conduct has either already resulted in harm or those whose conduct is likely to result in harm if allowed to proceed further. The function of tort law is to compensate an individual who is injured for the hurt he or she has suffered. With crimes, the state itself initiates criminal proceedings to protect the public interest rather than to compensate the victim. With torts, the injured party institutes action in order to recover damages. A private harm (tort) is almost exclusively concerned with the *result* of a hurt causer's action, whereas a public harm exists primarily in a perpetrator's *intention* to cause harm rather than in the actual result of his action. A private harm (tort) is so classified because it hurts an assignable individual(s), where "hurt" is understood to mean either physical pain or mental distress of a certain requisite intensity caused either by personal or by property damage. Although this hurt may be intentional, it is often caused by recklessness or negligence.

In contrast, a public harm (crime), although it usually hurts someone, need not actually hurt anyone. Neither every member of society nor any member of society need be hurt (injured, damaged) for society to be harmed. It suffices if at least one citizen is in a position to be hurt (injured, damaged). Society is harmed as much by the reckless driver who never maims or kills anyone as it is by the reckless driver who kills a toddler at play. Society is harmed by unsuccessful attemptors, solicitors, and conspirators whose criminal machinations are nipped in the bud as much as by those whose evil plan attains fruition.[20] Society is harmed in the former as well as the latter instances because not only actual harm but the threat of harm is "the brute negation of the minimum that all of us—from the most self sufficient to the most dependent—expect from life in organized society."[21] Unless society can provide its members with a minimum of security, society loses its raison d'être.

If this analysis is correct, then, on the one hand, woman-battering is a tort because an assignable wife/girlfriend is physically and psychologically hurt by her husband/boyfriend. On the other hand, woman-battering is also a crime because society is harmed by the man who believes his marriage certificate licenses otherwise unacceptable behavior. If women lived in an atmosphere of feeling threatened that their male companions could at any point harm them *and* that the men would not have to pay for so doing, even though the law pays lip-service commitment to protecting the rights of *all* its citizens, then society is harmed both in that the female population lives in fear of being harmed and in that the female population's rights are not being protected.

Because woman-battering is both a tort and a crime, the battered woman has the option either to bring civil suit (divorce proceedings) or to press criminal charges (assault and battery) against her batterer. In theory, each battered woman is allowed to resolve her problem in the way that best suits the circumstances of her particular situation. In practice, however, the battered woman is frequently lost in a bureaucratic maze, shunted back and forth by legal authorities between civil court and criminal court. This inexpeditious situation is not likely to improve unless battered women both know and insist upon their legal rights. Therefore, it is important that civil and criminal remedies for woman-battering first be understood in detail and then altered in ways that help rather than hinder the battered woman in her struggle for physical and psychological integrity.

The civil-law remedies for woman-battering are divorce and, in some instances, a preliminary injunctive order cautioning the batterer that if he assaults his wife while their divorce is pending, he will be punished for contempt of court. However, in most jurisdictions preliminary injunctive orders are either not filed at all or if filed,they are not enforced. Some divorce lawyers claim that such orders prompt husband-assailants to become more violent toward their wives or to cooperate less in the settlement of property or custody disputes. When divorce lawyers do file for injunctive orders, husband-assailants frequently escape punishment for transgressions of them because civil-court orders are not enforced unless both the prosecutor's office and the police chief's department take them seriously. Unfortunately, law enforcement officials tend to be cavalier about "refereeing" what they describe as "spats" between divorcing parties. Even when injunctive orders are stringently enforced, feminists claim that they do not always improve the condition of the battered woman who sues for divorce, and in some instances where, for example, her bullish husband sees the injunctive order as a red flag mocking his authority, it may make her lot much worse. Moreover, neither preliminary injunctions nor divorce are options for unmarried women whose live-ins or ex-live-ins beat them, or for already divorced women whose ex-husbands maintain an atmosphere of cruelty even after the divorce. Nevertheless, despite the limits of these civil remedies, feminists believe that they could be more effective were the courts more sympathetically disposed toward battered women. Indeed, what most puzzles feminists is the unsympathetic manner in which divorce courts have and still do treat battered women. Like victims of rape, victims of woman-battering are often put on trial alongside their assailants.[22]

Prior to the wide acceptance of no-fault divorces (circa 1970), many states allowed wives to produce evidence of brutality in order to establish their husband's culpability under the classification of extreme cruelty. In those cases where the court determined that the husband's battering constituted extreme cruelty, the wife was granted a divorce. In many cases, however, a woman was denied her divorce for one of four reasons: (1) she was lying; (2) her injuries were not so great as to warrant the subordination of the state's interest in preserving the institution of marriage to her individual interests; (3) she had verbally provoked her husband to beat her; or (4) her husband's cruel behavior was negated by her equally cruel behavior. Each of these reasons demands separate attention, if only to indicate the odds against a battered woman sailing smoothly through civil courts even today.[23]

The first reason traditional fault-oriented courts gave to justify a no-divorce decision was that the allegedly battered woman was a liar. The myth of woman as a lying temptress has been a pervasive myth in our culture (see Chapter 4). Thus feminists have not been surprised that the old divorce courts often dismissed battered women's accounts of life with their husbands as exaggerations. Frequently, judges disbelieved a woman's story simply because she had stayed with her husband anywhere from five to thirty years before filing for divorce. Many judges reasoned that no person could *willingly* live with such abuse for so long. Clearly, what judicial officials overlooked was the capacity of some women to endure an awful marriage in the hope that it will get better, or that they can make it better.

A second reason given by the old divorce courts for denying a battered woman her divorce was that a woman's interests in her own personal happiness are less important than the state's interest in preserving the institution of marriage—even when the manifestations of that institution do not live up to the ideal, indeed when the manifestations make a mockery of the institution of marriage. In 1963 the Supreme Court of Michigan denied a divorce to a battered woman whose husband periodically slapped her on these grounds:

> What we have here is bickering, shortness of temper, and vexatious conduct. Aggravation there has been, but not cruelty. The bonds of matrimony are not to be thus lightly cast aside. There is at stake, for our society as a whole, too much of the public welfare, too much of the public morals, in the preservation of family ties, to permit the spouses to come and go as tempers wax and wane. . . . The cruelty we demand . . . must[be in] the realm of the evil and the wicked, of brutality, of malignancy, of indignities endangering mental or physical health.[24]

In sum, unless a battered woman's injuries are cruel (whatever that may mean), it is a woman's duty to remain with her husband till death (probably hers) do them part. Yet, feminists ask why married women are *required* to put up with physical abuse that violates their legal rights. Were they not married to their batterers, they would not be expected to tolerate a push or a shove, let alone a kick or a punch. In response to this and related queries the courts have suggested that on occasion intimates are required to put up with more— that is, to forgive each others' trespasses. Were men and women not willing to overlook certain violations of their respective rights, they would not stay together and society would be imperiled because short-lived marriages are not conducive to societal stability.

Feminists reply by observing that if a woman chooses to forgive her batterer, that is her affair. But that it is quite another matter for a court of law to expect, or even demand, that she do so for the good of society. If society wishes its citizens to take rights seriously, it cannot also ask citizens, especially vulnerable citizens, to downplay or ignore their rights. When it comes to a harm like woman-battering, study after study shows that the longer a woman remains with her batterer, the greater are the odds that she will be grievously injured. Instances of battery escalate in frequency and intensity, and the woman who overlooks a slap is likely to be the eventual recipient of a thrashing.[25] In general, one forgives someone in the hopes that he or she will change his or her offending behavior. For a battered woman to forgive her batterer when there is every sign that he cannot or will not change his behavior is to do a disservice to oneself as well as the harm-doer. Far from encouraging battered women to "hang in there," society should encourage them to "get out." Indeed, psychologists and social workers are of the general opinion that unless a battered woman lets her batterer know that she will not tolerate physical abuse from him, she and he will have tremendous difficulty escaping the cycle of violence that will subsequently envelop them (husband beats wife, husband asks for forgiveness, wife forgives husband, husband beats wife).[26]

Traditional fault-oriented courts also denied battered women divorces when they determined that a wife had verbally provoked her husband into battering her. Although provocation has never, except in cases of retaliatory violence (Chapter 1), constituted adequate defense against a charge of criminal assault, the claim that a wife has provoked her husband into violence has in the past repudiated her claim of extreme cruelty in divorce cases. The reasons for this peculiar emphasis on provocation are obscure. The courts may have reasoned that intimacy lowers anger's boiling point, and that husbands and wives must take care not to test one another's patience. After all, it is one thing to tolerate strangers' idiosyncrasies or even more volatile behavior now and then; it is quite another to live with disagreeable behavior day in and day out. If a wife constantly finds ways to tell her husband that he's worth nothing, then if, after having exhausted "sweet reason," he responds to her taunts by hitting her, his violent behavior is either excusable or justifiable, for it is no more harmful than her behavior. Indeed, opine some courts, the batterer's behavior may be less harmful than his wife's, for contrary to children's wisdom, "names" can be just as harmful as "sticks and stones." Although feminists admit that some women can and do assault their husbands verbally, they nevertheless insist that even the wife who nags her husband from morning to night, who whines and complains, does not deserve blows and physical abuse. A husband's angry words are a response proportional to a nagging wife's verbal provocation; physical brutality is excessive. Because men are generally physically superior to their wives, wives are in immediate precarious physical danger from a batterer. Psyches are not as obviously vulnerable as bodies, so a husband's psychological integrity does not seem to be in as much danger as his wife's physical person is. Therefore, *verbal* provocation is an inadequate defense for woman-battering.[27]

A fourth reason traditional fault-oriented courts gave to justify a no di-vorce decision was that the battered woman had inflicted cruel behavior on her husband equal to the cruel behavior he had inflicted on her. Such behav-ior on the wife's part had to amount to something more than verbal provoca-tion. In *Metcalf* v. *Metcalf*, the Michigan Court of Appeals affirmed a lower's court ruling that the wife's "denial of sexual relations," her refusal to get the children off to school in the morning, her refusal to take her husband's telephone messages, her overnight absences, and her refusal to allow her husband "to experience the pleasure inherent in the sport of hunting deer" constituted a course of conduct tantamount to cruelty. The wife's counter-claim for legal separation based on allegations of physical abuse was denied on the grounds that any acts of cruelty committed by her husband were counterbalanced or neutralized by her "unreasonable conduct."[28] In response to cases such as this, feminists note both that only a sexist would classify Mrs. Metcalf's behavior as cruel, and that the cruelty of being denied a deer-hunting trip is not equal to the cruelty of being pummeled.[29]

Although this may seem like nothing more than interesting legal history, it is more than that. While the advent of no-fault divorce laws eliminated the "fault standard" in regard to the dissolution of marriages, it did not make fault irrelevant in regard to the adjudication of custody, child support, ali-mony, and property division. In an attempt to gain the sympathy of the court and to accomplish awards of larger support and alimony payments, today's battered woman will inform the court that her husband repeatedly beat her. The court will listen to her, but if her husband can establish either verbal provocation or cruel behavior on his wife's part, the woman will receive no special consideration. Unfortunately, it is relatively easy for a husband to convince current courts that his wife is the guilty party. As a result, a battered wife is unlikely to receive generous alimony payments in compensa-tion for the pain she sustained during a marriage that she tried so hard to keep intact.[30]

STANDARD CRIMINAL REMEDIES: THEIR LIMITS

Criminal remedies provide an alternative form of protection both for the woman who is not married to her batterer and for the woman who does not want to divorce her husband but change his behavior. In most states, woman battering falls under any one of a variety of assault statutes: assault and battery, assault and infliction of serious injury, felonious assault, assault with intent to do great bodily harm less than murder, assault with intent to commit murder, and assault with intent to maim. Most cases of woman-battering constitute simple assault and battery, but some cases constitute the higher degrees of assault, as when a husband punches his pregnant wife in the abdominal area, carves her face with a razor blade, or knocks her teeth out with a hammer.[31] As a victim of assault, it is within a battered woman's rights to demand that her batterer be arrested or otherwise served notice. Unfortunately, even though they are on the books, these remedies are not always enforced by police officers, prosecutors, and judges.

1. *Problems with Police Officers.* The police usually provide battered women with their first, most frequent, and most discouraging contact with the law. Police officers' behavior in responding to "domestic violence" calls reflects a pervasive assumption that "family problems . . . are non-criminal 'disputes' or 'disturbances,' essentially verbal in nature, not serious, and causing no one injury."[32] Although feminists admit that most family problems are noncriminal, they do not wish to give the impression that family violence is a rarity. The U.S. Task Force on Crime notes that the risk of a serious attack from spouses, family members, friends, or acquaintances is nearly twice as great as that from strangers, and the injury inflicted by intimates is likely to be more serious than that inflicted by strangers.[33] Nevertheless, police officers are inclined to trivialize sights and sounds that would shock most civilians. There are several reasons why police officers downplay domestic violence. First, to the degree that a male police officer believes that battered women are whiners, complainers, or nags, he may be prompted to put their plight into "proper perspective." Exchanges like the following one between an elder policeman who has witnessed many woman-batterings and a rookie cop who has seen his first battered woman are not uncommon:

> "Look son. I'm going to tell you something. I've been married probably longer than how old you are. . . . My wife feels as though I don't love her anymore, so at least once a month, I start an argument, I slap her around a little bit, and we have a perfect marriage. I've been married thirty-five years."[34]

Not only do feminists doubt that this type of marriage is "perfect," they doubt that the type of attention wives crave from their husbands is a slapping session. Second, police departments frequently teach their officers to take the batterer's side. Several widely used training guides for police recruits portray battered women as domineering wives who take delight in controlling their husbands, as demanding nags or sharp-tongued vipers who are driving their husbands crazy, or as drug addicts/alcoholics with little interest in their "role" as wife and mother. In contrast, these same guides portray batterers as men whose patience and generosity have been tested to their limits.[35] Although feminists are not suggesting that these guides be substituted with ones that portray battered women as saints or innocent damsels in distress and batterers as ogres or Nazi storm troopers, they are demanding that police manuals pay proper attention to empirical studies, which indicate that most batterers are extremely short tempered and that more than 70 percent of batterers are under the influence of drugs or alcohol when they beat their wives or girlfriends.[36]

A third reason why police officers trivialize woman-battering is that police dispatchers routinely place all family calls in the low-priority class of disturbance, without distinguishing between very dangerous and less dangerous disturbances. Feminists are aware that police officers must assign priorities to harms perpetrated in their precinct; given limited resources and limited manpower, felonies must take priority over misdemeanors and so on. What they object to, however, is the presumption that all woman-batterings are *per definiens* minor "ouches," when in fact some of them are life-threatening blows. Finally, police officers tend to avoid woman-batterers and battered women because almost one-fourth of the total number of police officers killed on duty die while handling family disturbance cases.[37] Feminists can appreciate these fears (battered women know them well), but they observe that police officers are morally obligated to intervene in dangerous situations.

Given these factors, it is no wonder that police departments have traditionally favored an *arrest-avoidance* policy in woman-battering cases. Until recently, a so-called stitch rule was in effect, whereby a battered woman was virtually ignored unless she required a substantial number of stitches. Because these sort of batteries constitute felonies, police officers felt duty-bound either to arrest the assailant immediately or to secure a warrant for his delayed arrest. In cases where a woman did not require hospitalization, police officers routinely classified her case as a misdemeanor and rarely arrested her batterer even when they caught him in the act of abusing his wife. Moreover, on the grounds that they did not want to add fuel to the fire, police officers sometimes failed to inform the battered woman of her right to file a complaint against her husband if she thought, contrary to police opinion, that arrest was the appropriate course of action. Instead, police officers urged the battered woman to secure a peace bond or restraining order, pointing out that an arrest warrant would ruin her chances for making a better life with a man upon whom she was perhaps economically and emotionally dependent.

Not knowing any better, many battered women assumed that peace bonds or restraining orders were their best option. Unfortunately, these bonds and orders (to which nominal monetary penalties and/or minimal prison sentences are attached)[38] are, by almost any lawyer's admission, not worth the paper they are written on unless they are enforced—and police officers rarely devote time or energy to enforcing them. Once a battered woman feels that those who are supposed to protect her do not in reality care at all about her, she may become despondent. Unless she has family, friends, or social workers who can support her emotionally and financially, she may resign herself to the whims of her batterers.

Largely as a result of feminists' efforts to draw attention to the adversities of battered women, police departments are abandoning their traditional arrest-avoidance policies. In their place, they are increasingly adopting one of two new approaches to woman-battering: (1) the "crisis-intervention" and "conflict-management" approach, or (2) the "proarrest" approach.

The crisis-intervention and conflict-management approach is largely the brainchild of Morton Bard. Convinced that training police officers in interpersonal skills could improve their management of domestic disturbances, Bard persuaded several police departments, most notably the New York Police Department, to give their officers crash courses in human relations. Police recruits were taught that violence directed at a wife by a husband should not be treated in the same way as violence between strangers because intrafamily violence is merely a symptom of a "troubled relationship." Like most "people in conflict,"[39] battering husbands and their battered wives supposedly want an "objective, skillful, and *benign authority* who can negotiate, mediate or arbitrate a constructive outcome."[40] Therefore, if a police officer is to be benign, he or she must be able to reconcile battling parties.

This police-officer-as-community-mental-health-worker approach was tried in a few jurisdictions, including New York City's 30th Precinct. Assigned to biracial teams, black and white police officers received training in psychology prior to their assignments. Although they performed other, routine patrol duties, they were always dispatched to family disturbances. Careful records were kept of each call so all team-members could apply similar methods of intervention/counseling to similar calls. Not only did the unit, in consultation with psychologists, mediate family disputes, it also made referrals for medical and social work assistance from up-to-date resource lists compiled by the officers themselves. Although domestic peace was not achieved in the precinct, the project was nonetheless proclaimed a success because there were no homicides in the families aided by the unit and no injuries to the policemen of the unit.[41]

While feminists agree that arbitration, mediation, and negotiation between volatile family members are sometimes worthwhile objectives, they do not agree with Bard either that families always want to stay together or that it is in their best interest to do so. Recent studies indicate that battered women generally remain with their batterers not because they are still in love with these violent men, but because of (1) complex cultural factors ("good women stay with their husbands no matter what"), (2) economic, legal, and social dependence on their batterers, (3) a feeling that they have no safe place to hide, and (4) a feeling that a bizarre symbiotic relationship over which they have a measure of control may be better than life alone in a totally alien and unpredictable environment. When such women are provided with outside emotional and economic support, approximately 70 percent of them express interest in protecting their right to live apart from their batterer, and that less than 30 percent see marriage counseling and/or individual and couple therapy as desirable alternatives.[42] Related studies show that children who formerly lived in violent, two-parent homes express enormous relief at living in a nonviolent, one-parent home.[43] Finally, psychologists believe that the sooner a battered woman comes to terms with the fact that her husband or boyfriend is not Prince Charming, the better off they as well as any involved children will be. Unless a woman lets her man know that one incident of battering is one incident too many, they may find themselves locked into an increasingly pathological relationship.

According to Lenore Walker, a woman must experience the cycle of battering twice before she becomes a true battered woman. The battering cycle is composed of three stages that occur in order. It begins with a "tension-building phase," punctuated by the actual act of violence, and concludes with a "calm, loving respite."[44] If a woman experiences the battering cycle once and responds either by calling the police or by leaving her husband, she serves notice to her husband: "Either you agree to see a therapist, or you will never see me again; our relationship is not worth the destruction of my body and/or psyche." In contrast, if a woman experiences the battering cycle once and responds by trying to be more patient, more understanding, more submissive, chances are that she will be abused a second time. Her husband may interpret her willingness to forgive him as a tacit admission of her guilt, as a sign of her partial or total responsibility for his brutal behavior.[45] The odds are good that the more often a woman is beaten, the more likely *she* is to blame herself for not being able to transform her husband's behavior, and the more likely she is to stay with her husband despite the costs to herself. Therefore, feminists conclude that the authorities sometimes err when they encourage battered women to "kiss and make up" with their abusive husbands. Unless legal remedies with primary ambitions other than reconciliation are available for all battered women, some battered women will be asked or even required to sustain relationships that are not worth sustaining.

Because arbitration, mediation, and negotiation are not universal panaceas for woman-battering, feminists currently favor a proarrest policy in those cases where the battered woman expressly requests that her batterer be arrested. To date, a few jurisdictions have responded to this request by amending their police-training manuals to include statements such as "A wife-beating is foremost an assault—a crime that must be investigated."[46] Unlike crisis-intervention and conflict-management manuals, which tend to take the side of the batterer and almost always describe arrest as the worst possible remedy for woman-battering, these proarrest manuals usually note:

A police arrest, when the elements of the offense are present, promotes the well-being of the victim. Many battered wives who tolerate the situation undoubtedly do so because they feel they are alone in coping with the problem. The officer who starts legal action may give the wife the courage she needs to realistically face and correct her situation.[47]

Feminists do not claim that incarceration is always or necessarily the best solution for all battered women's problems, but they do insist that a battered woman is within her rights to press criminal charges and that police officers are duty-bound to help her.

2. *Problems with Prosecutors.* Even if police officers are willing and able to do their duty, the battered woman who initiates criminal proceedings will not get very far unless the district attorney's office decides to support her efforts. Unfortunately, the prosecutor assigned to the case may move to drop it for one of four reasons, all of which hinge on whether the battered woman is perceived as a victim meriting sympathy.

Although woman-battering is classified both as a tort and as a crime, a prosecutor may believe that solution through the criminal process is not appropriate. One prosecutor comments:

> Because our society has not found adequate alternatives to arrest and adjudication for coping with interpersonal anger publicly expressed, we pay a price. . . . The congestion and drain on resources caused by an excessive number of such cases in the courts weakens the ability of the criminal justice system to deal quickly and decisively with "real" felons.[48]

If faced with an enormous case load of every felony and misdemeanor conceivable, some prosecutors are especially prone to employ so-called mediation policies or diversionary strategies. Although mediation policies— where both parties are asked to identify sources of frustration in their relationship and to suggest solutions to the problems they identify—can be useful in limited circumstances in which the violence is not chronic, and in which both parties are motivated to make changes in their relationship, where violence is chronic and one or both of the parties is not willing to make changes, mediation is usually counterproductive. Mediation agreements often trivialize the offense of woman-battering by requiring the wife to have meals ready, or to tidy the house carefully, or not to argue with her mate about his drinking problem. Although the husband might in return agree to try to curb his temper, such a commitment is unlikely to be successful so long as he is permitted to blame his violence on his victim ("She didn't do what she promised"). Giving a batterer the opportunity to blame his victim for having caused him to lose control results not only in her feelings of shame, embarrassment, or lost self-esteem, but in his conviction that his actions are vindicated. If his behavior were her fault, then he should have beaten her because she did something to deserve it.

An equally problematic approach to woman-battering is the employment of diversionary strategies, which range from issuing peace bonds to the batterer to referring the battered woman to a civil court, where she will be handed an injunctive order. To the degree that these bonds and orders are not enforced, batterers learn that prosecutors are, in effect, their allies. Helene A. Pepe of the Georgetown Law Center in Washington, D.C., recounts one incident in which a husband crumbled up an injunctive order. Knowing full well that such orders are rarely enforced, he forced his wife to eat it before he proceeded to beat her.[49] In a similar vein, Elizabeth Truninger of California documents accounts of police officers who enforce injunctive orders or peace bonds not by removing the batterer from the home that he used to share with his wife, but by escorting her from it.[50]

The second reason why prosecutors shy away from woman-battering cases is not unrelated to the first. From the prosecutor's point of view, woman-battering cases are not only low priority cases, they are a prosecutorial nightmare. The frequent failure of police departments both to keep records of family violence calls that do not result in arrest but which do show a pattern of abuse, and the failure to gather substantive information and evidence (such as photographs) when an arrest is made, increase prosecutors' reluctance to press charges in cases of woman-battering and reduce the likelihood of conviction in cases that are brought to trial. The prosecutor will have to convince the judge or jury that that nice-looking, respectable, confident, and collected man did in fact batter his wife. Given that the victim's bruises will probably have healed before the case comes to trial, that the defendant's version of the incident may make sense, and that there are probably no witnesses except perhaps the children, the prosecutor may find it impossible to convince the jury that "good, old Joe" is guilty beyond a reasonable doubt.

Although it is difficult to win a woman-battering case, such cases need not be brought to trial to be dealt with effectively. Whatever one thinks of plea-bargaining, it has proved useful in woman-battering cases. Debbie Talmadge, an assistant district attorney in the Santa Barbara Family Violence Program, has explained to many a battered woman that if her abuser thinks she will expose him in court, he will plead guilty so that he can reduce the penalty that will be imposed. In those instances where the battered woman conveys her resolve to her batterer, Talmadge has succeeded in obtaining a high rate of guilty pleas in return for a penalty that makes counseling a condition of probation. (If the terms of probation are violated, the batterer may then be sentenced to prison without further criminal proceedings.)[51] The criminal sanction can be used effectively against woman-batterers in ways that do not require drawn-out court battles or, in the event of conviction, the automatic incarceration of the batterer for a long period of time.

Another factor that causes some prosecutors to shy away from woman-battering cases is their perception that criminal proceedings are not in the best interests of the battered woman, especially if children are involved. If a battered woman prosecutes her husband in criminal court and he is imprisoned or forced to pay a large monetary fine to the state, the fine may be more than their *joint* bank account can withstand.[52] Moreover, not only her husband, but she and her children may be embarrassed by public court proceedings. Although a battered woman should consider these factors, prosecutors can help her avoid most of these problems by resorting to the creative use of plea-bargaining. In any event, it is one thing for a prosecutor to point out the problems inherent in criminal proceedings to a battered woman and quite another for him/her to decide unilaterally that criminal proceedings are not in her best interest even when she insists they are.

Finally, prosecutors slight woman-battering cases simply because many battered women who file complaints fail to follow through on prosecution. But feminists hasten to point out that it is not because battered women are "masochistic nuts" who like to be beaten. First, a battered woman may be pressured into dropping charges. Nancy Sich, an assistant district attorney in Santa Barbara, writes in an unpublished paper entitled "Family Violence: The Prosecutor's Challenge," that half of the abuse victims who came to her office to drop charges were accompanied by their abusers, who had threatened them into requesting dismissal.[53] Second, a battered woman may not understand the contemporary criminal justice system, especially practices such as plea-bargaining, probation, and suspended sentences. She may wrongly think that every criminal case goes to trial, that she will be required to testify and be subjected to merciless interrogation on the stand, and that if her batterer is convicted he will be given a lengthy jail sentence. Third, when a case takes months to process, a woman may tire of the whole procedure. She may drop charges because too much time will be lost from work, or because childcare will have to be arranged for numerous court appearances. Finally, the emotional difficulty of prosecuting a man she has lived with and may still love, a fear of reprisal, or the recognition that she is financially dependent on her husband's earnings often leads a battered woman to back down before a case gets to court.

Although feminists are convinced that most battered women would carry through their initial decision to prosecute if they were given strong prosecutorial support, they do not think that all women would or should do so. Women who have economic or emotional reasons for dropping a prosecution cannot, in the final analysis, be helped by the district attorney's office. These women need social services and psychological assistance, neither of which prosecutors can provide. Unless someone helps these battered women find food, clothing, shelter, and jobs, and unless someone helps them sort out their tangled web of emotions, these battered women may never be in a position freely and informedly to decide whether or not to apply criminal remedies against their batterers.

3. *Problems with Judges:* Even where conscientious police officers and prosecutors are determined to bring woman-batterers to court, certain judges, like certain police officers and prosecutors before them, tend to trivialize the offense of woman-battering by letting batterers off easily. This is especially true of judges who preside over family courts, which are permitted to dispose of intrafamily offense through civil suits with a civil procedure, even though they are recognized as violations of the criminal law. Frequently, family-court judges take the side of the batterer rather than the battered victim, implicitly suggesting that the woman who brings her husband to court is a vindictive shrew who only wants to malign her husband's reputation or to give him a hard time.

A mother of three, married for twenty-six years, who had gotten three family-court injunctions in ten years against her husband's violence, complained that not only her husband, but the judge told her the "piece of paper didn't mean a damn thing."[54] To save herself and her children, she finally moved out of her apartment. Finding refuge at a battered women's shelter, she dared not go back home for any of her possessions or those of her children. When the director of the shelter suggested that she secure a court order removing her husband from the apartment, the judge in charge of the case opined that "there is nothing more pathetic than to see a husband going to his home—usually in the company of a policeman—to collect his meager belongings."[55] The judge refused the battered woman's request. Because the battered woman had no financial assets, was unemployed, and was without supportive relatives, landlords were not interested in taking a gamble on her. Although this woman and her children were eventually taken in by a generous family, it is not uncommon for such displaced persons to wander the streets or to set up house in the backseats of automobiles.

Like family-court judges, criminal-court judges frequently trivialize woman-battering cases and/or sympathize with the batterers. In the late 1970s, for example, Seattle judges routinely imposed suspended one-month sentences and fines of no more than fifty dollars on defendants who pleaded guilty to charges of "causing a disturbance." The seriousness of the actual offenses had no apparent effect on the sentence, and not one assailant went to jail.[56] This is not to suggest that every woman batterer should be jailed, but it is to point out that unless judges take a firm hand with woman-batterers, all the conscientious work of police officers and prosecutors is for naught. When woman-batterers are merely slapped on the wrist by the courts, they are unlikely to change their behavior.

The Search for More Effective Legal Remedies

Well aware of the flaws in civil and criminal remedies for woman battering, feminists have responded to these limitations with one or more of three, novel strategies. The first approach is litigation against prosecutors and litigation against police and court employees. Generally the district attorney or prosecutor has broad discretion to decide which cases to prosecute. Nonetheless, the equal-protection clause imposes constitutional limits on this discretionary power. Prosecutors cannot refuse to enforce state criminal laws on behalf of a particular group of people if they enforce these laws on behalf of similarly situated people. During the ninteenth century, for example, police officers and prosecutors refused to enforce the law against members of the Ku Klux Klan who assaulted blacks, even though they enforced the law against members of the Ku Klux Klan who assaulted whites. There is an analogy between prosecutorial refusal to enforce the law to protect blacks and prosecutorial refusal to protect battered women. If prosecutors prosecute all batterers except for woman-batterers, then battered women are left without the equal protection of the law. Therefore, battered women can sue prosecutors for dereliction of duty if they routinely refuse to initiate criminal proceedings against woman-batterers.[57]

In *Raguz* v. *Chandler,* several battered women won a class-action suit against Cleveland prosecutors.[58] As a result, prosecutors were required to consider each case of women-battering on its own merits, to ask detectives to investigate even when no arrest was made, to advise police officers that woman-batterers will be prosecuted, and to permit each battered woman to request review of a prosecutor's decision not to prosecute in her case. Similarly in *Bruno* v. *Codd,* twelve New York City women who had been beaten by their husbands sued nineteen defendants, including the police commissioner, the chief clerk of the family court, and the director of probation.[59] The women alleged that all these officials failed to provide them with protection against their abusive husbands. In particular, they objected to New York's 1962 Family Court Act, which declared that women whose husbands beat them need "practical help" rather than "criminal punishment" for their attackers. As a result of this act, family court was given the power to issue injunctive or restraining orders to battered women whose husbands perpetrated against them such crimes as assault, reckless endangerment, or disorderly conduct.[60] The maximum penalty (rarely imposed) for violation of such orders was six months' imprisonment. Under this system, police officers routinely refused to arrest a husband unless his wife had secured a family-court order, but family courts routinely refused to issue such orders, demanding that the wife first exhaust less forceful alternatives, such as "kissing and making up." Although all the defendants in this suit argued that they had not violated their duty, the Manhattan Supreme Court refused to dismiss the charges against them. Eventually, the New York City Police Department entered into a voluntary agreement with the twelve women. The police agreed to treat woman-battering like any other assault. Specifically ruled out as reasons for nonarrest in the case of felonies and police-witnessed misdemeanors were "the fact that the parties are married, the fact that the woman had not previously sought an order of protection from family court or the officer's belief that mediation and reconciliation are more appropriate."[61] In addition, the police promised to stay at the scene of the attack long enough to stop the violence and to help the battered woman secure any needed medical treatment. Although such suits are costly, time-consuming affairs, when they are successful, they prompt other negligent departments and agencies to engage in programs of preemptive self-reform.

A second approach and by far the most standard taken by feminists has been to develop laws and policies that deal specifically with woman battering. In an effort to tailor a response to the unique problems of a victim who is to some extent either fearful of her batterer or still emotionally and financially dependent on him, those legal remedies distinguish woman-battering from other assaults, batteries, and harassments. This approach is in many ways opposite to the one used in rape law reform, which seeks to include rape under the general category of assault. Still, these reform attempts are related in that they both seek to undermine the false view that women want, need, or deserve to be hurt by men—a view that has traditionally hindered effective legal action on behalf of female victims of rape and woman-battering.

In an effort to ameliorate the plight of battered women who fear for their physical safety, nine states have enacted statutes that specifically authorize the imposition of certain conditions on the pretrial release of defendants in woman-battering cases.[62] For example, a temporary protection order may be issued requiring the man to refrain from causing or attempting to cause physical harm to the woman, or to refrain from entering her home, school, or place of employment. The order remains in effect only until the disposition of the criminal charge upon which it is based. If the order is violated, the batterer may be held in contempt of court and sentenced to a maximum of ten days in jail, or another order may be issued. The limitations of this approach are obvious. Unless the woman separates from her husband or divorces him, she may be forced to confront him after his release from prison or after he fulfills the condition of this probation. She can obtain an injunctive order against him if she still fears him, but these orders are not always enforced. And even if a woman does divorce or separate from her batterer, he may continue to plague her no matter how many court orders she secures. Indeed, he may make her life miserable by adhering to the letter of the law while violating its spirit—continually showing up at those old, familiar places, such as the local supermarket or movie theater. As it stands, there is little that the law can do for such a woman. Committed as it is to each and every person's freedom, the law cannot preventively detain a former batterer on the grounds that he may possibly inflict a harm in the future. Unless the former batterer actually violates a court order or a statute, the woman whom he cautiously torments will probably have to live with his intrusions into her psychic space.

Interestingly, the law has been more successful in devising ways to meet the needs of women who wish to remain with their batterers than in devising ways to meet the needs of women who wish to separate permanently from their batterers. In a limited number of cases, prosecution is deferred or suspended if the batterer agrees to enter a program of psychological counseling. If he successfully completes the program, charges are dropped and the defendant's arrest record may be wiped clean. If the defendant fails to comply with the terms of his contract, prosecution is resumed. Because deferral usually occurs before any adjudication of guilt, the protection of the defendant's rights requires his voluntary participation. The defendant always has a right to have the offense adjudicated, and the courts have no power to impose penalties for an offense charged unless a conviction is obtained. Because the conditions of deferral (such as seeing a psychiarist) are frequently the same as some of the therapeutic sanctions that might be imposed after a criminal conviction, the protection of the batterer's rights require that his consent be obtained.[63] However, even if the batterer consents, deferral should not occur if the battered woman does not want anything to do with her batterer, if she feels that prosecution and incarceration is more appropriate, or if she is afraid for her safety and does not want her batterer to be released. The option to veto deferral gives the battered woman, perhaps for the first time, control over the conduct of the batterer. This changes the balance of power between the parties, gives the abuser a clear message that he has violated the victim's rights, and encourages the victim to make decisions about her life.

The third approach that feminists have favored is cooperation between "women-centered" police officers, prosecutors, and judges on the one hand and directors of battered women's shelters and crisis helplines on the othe. Where legal and extralegal personnel work together, they are better able to determine what kind of help a battered woman needs. The problem with this mode of dealing with an individual victim of battery is one of priorities and resources. Few jurisdictions are both able and willing to allocate adequate legal personnel for those innovative and helpful efforts. Similarly, most shelters and helplines run on a shoestring budget and find it difficult to provide women with adequate short-term relief (such as overnight bed and board), let alone with meaningful long-term assistance. According to feminists, unless battered women become a national priority of sorts, their condition will not be significantly ameliorated. In short, unless battered women, who both want and need economic and emotional support receive it, they will not be able to escape whatever hold their batterers have on them.

The Connections Between Woman-Battering and Spouse Murder

Even though none of the legal approaches advocated by feminists has been or can be entirely successful, they are an attempt to come to grips with a problem that is escalating. Frustrated by the law's feeble and fleeting efforts to protect their rights and sometimes those of their children, more and more battered women are killing their husbands in "self-defense." During 1976 in Chicago, 40 percent of the 132 women detained in Cook County Jail on charges of killing their male partners had been assaulted several times by the men they killed.[64] Cases such as that of Roxanne Gay and Francine Hughes have attracted national attention to these frightening statistics. In 1976 Gay stabbed her husband, a professional football player, to death as he lay asleep in their home in Camden, New Jersey. She claimed in her defense that he had beaten her frequently, and that she killed him anticipating that his next assault upon her would likely result in her death. After a four-day sanity hearing to determine her fitness to stand trial for homicide, she was judged insane and then committed. This was a confusing case because the defense both insisted on the justification of self-defense (Roxanne had a *right* to kill her bully husband) and the excuse of insanity (poor little Roxanne was not to blame for killing her husband).[65] The Hughes case is a bit more chilling than the Gay case. Hughes admitted that, as her ex-husband slept, she killed him by pouring gasoline on his bed and setting it ablaze. Her defense was that after their divorce he moved back into their home over her protests and resumed the beatings he had inflicted while they were married. The jury decided that her deliberate arson was an act of temporary insanity and acquitted her.[66]

What is significant about these homicides is that although juries are willing to *excuse* battered women who kill their husbands, they are not inclined to *justify* or vindicate battered women who kill their husbands. A defendant who claims self-defense asks the trier of fact to find that a homicide was justified.[67] Justified behavior is correct, not only tolerated but also approved of by the law. Inquiries about justifications focus on the circumstances of the act rather than on the actor. In contrast, an excusable act is one that, although wrong, should be tolerated because of the individual circumstances of the case. The agent pleading an excuse says, "I didn't know what I was doing" or "I couldn't help myself." Influenced by a long heritage that teaches that families are happy havens, the trier of fact will prefer to see the act of a woman who kills her husband as unreasonable. In general, women will be excused for acting in the heat of passion or on grounds of insanity. Of these two excuses insanity is sometimes perceived as a perfect plea for women because it emphasizes their supposed mental weaknesses. Feminists observe that this "perfect plea" often has less than ideal consequences for battered women. Women who secure acquittal on grounds of insanity are often in-voluntarily committed to mental health institutions, although often they are not crazy but simply desperate women who have exhausted (what seems to them at least) every alternative way of dealing with their batterers.

Cases, statistics, and observations such as these are forcing the law to reconsider definitions of self-defense and provocation in light of the unique predicament of the battered woman. Each of the three traditional require-ments for a self-defense plea—the defendant did not use excessive force, ignore a requirement to retreat, or act before a crisis of appropriate magni-tude was imminent—need to be rethought if the law is to deal justly with homicides committed by women trapped in a pattern of repeated violence with male assailants physically stronger than they. The excessive-force rule teaches that the right to kill in self-defense requires that person x reasonably believe that person y will inflict fatal or serious physical injury and that only deadly force will repel this attack. This requirement may unduly burden a battered woman. For example, when it comes to minor assaults, person x is required to submit to an ordinary battery and have his remedy in court rather than endanger the life of person y, the assailant. This formula does not preclude defense by nondeadly means—y hits x, x hits y back—but in a battle between spouses of unequal size and strength, "hitting back" is not usually one of the woman's options. When it comes to serious assaults, deadly force may be used to combat deadly force—that is, force that could cause death, a protracted impairment of physical health, or serious disfigurement. Since many woman batterers inflict deadly force, their victims may respond with deadly force. Unfortunately, judges and jurors often rule that a battered woman applied more force than was necessary to preserve her physical integrity.[68]

In this connection, lawyer Maria Marcus describes a case in which a woman was charged with murdering her husband. She testified that her husband had battered her on numerous occasions, and early on the night of the homicide he threatened to beat her. Later that night he threatened to kill her, advancing upon her with a knife. As he advanced toward her, she picked up a gun and fired a warning shot into the air. When the warning shot failed to stop him, she shot and killed him. The jury found the woman guilty of manslaughter.[69] According to Maria Marcus, the jury erred because it looked at the case not from the point of view of a reasonable battered *woman*, but from the point of view of a reasonable *man*. The jury failed to take into account the disparity in strength between the battered woman and the deceased, and it failed to consider whether the battered woman could really have fought off the deceased's attack without the use of a gun.

In a similar case, *State* v. *Wanrow*, the Washington Supreme Court insisted that the perceptions or beliefs of the battered woman—not the perceptions or beliefs of some hypothetical or actual man—are the key factors in determining whether or not a battered woman acted reasonably:[70]

> The impression created—that a 5'4" woman with a cast on her leg and using a crutch must, under the law, somehow repel an assault by a 6'2" intoxicated man without employing weapons in her defense [was a misstatement of the law that was underlined by] the persistent use of the masculine gender leav[ing] the jury with the impression [that] the objective standard . . . is that applicable to an altercation between two men.[71]

Not surprisingly, feminists applaud the *Wanrow* decision, arguing that the equal-force rule must be reinterpreted, taking into account the current physical strength inequalities between the sexes and recognizing that often only an armed woman can approach a force equal to that of an unarmed male assailant.

The second requirement for self-defense, the duty to retreat, is even more problematic for battered women, according to lawyer-feminist Marcus. The common law required those pleading self-defense to retreat from any setting *other than the home* in preference to using deadly force. The doctrine that a person is never required to flee from his or her "castle" is based on the rationale that liberty is imperiled if a law-abiding citizen can be forced out of a place where he has every right to be. In the conjugal context, both the battering man and the battered woman are in their own dwelling. Under such circumstances, must the battered woman attempt flight before she can kill in self-defense or may she kill in self-defense without attempting flight?

Although a few courts have ruled that wives are obligated to retreat from their husband's castles,[72] most courts have agreed that retreat should not be required of a battered wife:

> Her opportunities to flee are usually severely limited. The husband may have the car; there may be children in the home to be considered; and the unaccompanied female at night is greeted with suspicion if not refusal of admission by hotel and motel clerks who fear not only her possible profession but if convinced of her true plight are fearful of her being followed by a vengeful husband who would create a scene.[73]

Although feminists are relieved that self-defense is permissible in the home, or "castle," they are nonetheless distressed that battered women often stay put only because there is nowhere else to go.

The third requirement for self-defense, the immediacy of the threat, is also controversial. The so-called imminent-danger rule, which focuses on the circumstances immediately before the incident and does not take into account harm done in the past or threatened in the future, is inherently disadvantageous to women who, if they wait until they are in immediate danger from their husbands, are likely to be hurt because of a physical strength disadvantage in a direct confrontation.[74] In view of this, feminists have suggested that "judges in domestic homicide cases should provide a modified instruction on self-defense, replacing the imminent danger requirement with the certainty of harm in the future."[75] If a battered woman can prove that her husband would surely have seriously harmed or killed her in the future, then she may, like Roxanne Gay or Francine Hughes, kill her husband in anticipatory self-defense. Not surprisingly, this suggestion has not been met with enthusiasm. Two sound reasons are given for not justifying deadly defensive force if the danger to be countered is not occurring at the time of the force's exertion: The assailant may voluntarily change his mind, or he might be "legally prevented" from carrying out his intentions.[76] With reference to the first reason, it is difficult to be certain whether a batterer will in fact perpetrate a serious harm in the future, nevertheless an assailant is not likely to change his mind where he has established a "recidivistic pattern of violence."[77] With reference to the second reason, feminists admit that it is important that citizens not take the law into their own hands. They largely agree with William Blackstone:

> This right of natural defense does not imply a right of attacking; for, instead of attacking one another for injuries past or impending, men need only have recourse to the proper tribunals of justice. They cannot, therefore, legally exercise this right of preventive defense, but in sudden and violent cases; when certain and immediate suffering would be the consequence of waiting for the assistance of the law.[78]

What Blackstone fails to consider are those situations in which serious injury is virtually certain, but the assistance of the law is withheld. Francis Wharton, a legal expert postdating Blackstone, notes that where there is no legal remedy forthcoming,

> it has sometimes been said that if A's life be made wretched by the reckless and desperate enmity of B, . . . whom no other process can be used to check, then A is excused in taking this violent but only possible way of saving his own life, by sacrificing that of B. But it is otherwise where there is opportunity to invoke the interposition of the law.[79]

Although feminists are inclined to argue that Wharton's rule applies to those cases of woman-battering in which civil and criminal justice personnel do not enforce assault and battery statutes against batterers, they are not convinced that a major weakening of the imminent-danger rule is necessarily advisable. If battered women were routinely acquitted for their anticipatory slayings of their batterers, the deterrent effect of the law of homicide would be weakened and women would be tacitly encouraged to perpetuate acts of violence. If women are unable to get adequate help from the law to extricate themselves from violent relationships with their batterers, or to restructure these relationships before they become unbearable, women may increasingly turn to violence as the only apparent resolution and cast themselves on the mercies of the courts. But spouse murder, whether the victim is the husband or wife, is clearly not something that should be excused lightly or justified routinely. Still, if society does not offer to help battered women help themselves in more positive, less destructive ways, it cannot expect the incidence of intrafamily homicide to decrease. Indeed, it can blame itself for its increase.

Conclusion

What battered women most need is independence from the men who batter them. At first this independence may mean nothing more than access to a women's shelter. Ultimately, however, independence must mean more than this. As Judge Lisa Richette of Philadelphia said at the United States Civil Rights Commission Hearings on Domestic Violence in January 1978, "All the shelters in the world would not provide support for women unless all society is reorganized to end sexism."[80] Until a woman has the skills and financial resources to make a life of her own, she can never be certain whether she would be better off without her batterer, and until a woman understands that she is not to blame for her batterer's behavior, she will never be free of him.

It is not easy for a battered woman to get over her guilt, especially if she has been socialized to be nurturant—to be the giver rather than the receiver. This point is well illustrated in a letter from a woman battered by her husband:

> For most of my married life I have been beaten. . . . Early in our marriage I went to a clergyman, who, after a few visits, told me that my husband meant no real harm, that he was just confused and felt insecure. I was encouraged to be more tolerant. . . . Next time I turned to a doctor.
>
> I was given little pills to relax me and told to take things a little easier. I was just too nervous. . . . I turned to a professional family guidance agency. I was told there that my husband needed help and that I should find a way to control the incidents. I couldn't control the incidents—that was the whole point of my seeking help.[81]

No woman should be expected to control her man's anger, but every man, and every woman for that matter, should come to understand the causes of the battering cycle. People react to internal stress (feelings of insecurity, inadequacy, or vulnerability) and external stress (interpersonal conflicts, unemployment, or illness) in different ways. Some people laugh or cry; others overeat, talk too much, or work too long; still others engage in violence. All these behavioral manifestations are learned responses to stimuli. Somewhere along the line, the batterer learned certain cultural and social values about masculinity and his role in the family that support his aggression and violence toward women. Similarly, somewhere along the line, the battered women learned certain cultural and social values about femininity and her role in the family that support not only her submission to men, but her willingness to serve them.

Obviously, it is neither easy for a man to unlearn his abusive behavior nor simple for a woman to unlearn her victimlike behavior, especially when society continues to socialize aggressive men and passive women. The process is slow, painstaking, and sometimes unsuccessful. But the effort must be made. In the interim, to protect not only the rights of women but also the law's own integrity as an orderly alternative to vigilante justice, the law must deal with woman-battering by enforcing existing laws and by making new laws tailored to the unique situation of the battered woman.

Notes

1. Elizabeth M. Schneider, "Equal Rights to Trial for Women: Sex Bias in the Law of Self-Defense," *Harvard Civil Rights—Civil Liberties Law Review* 15, no. 3 (Winter 1980):624.

2. Ibid., p. 626.

3. Anne L. Ganley, *Court-Mandated Counseling for Men Who Batter: A Three-Day Workshop for Mental Health Professionals* (Washington, D.C.: Center for Women Policy Studies, 1981), p. 8.

4. Ibid., pp. 9–15.

5. Ibid., p. 10.

6. Ibid., p. 13.

7. Ibid., pp. 298–353.

8. Muhammad I. Kenyatta, "The Impact of Racism on the Family as a Support System," *Catalyst: A Socialist Journal of the Social Services* 2 (Winter 1980):39.

9. Jean Bethke Elshtain, *Public Man, Private Woman* (Princeton, N.J.: Princeton University Press, 1981), p. 335.

10. *Bruno v. Codd,* 90 Misc. 2d 1047, 1048, 396 N.Y.S. 2d 974, 975 (Sup. Ct. 1977), rev'd in part, appeal dismissed in part, 64 A.D. 2d 582, 407 N.Y.S. 2d 165 (1978), aff'd, 47 N.Y.S. 2d 582, 393 N.E. 2d 976, 419 N.Y.S. 2d 901 (1979).

11. *Bradley v. State,* 2 Miss. 156, 158 (1 Walker 1824).

12. Lenore E. Walker, *The Battered Woman* (New York: Harper & Row, 1979), p. 12.

13. William Blackstone, *Commentaries on the Laws of England,* bk. 4 (Philadelphia: R. Welsh & Co., 1897), p. 1602.

14. Ibid.

15. *State v. Black,* 60 N.C. 162, 163, 86 Am. Dec., 436 (1864).

16. Ibid.

17. Ibid.

18. Terry Davidson, *Conjugal Crime: Understanding and Changing the Wife-Beating Pattern* (New York: Hawthorn Books, 1978), p. 102.

19. *Commonwealth v. McAfee,* 108 Mass. 458, 11 Am. Rep. 383 (1871).

20. Jerome Hall, *General Principles of Criminal Law,* 2d ed. (Indianapolis: Bobbs-Merrill, 1960), p. 240.

21. Herbert Parker, *The Limits of the Criminal Sanction* (Stanford, Calif.: Stanford University Press, 1968), pp. 297–98.

22. Sue E. Eisenberg and Patricia L. Micklow, "The Assaulted Wife: 'Catch 22' Revisited," *Women's Rights Law Reporter* 3 (Spring/Summer 1977): 151–53.

23. Ibid., p. 152.

24. Ibid., cf., *Williams* v. *Williams,* 351 Mich. 210, 212, 88 N.W. 2d, 483, 484 (1957).

25. Ibid., pp. 144–45.

26. Walker, *The Battered Woman,* pp. 51–54.

27. If a wife hits her husband first, especially if she hits him with an object, then he may be justified to hit her back with proportional force.

28. Eisenberg and Micklow, "The Assaulted Wife," p. 152.

29. This case, more than others, reveals the implicit value schema of Anglo-American courts.

30. Eisenberg and Micklow, "The Assaulted Wife," p. 153.

31. Ibid., pp. 147–49.

32. New York City Police Department, *Police Student's Guide—Social Science,* sec. 8, para. 41 (undated).

33. *U.S. President's Commission on Law Enforcement & the Administration of Justice, Task Force Report: Crime and Its Impact—An Assessment* (Washington, D.C.: U.S. Government Printing Office, 1967), p. 15.

34. Jennifer Baker Fleming, *Stopping Wife Abuse* (New York: Anchor Books, 1979), p. 151.

35. Law Enforcement Assistance Association, "The Function of the Police in Crisis Intervention and Conflict Management, A Training Guide" (*LEAA,* National Institute of Law Enforcemment and Criminal Justice, 1975), app. 1–11, 1–17, 1–23, 1–24.

36. Eisenberg and Micklow, "The Assaulted Wife," p. 144.

37. Fleming, *Stopping Wife Abuse,* p. 173.

38. Eisenberg and Micklow, "The Assaulted Wife," pp. 150–51.

39. Fleming, *Stopping Wife Abuse,* p. 173.

40. Ibid.

41. Marjory D. Fields, "Wife Beating: Government Intervention Policies and Practices," in *Battered Women: Issues of Public Policy (1978),* U.S. Commission on Civil Rights (Washington, D.C.: U.S. Government Printing Office, 1978), p. 139.

42. Fleming, *Stopping Wife Abuse,* pp. 178–79.

43. Walker, *The Battered Woman,* pp. 30–31.

44. Ibid., pp. 55–57.

45. Fleming, *Stopping Wife Abuse,* p. 174.

46. Fields, "Battered Women," p. 165, n. 81.

47. Ibid., n. 82.

48. Vera Institute of Justice, *Felony Arrests: Their Prosecution and Disposition in New York* 31 (1977), p. xv.

49. Terry Davidson, *Conjugal Crime* (New York: Hawthorn Books, 1978), p. 87.

50. Ibid., p. 78.

51. Center for Women Policy Studies, "Prosecutors Discourage Battered Women from Dropping Charges," *Response* 3 (December 1979):1.

52. Eisenberg and Micklow, "The Assaulted Wife," p. 158.

53. Center for Women Policy Studies, "Prosecutors Discourage Battered Women," p. 1.

54. Davidson, *Conjugal Crime,* p. 79.

55. Ibid.

56. Fields, "Battered Women," p. 188.

57. Laurie Woods, "Litigation on Behalf of Battered Women," *Women's Rights Law Reporter* 5, no. 1 (Fall, 1978):18.

58. No. C74–1064 (N.D. Ohio, filed 1974).

59. 396 N.Y.S. 2d 1974 (Sup. Ct. N.Y. County, 1977).

60. Women who were not legally married to their assailants were not eligible for orders of protection but could go to criminal court, where the defendant might face penalties of up to seven years.

61. Fleming, *Stopping Wife Abuse*, pp. 225–26.

62. *Ariz. Rev. Stat.* §13–3601 (C) (Supp. 1980); *Me. Rev. Stat. Ann.* tit. 15, §301 (Supp. 1980–1981); *Mass. Gen. Laws Ann.* ch. 276, §42A (West 1972 and Supp. 1980–1981); *Minn. Stat. Ann.* §629.72 (Supp. 1980); *N.Y. Crim. Proc. Law* §530.11 (McKinney Supp. 1980–1981); *N.C. Gen. Stat.* §15A–534.1 (Supp. No. 5, 1979); *Ohio Rev. Code Ann.* §2919.26 (Supp. 1979); *Wash. Rev. Code Ann.* §10.99.010 (Supp. 1980–1981); *Wis. Stat. Ann.* §969.02 (West 1979).

63. Punishment does not necessarily mean incarceration. Frequently, it takes the form of probation with mandated therapy.

64. "Study of Female Killers Finds 40% Were Abused," *New York Times,* December 20, 1977, p. 20.

65. Jerrold K. Footlick, "Wives Who Batter Back," *Newsweek,* January 30, 1978, p. 54.

66. Ibid.

67. Paul H. Robinson, "A Theory of Justification: Societal Harm as a Prerequisite for Criminal Liability," *University of California at Los Angeles Law Review* 23 (December 1975):266, 275.

68. Maria L. Marcus "Conjugal Violence: The Law of Force and the Force of Law," *California Law Review* 69 (July 1981):1704–05.

69. *People* v. *Jones,* 191 Cal. App. 2d 478, 12 Cal. Rptr. 777 (2d Dist. 1961).

70. *State* v. *Wanrow,* 88 Wash. 2d 221, 559 P. 2d 548 (1977).

71. Ibid., 240, 558.

72. *Commonwealth* v. *Shaffer,* 367 Mass. 501, 511, 326 N.E. 2d 880, 883 (1975).

73. *People* v. *Cameron,* 53 Cal. App. 3d 786, 792, 126 Cal. Rptr. 44, 48 (5th Dist. 1975).

74. Marcus, "Conjugal Violence," pp. 1709–11.

75. Ibid., p. 1730.

76. Ibid., p. 1710.

77. Ibid.

78. William Blackstone, *Commentaries,* p. 184.

79. Francis Wharton, *A Treatise on Criminal Law,* 9th ed. (Philadelphia, 1885), p. 460.

80. Schneider, "Equal Rights to Trial for Women," p. 627, n. 17.

81. Dorie Klein, "Violence Against Women: Some Considerations Regarding Its Causes and Its Elimination," *Crime and Delinquency* 27 (January 1981):76.

CHAPTER 6

BLACK PERSPECTIVES ON WOMEN, SEX, AND THE LAW

An exhaustive analysis of women, sex, and the law would require looking at all groups (Latin-American, Asian-American, Native-American, Afro-American) that are not part of the Anglo-American or European-American tradition when it is narrowly conceived. Yet, this chapter will concentrate on black women, and readers should make whatever adjustments are necessary as they reflect upon the experiences of other nonwhite women, or women of color.[1] Because black women are often disadvantaged not only by their gender, but also by their race and sometimes their class, the issues of pornography, prostitution, sexual harassment, rape, and woman-battering have different implications for them than for advantaged white women. Sex-related issues have not been priority issues for black women, even though black women are featured in pornography, pimped, harassed, raped, and battered just as frequently, if not more frequently, than white women.

One explanation for this deemphasis on sex-exploitative issues is that for black women racism and classism are sources of oppression more hurtful than those either threatened or delivered by sexism. Jill Lewis comments:

The relationships of Black men and women have developed and been sustained in a context of survival and struggle. They have been allied against White domination and the savage brutality it has entailed. The history and culture of Black men and women have therefore evolved in large part in opposition to the dominant culture and its codes and laws. The struggle for survival and for the most elemental human rights has meant a collaborative opposition to and disruption of the structures "White" culture valued. The different conditions, tactics, and collaboration experienced within Black history created forms of support, collusion, mutual respect, and reliance between men and women in the Black community.[2]

As many black women see it, now is not the time to attack black men on account of their sexism. The battle against sexism must remain largely unfought until the struggles against racism and classism are over. A second explanation produced to explain black women's relative calm in the face of increasing sexual violence against all women is that black women are less sexually inhibited and thus less indignant than their white counterparts. Unlike white women, who supposedly read degrading meanings into virtually all sexually-explicit material and who take umbrage at anything physical, black women are supposedly more earthy: Sex is sex and women can enjoy it as much as men.

The first of these explanations depends on a world view according to which fighting for the integrity of one's race as a whole is somehow more of a priority than fighting for the integrity of one's gender or one's class as a whole. This is, to say the least, a controversial world view. Radical feminists and classical Marxist feminists, for example, both take exception to it. According to the radical feminist, the physical subjection of women by men was historically the most basic form of oppression, prior rather than secondary to the institution of private property and its concomitant, class oppression. Moreover, the radical feminist also maintains that the sexual politics which develop within the biological family provide a paradigm for understanding all other types of oppression such as racism and classism. In contrast, the classical Marxist feminist believes that the economic oppression of propertyless workers (the exploited) by propertied owners (the exploiters) was historically the most basic form of oppression, prior rather than secondary to the institution of the family and its concomitant, gender oppression. In sum, whereas the radical feminist believes that the struggle against capitalism and against racism must take second place to the more fundamental battle against sexism, the classical Marxist feminist believes that the struggle against classism is more important than the battles against racism and against sexism.

In contrast to radical feminists and classical Marxist feminists, most of whom are white,[3] black feminists such as Audre Lorde point out that each woman must decide for herself whether it is the circumstances of her race, class, or gender that most oppresses her, and that women must support each other in their individual struggles for liberation, whether that liberation is from racism, classism, sexism, or some combination thereof.[4] In short, a woman's priorities depend on her concrete circumstances. For most black women, issues of race will remain a priority for some time. Slavery was a legal institution until a century and a quarter ago, the Civil Rights movement is recent history, the Ku Klux Klan still burns crosses, and the average black person remains close to the bottom of the socioeconomic ladder. Not only must white feminists understand this, they should—if only to express their solidarity with black women—join in the struggle against racism. Only when racism is not an issue for the black woman will she be able to give her wholehearted attention to issues of gender.

The second explanation for black women's matter-of-fact attitude toward sex-related issues is based on the notion that black women are less sexually puritanical than white women. Although those who make this point intend to compliment black women ("It's a good thing that all that awful Puritanism didn't seep into your soul"), the compliment is not unobjectionable. In fact, it is implicitly racist because it feeds the old myths and stereotypes that portray black women as licentious, loose, immoral, and promiscuous. It stands to reason that to the extent black women are socialized differently from white women, their perspectives on sex-related issues will be different from those of their white counterparts. Nevertheless, since in America black and white patterns of socialization are not markedly different, especially among blacks and whites from the same socioeconomic class, black and white women's intuitions about sex-related issues will probably be similar. To suggest anything else is to imply that because of their higher sensibilities and standards white women want and need to be protected from pornographers, pimps, sexual harassers, rapists, and woman-batterers, but that on account of their lower sensibilities and standards black women neither want nor need such protection. Clearly, any such implication is intolerable; it would constitute a throwback to mid-nineteenth-century America, to an America that treated black women very differently from white women. Said the black feminist and abolitionist Sojourner Truth in 1851:

> That man over there says that women need to be helped into carriages and lifted over ditches and to have the best place everywhere. Nobody ever helps me into carriages or over mud puddles or gives me the best place. And ain't I a woman? . . . I have borne thirteen children and seen most of 'em sold into slavery, and when I cried out with my mother's grief, none but Jesus heard me, and ain't I a woman?[5]

Keeping Sojourner Truth's challenges in mind, this chapter discusses the adjustments Anglo-American law must make if it is to show black women and other women of color the same respect and consideration it is trying to show white women.

Pornography

Degrading pornography represents depersonalized sexual changes devoid or nearly devoid of mutual respect. In other words, such pornographic descriptions and depictions display sexual exchanges in which the desires and

experiences of at least one participant are not regarded by the other partici-
pant(s) as having a validity and importance equal to his/her/their own. This
characterization applies equally to sexually explicit material that degrades
both men and women, blacks and whites, homosexuals and heterosexuals.
Of course, it is easier to convince people that coercive or violent (thanatic)
pornographic representations better display depersonalized sexual exchanges
devoid or nearly devoid of mutuality than do nonviolent ones. Perhaps this
is because in this culture violence is an unambiguous sign of disrespect—
indeed of ultimate disrespect where loss of life is involved. In large measure
this is why feminists have focused their antiporn campaign on gyno-
thanatica, or violent, women-degrading pornography. There is simply too
much controversy among people about whether certain nonviolent but arguably women-degrading descriptions (a *Playboy* centerfold) are *really*
women-degrading.

Significantly, of all the sex-related issues discussed in this book pornography is the one that has stirred the black community the least. Faced with
problems such as lack of adequate food, shelter, clothing, education, and
jobs, many black women feel that the feminist antipornography campaign
is an instance of misplaced outrage, a spewing of venom that only white
middle-class women can afford. Tracey Gardner, a black woman, believes
that like some white women, some black women have dismissed the antiporn
campaign as self-indulgent without appreciating what the "fuss" is all about.
In fact, Gardner attributes the disinterest of black women in the antiporn
movement largely to lack of information and exposure:

> Most women in this country, white and Third World, are unaware of
> the nature of hard-core pornography and how widespread it is. I know that
> if any woman of color were to see some of the brutal and deadly hard-core
> pornography around, she would be outraged by it no matter what the color
> of the woman being exploited was.[6]

In short, many women—black as well as white—think they know what
pornography is. They may have seen copies of *Playboy* or *Jiveboy;* they may
have attended an X-rated movie; they may have heard about urban "combat
zones" or even visited them. But it is unlikely that these same women have
also seen gyno-thanatic horrors like *Snuff* or that they have spent many hours
cruising New York City's Forty-Second Street or its equivalents. Moreover,
few women have analyzed pornography in any depth. Those who have
observe that there is a whole genre of pornography that heaps racist representations upon sexist representations.[7]

In this society women-degrading pornography, even non-women-
degrading pornography (erotica), can be racist on several accounts. Magazines such as *Jiveboy,* which is targeted for the black male population, are filled
with images of white women or light-skinned black women coupled with

dark-skinned black men. In some instances, this sexually explicit material is not women-degrading because it displays black men and white women who seem to care about each other's desires and experiences as sexual beings. But such erotic material is often implicitly racist because it suggests that black men find white women irresistible, that black women are not sufficiently attractive to merit black men's attention, and that despite the "black is beautiful" slogan, black men still dream of white-skinned, blue eyed, blonde women. If the supply of black men were more abundant, black women might not be as distressed as they are by black men's fantasies about white women. However, the pool of marriageable black males is small.

Black women 25 years old and over are more than twice as likely as white women to remain never married. The situation grows far more grave among the college-educated where—within the urban population 19 to 44 years old—for every 100 males there are 54 extra females without a mate or forced to share somebody else's.[8]

Given these statistics, it is difficult for many black women to look at depictions of black men and white women enjoying sex together and see there a representation of black men and white women transcending racial differences through tenderness and affection. What they see instead is black men choosing white women over black women. There is nothing the law can or should do about these wounds to black women's psyches, but feminists can and should point out that when pornography is racist, there is reason enough to object to it even though it is not women-degrading. Most often, however, the type of porn *Jiveboy* peddles will, when it is racist, also be women-degrading. Either it will show black men degrading white women by forcing them to perform sexual acts they object to (here the racist message is that when a black man finally gets a white woman, she must do his bidding "or else"), or it will show black men degrading black women, frequently in worse ways than white women (for example, by excreting or urinating upon them). The racist message here is that black men do not take pride in anything or anyone black. In her moving essay "Coming Apart," Alice Walker describes a black man's coming to terms with his reliance on women-degrading pornography:

What he has refused to see. . . . is that where white women are depicted in pornography as "objects," Black women are depicted as animals. Where white women are at least depicted as human bodies if not beings, Black women are depicted as shit. He begins to feel sick. For he realizes that he has bought some if not all the advertisements about women, Black and white. And further, inevitably, he has bought the advertisements about himself. In pornography the Black man is portrayed as being capable of fucking anything . . . even a piece of shit. He is defined solely by the size, readiness and unselectivity of his cock.[9]

In degrading women, the black man also degrades himself.

In the same way that magazines like *Jiveboy* can be racist without being women-degrading, so, too, are magazines like *Playboy,* which is targeted for the white male population. Whereas white women are frequently displayed as Frosty Snow Queens, inaccessible to the likes of mortal men, black women are often displayed as Bubbling Brown Sugars who will share their sweetness indiscriminately. More often, however, the material in these magazines is women-degrading as well as racist. It will, for example, show white men lording it over black women, as in a recent advertisement that portrayed two black women naked and in chains and a white man standing over them with a whip. Or it will show black women dressed up as wild animals simply begging their white masters to tame them. But whether or not black women find themselves spread across the pages of *Jiveboy* or *Playboy,* more than likely they will be defamed on account of their race as well as their sex. Black women can no more escape the abuse their race brings them than the abuse their gender subjects them to.

What this all suggests is that unlike the enormous and splintered group "women," the more unified and less numerous group "black women" may be able to initiate successful group defamation suits against those who have excited adverse feelings against them or diminished the esteem in which they are held by purveyors of racist gyno-thanatica. If a court were vacillating as to whether or not black women had been defamed on account of their gender, the fact that they had also been defamed on account of their race could influence its ultimate ruling in an antipornography suit. And since the pornography industry is largely controlled by white men, black women would not need to feel that in attacking the purveyors of racist gyno-thanatica they were attacking their own men, who, like them, are degraded on account of their skin color.

This is not to say, however, that black men are innocent spectators or bystanders. Like white men, black men buy pornography. But because black men are less politically and economically powerful than white men, their ability to live out their violent, women-degrading sexual fantasies is more limited than that of white men, if only because black men are more likely to go to prison for their transgressions than white men. Moreover, there is reason to think that pornography does not have as firm a grip on the imagination of Afro-American men as it does on the imagination of most Anglo-American or European-American men. Tracey Gardner comments:

> Pornography speaks to the relationship *white* men and women have always had with each other. Because they have been forced to live under the values of white people, the identity of Afro-Americans has been distorted and belittled to the point where pornography also speaks in part to our relationship.[10]

Any such claim would be difficult to prove, but this particular claim seems plausible. If, for example, Susan Griffin is correct in assuming that the pornographic imagination thrives only in cultures that are obsessed by dualities such as that of mind versus body or nature versus culture,[11] then pornography would not bloom in nondualistic cultures such as those of West Africa.[12] In any event, gyno-thanatic pornography is not, as some insist, a universal or essential phenomenon without which all the excitement would go out of human sexual fantasy. The notion that sexuality and aggression (violence) are inextricably linked is a notion that Western culture needs to outgrow.

Prostitution

Some women are forced into prostitution as a result of either individual coercion (a pimp's threats) or institutional coercion (economic necessity), and other women freely choose the life. Feminists agree that prostitution should be decriminalized. Whether or not a woman has *freely* chosen to be a prostitute, she should not be penalized for being a prostitute *if* prostitution is not harmful to others, immoral, or necessarily offensive. However, there are implications in decriminalizing prostitution, especially for those women who become prostitutes as a result of coercion.

Most black prostitutes are streetwalkers rather than call girls. Whereas call girls come from at least middle-class environments,[13] streetwalkers are generally drawn from the ranks of the lower class,[14] especially those segments of the lower class that are unemployed.[15] Since many black people still find themselves at the lower end of the socioeconomic ladder, black prostitutes will frequently have to walk the streets. Although blacks comprise about 11 percent of the general population, 53 percent of the prostitutes arrested in urban areas are black.[16] There are at least two possible explanations for this statistic: (1) either police officers tend to pick up black suspects more frequently than white suspects; or (2) the disproportionate number of black women arrested for prostitution reflects the "actual ratio" of black and white prostitutes on the streets in urban areas.[17]

Social commentators who are persuaded by the latter explanation disagree as to why black women become prostitutes. There are those who claim that unlike white women, black women are naturally promiscuous. Consequently, they are supposedly attracted to prostitution as a profession because they may as well profit from doing what they would do anyway. That this is not the case, despite the racist speculations of some white people about super-sexy black women, is amply attested to by many black prostitutes. Comments one black streetwalker:

You can say whoring is business. Or a means to an end. But it's not that cut and dried. It's important for you to know that most women who turn tricks have to be loaded on something. You don't have any woman out there selling this commodity and doing this trading who's not loaded on something. They're not that hip to business. And they're not that void. Like you gotta have something. If you're not high on dope it's something else.

Every time I went to turn a trick I had to fix before and after. There's a price a woman pays.[18]

According to her explanation, promiscuity is not the motivating factor behind this black prostitute's action. If she needs drugs to get herself through a day's work, then one of two conclusions may be drawn: (1) she needs the drugs and will do whatever is necessary (here, prostitution) to keep herself supplied with drugs; or (2) she does not "freely" prostitute herself, but for some conscious or unconscious reason she must prostitute herself, and she needs the drugs to help her endure the troubles of her life, including the troubles of *having* to be a prostitute.[19]

There are those social commentators, like Charles E. Silberman, who claim that some black women turn to prostitution and other related professions because their occupational options are so limited:

It should not be surprising that many poor people choose the routes to success that seem open to them. To youngsters growing up in lower-class neighborhoods, crime is available as an occupational choice, much as law, medicine, or business management is for adolescents raised in Palo Alto or Scarsdale—except that lower-class youngsters often know a good deal more about the criminal occupations available to them than middle-class youngsters do about their options. . . . Thus the fabric and texture of life in urban slums and ghettos provide an environment in which opportunities for criminal activity are manifold, and in which the rewards for engaging in crime appear to be high—higher than the penalties for crime, and higher than the reasons for avoiding it.[20]

Although Silberman's point has been criticized as implicitly racist because it seems to suggest that crime is a way of life for blacks, it can be given a nonracist reading. Anyone, black or white, growing up in a poor neighborhood will probably be tempted to engage in crime if it promises him or her a means of survival or better. This is not to claim that all or even most poor people will succumb to the lure of certain types of crime, but the temptation will be there and it may be difficult to resist. Since black women face great discrimination in education, jobs, and federal aid, their resistance may be particularly low. And because prostitution can offer them, if nothing else, a relatively steady income, some black women may hit the streets.

If prostitution were decriminalized, the number of black prostitutes and black pimps would probably increase, unless of course black women and men were suddenly showered with educational and vocational opportunities. As noted in Chapter 2, however, decriminalization would in theory benefit prostitutes by freeing them from the pimps who supposedly exploit them. Currently, many streetwalkers put up with abusive pimps because these men provide them with protection against robbers and other assailants. Pimps also provide them with bail and lawyers in the event of their arrest. Removing the threat of criminal penalties from prostitution would to some extent lessen the prostitutes' dependence on pimps. If promised police protection not only from violent patrons but from exploitative pimps, prostitutes would be free to work the streets alone or in conjunction with one another.

Unfortunately, it is difficult for some streetwalkers to free themselves from a pimp's psychological control, especially if he has been able to fill their need for affection and status. This seems to be the case with many black prostitutes. They may consider it an honor to be actively recruited by a wealthy and perhaps handsome pimp for a particular stable, and they may delight in someone paying attention to them. The honor of course, is a dubious one. Comments one black prostitute:

> Black men might do a lot about prostitution if they thought they could stop white men from coming uptown and turning a trick. They could stop putting black women out on corners. . . . Most of those guys uptown that keep sticking black women out on corners get into their El Dorado and go downtown, and spend most of her money on some eighteen or nineteen-year-old little white girl. She's a lady 'cause she went to a fancy school and her folks are white bread. That's racism. Doing Whitey's thing. Charlie's nigger. Fucking Charlie's daughter. . . . Since childhood that's what he's seen Charlie do. Can't do nothing else, 'cause Charlie's his role model. He has no others. The white man is the *only* man.[21]

By patronizing white prostitutes (that is, fucking like white men), and by doing business with white men, such as selling black hookers to white men (making a livelihood not only off white men but *like* white men), the black man, in this instance the black pimp, emulates the white man. But by emulating white men's weaknesses, black men frequently do harm to women. In particular, the black man who seeks out white prostitutes can harm women in one of two ways. On the one hand, if a black man patronizes a white prostitute merely to get back at white men for having sexually abused black women during the slave era, then the black man uses a white woman's body as a means to prove that he can have anything or anyone the white man has. On the other hand, if a black man patronizes a white prostitute not so much because he has an idiosyncratic penchant for a peaches-and-cream complexion as because he accepts the media's message that white women are more beautiful than black women, then he helps erode black women's self-image. Likewise, a black man can harm the class "women" by pimping *black* women. a black man sells black women to white men merely to make "Whitey" pay dearly for what he once took without asking, or simply to make easy money, then the black man acts in a way that shames his ancestors, who, had it not been for their chains, would have fought the white slaveowners who bought black women to work not only in their fields, but in their beds.[22]

Whether or not prostitution is decriminalized, there is little, if anything, that the law can or should do to relieve the pathos of this racist triangle. The law can, however, see to it that prostitutes (black as well as white) are protected from men (pimps or patrons) who abuse them. And if Kathleen Barry is correct, this is demanding work. As she sees it, only the happiest of hookers manages to escape her share of sadistic johns. Barry comments: "I hope no one is under the illusion that what the johns want from these women is a normal sexual experience. What they are looking for is horrendous, violating and, many times, life-threatening."[23] Thus if prostitution is decriminalized, old laws will have to be rigorously enforced against pimps or johns who abuse prostitutes, and new laws will have to be passed promising pimps imprisonment for recruiting minors, especially runaway girls as young as nine into the life.[24] If any sense is to be made of the claim that women freely choose to prostitute themselves, then those entering the life should be mature enough to make a sound decision about their future. Young girls, especially if they are without the support of family and friends, are generally incapable of making such a major decision. To allow an experienced, worldly-wise pimp or madam to take advantage of ignorance, hunger, or loneliness is to deprive these minors of the brighter future they might have had if they had been less deficient in knowledge and power.

Unfortunately, since police officers, prosecutors, and judges have not handled either rape victims or battered women respectfully and considerately, there is little reason to think that they will rank abused prostitutes as one of their top priorities. Indeed, if prostitution is decriminalized, criminal justice personnel may adopt a "she-had-it-coming to-her" attitude. And unless racism is suddenly eradicated, past experience indicates that abused black prostitutes will probably be treated more callously than abused white prostitutes by law enforcement agencies. Clearly, decriminalization is only a necessary condition for the amelioration of prostitutes' lives; it is far from a sufficient condition. Without the assistance of social agencies and without self-help measures such as unionization, decriminalization will not automatically improve the lot of prostitutes dramatically. It is one thing for a prostitute to get the law off her back; it is quite another for her to get abusive pimps and patrons out of her life.

Sexual Harassment

Cases of sexual harassment (unwanted sexual attention) are of two sorts: nondiscriminatory and discriminatory. Nondiscriminatory sexual harassment occurs when the harasser has no institutional power or authority over the women whom he harasses. Discriminatory sexual harassment occurs when the harasser is in a position of authority or power that allows him either to make better or to make worse the educational or occupational opportunities of the women whom he harasses.

Women react to nondiscriminatory sexual harassment in a variety of ways. Women who have been taught by their mothers "that sex is dirty, that it is not a subject for polite conversation, that masturbation is unnatural, and that sex will get you in trouble,"[25] are apt to want less in the way of sexual attention than women who have been reared in homes that have a more related attitude toward sex and teach that "sex is desirable, sex is satisfying, sex is 'good,' and everyone gets involved sooner or later."[26] But whether a woman is raised in a home of sexual restraint or of sexual exuberance, she will learn how to draw the line between wanted and unwanted sexual attention. In many black communities, for example, young men and women engage in an elaborate dating ritual during which the men give the women small gifts in return for small sexual favors (kisses or hugs) and large gifts in return for large sexual favors (intercourse). This is a time-consuming process. Gloria Joseph comments:

> If a male starts talking *sex* right away, with no rapping or presents, it's not considered respectable. So in most cases, games are played to keep the image of respectability (an important necessity for the woman) and games are played to keep women on the string (an important notion for men). It may take three weeks or more or less for the fuck to be achieved.[27]

Should the man rush the "fuck" or any of the stages leading up to it, he will be treated as a harasser even if he is not called that. And if he gets completely out of hand, the woman involved will have available to her the same legal remedies that are available to any white woman who finds herself in a similar situation: the criminal law of assault and battery or tort law. At least this is the theory. In practice, a black woman is not likely to do much, if anything, about nondiscriminatory sexual harassment, especially if her harasser is black. She will tend to take care of such annoying matters on her own, either by telling her admirer that she will not stand for such behavior or by getting her father or one of her brothers to make her feelings perfectly clear.

In contrast, when it comes to discriminatory sexual harassment, black women have been leaders in the efforts to stop its incursions into the workplace and into academia. That this should be the case is not surprising. Although black women identify 53 percent of their harassers as white and 47 percent as black, most of their black harassers are co-workers, while most of their white harassers are employers or supervisors.[28] Since harassed women are more likely to take employers, supervisors, or other powerful men to court, harassed black women rarely waste their time, energy, and limited financial resources on relatively powerless black harassers. They prefer to do battle with their white harassers, using racism as an added bonus in their legal case against a white sexist.

Black women's consideration for black men's sensitivities is particularly generous given that black women occupy the least advantaged position in society. Comments Catherine A. MacKinnon:

> When black women enter the labor market of the dominant society, they succeed to the secondary place of white females (remaining, in addition, under the disabilities of blacks), while black men succeed at least to some of the power of the male role. Indeed, many of the demands of the black civil rights movement in the 1960s centered upon just such a recovery of "manhood."[29]

Poor black women are especially vulnerable to sexual harassment because of their negative image as promiscuous women available for the asking and because of their pressing need for education and employment. Given these two facts—one related to their race and the other related to their class—poor black women are especially angered by well-heeled white men who sexually harass them.

Black women rightly resent the racist imputation that they are all whores. Shocking as it may seem, black women are frequently treated in a particularly demeaning manner. Not atypically, a medical administrator who was interviewed for a job was asked if it were true, in the black neighborhood in which she and her family lived, that "all the women were prostitutes." After she was hired, her white supervisor asked that she go to bed with him and several of his colleagues at once.[30] Properly angered, the black woman resigned and decided to take her harasser to court, where she won a Title VII case against him.

Even more significantly, black women, like all people, resent those who threaten to take what they are entitled to. As a class, black women have to work longer and harder to achieve relative success. For an employer to deprive any of these women of the fruits of their labor simply because they refuse to engage in sexual hanky-panky with him is an egregious violation of minimal justice. Properly angered by such unfair treatment, black women tend to confront their sexual harassers whenever it is reasonable for them to do so. Although disadvantaged black women have the most to lose by protesting—whatever little they have worked hard to achieve—paradoxically, it is also true to say that they have the least to lose by protesting. In this connection, Catherine MacKinnon observes:

> Since they [black women] cannot afford any economic risks once they are subjected to even a threat of loss of means, they cannot afford *not* to risk everything to prevent it. In fact, they often must risk everything even to have a chance of getting by. Thus, since black women stand to lose the

most from sexual harassment, by comparison they may see themselves as having the least to lose by a struggle against it. Compared with having one's children starving on welfare, for example, any battle for a wage of one's own with a chance of winning greater than zero looks attractive.[31]

Disadvantaged black women's desperation may breed a certain type of courage, a courage many advantaged white women lack. Court battles do not strike advantaged white women as particularly attractive unless the chances of winning are extremely high. Unlike many disadvantaged black women, many advantaged white women have the option of moving on to other equally lucrative jobs or the option of staying home and letting their husbands support them. Consequently, sexually harassed, advantaged white women are more prone than sexually harassed, disadvantaged black women to quit their jobs without making a "fuss." Black women are sensitive to the power politics involved in sexual harassment. In those cases where their harassers are white men, black women generally observe that their harassers use sex as an excuse not only to control their *individual* bodies but also to exercise power over all of them as a *class* of persons: as women (sexism) or as blacks (racism) or as disadvantaged blacks (classism). In short, black women tend to describe sexual harassment as a systematic abuse of power rather than a random occurrence of sexual lust. That black women's reports of sexual harassment by white male superordinates reflect a "sense of impunity that resounds of slavery and colonization" is, in this connection, highly significant.[32] Sexual harassers tend to take advantage of those whom they perceive as most vulnerable, and whether we care to face it or not, black women enflesh the vulnerability of their people's slave past.

This is not to claim that white women are not harassed by black men as well as white men.[33] It is to suggest, however, that the sexual harassment of a black woman by a white man is qualitatively different. When a white woman is sexually harassed by a black supervisor or employer, chances are that she will perceive the harassment as a random occurrence directed at her in particular. Since black men do not have a long history of systematic discrimination against white women, she will probably not describe her unfortunate experience as one of those things likely to happen to *white* women who enter the workplace or academy. Moreover, if she is at all familiar with the effects racism has had on our legal system, a white woman may anticipate a supportive response should she decide to bring her black harasser to the authorities' attention. In the same way that the law shows special, though unjustified, concern for white women who are raped by black men, it is likely to show special, though unjustified, concern for white women who are sexually harassed by black men. Indeed, Catherine MacKinnon reports that sometimes sensitive white women consciously resist reporting sexual harassment by black men to authorities precisely because they feel the reaction would be supportive for "racist reasons."[34] In contrast, when a black woman is harassed by a white man, she will be more prone to describe her unfortunate experience as one of those things bound to happen to *black* women who enter the workplace or academy. Although she may anticipate snags in her legal battle against her white harasser, the black woman may nevertheless feel obligated to her white harasser to demonstrate that no woman, especially no black woman, is his for the taking.

Rape

Of all the issues examined in this book, rape is the issue that most frequently divides black from white feminists. In her recent book, *Women, Race & Class,* Angela Davis points out that white feminists ranging from Susan Brown-miller to Jean MacKellar to Diana Russell have resuscitated the "old racist myth of the Black rapist" who yearns to abuse white women sexually.[35] All three of these feminists, but especially MacKellar and Russell, imply that the typical racist is a man of color or, if he is white, a poor or working-class man. MacKellar, for example, claims that 90 percent of all reported rapes in the United States are committed by black men,[36] even though the FBI's corresponding figure is 47 percent.[37] Similarly, of the twenty-two cases of rape Diana Russell describes, more than 50 percent involve women who have been raped by men of color, even though only 26 percent of the original ninety-five cases she studied involved men of color.[38] By skewing their statistics in such ways, Davis observes, MacKellar and Russell obscure the real social causes of rape, which may have little to do with the color of one's skin or the size of one's check book. Since only a small fraction of rapes are ever reported, it could be that more women report poor or black rapists than rich or white rapists. Although this is conjecture, it is not idle speculation. The law is not always a raped woman's best friend, and the law prefers not to catch rich, respected, or powerful men in its snares. Therefore, a woman who is raped by a pillar of the community, especially a white pillar, is likely to leave bad enough alone by not reporting her rapist to the authorities. As a result, there is no way of estimating how many women are raped by nice doctors, lawyers, professors, and businessmen.

According to Davis, what is most distressing about Brownmiller's as well as MacKellar's and Russell's respective accounts of rape is what they all have in common: a tendency to describe black men as exceptionally violent when it comes to their relationships with women, especially white women. In her depiction of poor black men, Brownmiller, author of *Against Our Will: Men, Women, and Rape,* insists that "Corporate executive dining rooms and climbs up Mount Everest are not usually accessible to those who form the subculture of violence. Access to a female body—through force—is within their ken."[39] Similarly, in her book *Rape: The Bait and the Trap,* Jean MacKellar claims that "Blacks raised in the hard life of the ghetto learn that they can get what they want only by seizing it. Violence is the rule in the game for survival. Women are fair prey: to obtain a woman one subdues one."[40] Finally, Diana Russell adds her voice to this chorus with the most racist note of all: "If some black men see rape of white women as an act of revenge or as a justifiable expression of hostility toward whites, I think it is equally realistic for white women to be less trusting of black men than many of them are."[41]

As Angela Davis sees it, these three feminists are either deliberately or inadvertently contributing to white society's irrational fear of the black man. Davis takes particular exception to certain passages in *Against Our Will*. According to Davis, Brownmiller implies that the philosophy of Eldridge Cleaver, who called rape an "insurrectionary act " against "white society," is one shared by the black man down the street.[42] Comments Davis: "It seems as if she [Susan Brownmiller] wants to intentionally conjure up in her readers' imaginations armies of Black men, their penises erect, charging full speed ahead toward the most conveniently placed white women."[43] Of course, if this is Brownmiller's intention—and one would like to think that it is not— then it feeds the flames of the racist fire that continues to warm the passions of bigoted people.

In the nineteenth century, thousands of black men were lynched by white men. For several years these lynchings were justified as necessary to prevent "Negro conspiracies, Negro insurrections, Negro schemes to murder all the white people, Negro plots to burn the town and to commit violence generally."[44] When it became all too obvious that no such conspiracies, insurrections, schemes, or plots were brewing, another reason was offered to justify white society's lynching of black men: to save white women from black men's sexual assaults. Tragically, these sexual assaults were usually imagined, if not by white women then by white men. Nevertheless, the lynchings continued despite the concerted efforts of black Anti-Lynching Crusaders like Ida B. Wells, Mary Church Terrell, and Mary Talbert, all of whom did their best through the 1890s and early 1900s to expose these "justified lynchings" for what they really were: unjustified murders of innocent black men. Not until 1930, when white women, under the leadership of Jessie Daniel Ames, established the Association of Southern Women for the Prevention of Lynching, did the tide of lynching reverse itself and abate. These white women refused to "allow those bent upon personal revenge and savagery to mount acts of violence and lawlessness in the name of women."[45] Although these white women are to be commended for their convictions and courage, it is regrettable that it took white women forty years to answer the repeated pleas of their black sisters. This is a pattern of behavior that persists to this day. White women do not always respond as quickly to issues of racism as they should. They sometimes overlook the fact that solidarity between a black woman and a white woman need not always consist in fighting together for sexual equality. On occasion, sisterhood will consist in fighting together for racial equality.

Currently, black women are very reluctant to press for stringent rape laws. Although black women, no less than white women, wish to deflate the myth that all women are liars, they do not wish to deny that some women, like some men, perjure themselves on the witness stand. In particular, they remind white women that judges and jurors, especially white judges and jurors, are more apt to believe a white woman who claims that she has been raped by a black man than a black woman who claims that she has been raped by a white man. A notorious case in which a racist court listened to the false testimony of two white women is the Scottsboro Nine Case, which resulted in the lengthy incarceration of nine innocent black men. More recently, a racist court falsely convicted a black man named Delbert Tibbs of raping a white woman. Only months after she had been acquitted of the murder of a white prison guard who had raped her in her cell, Joann Little, a black woman, rallied to the side of Tibbs, whom she had never met. Although Ms. Little asked the white feminists who had fought for her to fight for Tibbs, they were initially reluctant to support Tibbs's cause. Unfortunately, many black women read their hesitation as another instance of white feminists' inability or refusal to bother themselves with black people's concerns, in this case the concern that stringent rape laws will be enforced against black men but not against white men.[46]

This is of course a concern that is rooted in reality. For example, since 1930, of the 455 men who were legally executed in the United States for a rape conviction, 89 percent were black. In a majority of these cases, the rape victim was a white woman. In Florida alone, between 1940 and 1964, 6 white men who raped white women were executed in comparison to 45 of 84 blacks who were executed for raping white women. Significantly, no rapist, white or black, who violated a black woman received the death penalty.[47] In view of such statistics, black women want to be assured by white feminists that the new rape laws will be enforced fairly against white as well as black men, and that the penalties for rape will not be disproportionate as compared to the penalties meted out for equally serious crimes perpetrated upon members of the black community.

None of the above, however, is meant to imply that most rapes are interracial. Indeed, most rapes are intraracial; and there is no reason to think that there are fewer rapes per capita in black communities than in white communities. It is interesting that even when it comes to black-on- black rape, black women have not made rape a priority. Essie Green Williams of the National Black Feminist Organization offers at least three explanations for this phenomenon. First, seen in its political context, rape is "just another desperate act among many—a way to act out hostility, frustration, and anger."[48] Ms. Williams has said, "I think black folks over the years have felt rape to be so much a part of their everyday lives, so when you talk to a black woman about rape, it's crucial, but so many things are crucial—at least you're still alive."[49] In sum, many black women—and here we are speaking about poor black women—can stand being raped, harassed, prostituted, and visually degraded, provided that they and those whom they love are allowed to live. These women are not going to exert energy compaigning against rapists when they and their children are engaged in a daily struggle for mere survival. Second, black women realize that if white rape victims are treated callously by the criminal justice system, they are likely to be treated cruelly by it. Most black women do not notify the police when they have been raped for fear they will be scoffed at or ignored by white policemen.

Finally, like pornography, prostitution, and, to a lesser extent, sexual harassment, black-on-black rape is a very touchy issue between black men and black women. Essie Williams observes:

> Rape is one of the issues that are going to have to be addressed in the black community as more women become aware of what the movement is all about, but as an issue it is going to touch on some aspects that you don't want out there. It will be very difficult, very painful to address, because what you're talking about is violence against each other. What happens when people are oppressed is that they take it out on each other instead of against the oppressor. Not everybody is going to make that political connection, and so some people in the black community will feel that the whole issue of rape is a put-down and that these problems within the community should not be exposed.[50]

But in the same way that middle- and upper-class white women have to confront the fact that white employers, executives, politicians, doctors, and professors rape women, lower-class black women have to admit to themselves that black blue-collar workers rape women. Similarly, lower-class white women and middle- and upper-class black women have to acknowledge the rapists in their respective communities. Unless each class and each race examines the phenomenon of rape as it manifests itself throughout society, we will never learn all the reasons for rape or how it can be eliminated.

Woman-Battering

Like rape, woman-battering is a problem that embarrasses black men and black women. That this should be the case is not surprising. Woman battering is a problem that embarrasses white men and white women, Hispanic men and Hispanic women, and so on. Nevertheless, unless woman-battering is confronted whenever and wherever it occurs, it will continue to erode male/female relationships.

As black and other minority women perceive the issue, several myths about women-battering that need to be disspelled. Chief among them is the myth that teaches that nonwhite people are inherently more violent than whites. As a result of this false view, violence among minorities and the lower classes is seen as inevitable. Indeed, police trainees are frequently told that physical violence is an acceptable part of life among "ghetto residents":

> Although the prevailing American culture tolerates a minimum of physical force as a reaction to anger, such physical force is the common response among certain ethnic groups. Therefore, whether or not the use of such force can be considered serious depends in part on the cultural background of the people using it.[51]

Supposedly, there is no reason to rush to the aid of a black woman who is being battered by her husband, for she and he are just "working things out of their systems." This is clearly racist nonsense. There is little evidence for the belief that the lower class or the minority family is inherently more violent than the middle class or the white family. In fact, a nationwide survey conducted for the National Commission on the Causes and Prevention of Violence by Louis Harris and Associates found that approval of violence increases with income and education:

> Overall, one fifth of all Americans approve of slapping one's spouse on appropriate occasions. . . . Among those with eight years of schooling or less, 16 percent approve of a husband's slapping his wife, but the comparable figure is 25 percent among the college-educated. . . . We suggest that altercations among the poor are simply more likely to become police matters . . . lower-class people are denied privacy for their quarrels: neighborhood bars, sidewalks, and crowded, thin-walled apartment afford little isolation. The privacy of the middle-class lifestyle preserves an illusion of greater domestic tranquility; but it is, apparently, only an illusion.[52]

Even if woman-battering is no stranger to white suburbia, when women of color are battered by the men they live with, their bruises and cuts hurt just as much as those sustained by white women; and they, no less than white women, need to be protected from abusive men.

The battered black woman finds herself in racist binds that do not affect battered white women. Black women are even more prone than white women to excuse their husbands' violent behavior. All battered women have a tendency to blame themselves for provoking their husbands, for not being kind, patient, and long-suffering enough, but this tendency is more marked in black women, who know only too well that in this society life is harder for black men than for white men: "If he can't have things his way out in Whitey's world, at least he can have them his way at home," reasons many a black woman. Unfortunately, his way is not always tolerable; in fact, his way is sometimes intolerable. Like the white man's privileges, the black man's burdens constitute neither an excuse nor justification for woman-battering. And like the white woman, the black woman owes it to herself to demand proper respect and consideration from all men no matter what their race or class may be.

Black women are more likely than white women to wonder whether a policy of arrest is the best strategy to follow when it comes to woman-battering. Because the law has dealt more harshly with black rapists than white rapists, there is reason to believe that it will deal more severely with black woman-batterers than white woman-batterers. Even though it is true that arrest has traditionally been used as an "establishment tool against minorities," it is unlikely that police officers, prosecutors, and judges will rush to the defense of black women who have been beaten by black men.[53] Unless criminal justice personnel have ulterior reasons to arrest a black woman-batterer ("He's a troublemaker"), they will probably leave his wife or girlfriend to fend for herself.

Black women are more unlikely than white women to pursue legal remedies. Although the law has not been particularly solicitous about women, it has been more concerned about white women's interests and rights than black women's. As a result, many black woman are ambivalent about the role of the law in their lives. Comments Kenyari Bellfield of the Harriet Tubman Women's Shelter in Minnesota:

> The effects of racism and sexism seem too great to tackle in the face of having been victimized by a loved one. The woman often times feels powerless to change her situation, tending to feel she is being forced to tolerate the situation longer because the very system which has historically served to subjugate and oppress her is the only system which can save her from the immediate abusive system.[54]

In short, although the battered black woman wants the law to help her, she may not trust it. The law has hurt her and her people too grievously in the past for her to forgive its sins quickly. Similarly, although the battered black woman wants the relevant social agencies to help her, she may not trust them. Too often a battered black woman has gone to a women's shelter only to be subjected to unnecessary red tape or to the thoughtless comments of "well-intentioned" white women: "Why, I'd never let my husband do *that* to me!" Unless legal and extralegal personnel confront their own sexism, racism, and classism, the plight of battered black women is likely to remain serious indeed.

Conclusion

The experience of sexual degradation or abuse is hurtful for any woman regardless of race or class, but it is particularly distressing for women of color, especially if they are members of the lower class. Chances are that if a poor black woman's complaint of sexual abuse is not dismissed on account of her gender, it will be dismissed on account of either her race or her class. Black women and other women of color have been slighted by Anglo-American law. In the same way that the myth of the violent black man has caused black men to suffer the law's savagery, the myth of the promiscuous black woman has caused black women to suffer the law's neglect. Indeed, as Angela Davis sees it:

> Once the notion is accepted that Black men harbor irresistible and animal-like sexual urges, the entire race is invested with bestiality. If Black men have their eyes on white women as sexual objects, then Black women must certainly welcome the sexual attentions of white men.[55]

This notion has led to another, related notion: that black women welcome the sexual attentions of any and all men, and that it is impossible to harass, rape, or prostitute a black woman. Supposedly, nothing is too degrading, demeaning, or disgusting to a woman of color. This attitude has caused many police officers, prosecutors, and judges not to do their duty insofar as black women are concerned. Although the law cannot destroy racist myths, it can promise to preserve black women's, as well as black men's, life and liberty. Unless the law makes and keeps this promise, black women will find themselves with little worth the law's equal protection.

Notes

1. Many nonwhite feminists prefer to refer to themselves as "women of color." This expression highlights the fact that one does not have to be black to be disadvantaged. Yellow, red, or brown skin remains a liability in any white-dominated society.
2. Jill Lewis, "Sexual Division of Power: Motivations of the Women's Liberation Movement," in *Common Differences: Conflicts in Black and White Feminist Perspectives,* by Gloria I. Joseph and Jill Lewis (Garden City, N.Y.: Doubleday, Anchor Books, 1981), pp. 44–45.
3. Most women who have written about radical feminism (Mary Daly, Janice Raymond, Shulamith Firestone, Susan Brownmiller) and most women who have written about Marxist/socialist feminism (Juliet Mitchell, Zillah Eisenstein, Nancy Chodorow) are white.
4. Audre Lorde, Address to Feminist Alliance, Williams College, November 16, 1982.
5. Gloria I. Joseph, "White Promotion, Black Survival," in *Common Differences,* p. 27.
6. Tracey Gardner, "Racism in Pornography and the Women's Movement," in *Take Back the Night,* Laura Lederer, ed. (New York: William Morrow, 1980), p. 112.
7. Susan Griffin, *Pornography and Silence: Culture's Revenge Against Nature* (New York: Harper & Row, 1982).
8. Gloria I. Joseph, "Styling, Profiling, and Pretending: The Games Before the Fall," in *Common Differences,* p. 219.
9. Alice Walker, "Coming Apart," in Lederer, ed., *Take Back the Night,* p. 103.
10. Gardner, "Racism in Pornography," in Lederer, ed., *Take Back the Night,* p. 112.
11. Griffin, *Pornography and Silence.*

12. Gardner, "Racism in Pornography," in Lederer, ed., *Take Back the Night,* pp. 106–8.

13. M. Anne Jennings, "The Victim as Criminal: A Consideration of California's Prostitution Law," 64 *California Law Review* (July 1976):1253.

14. Ibid.

15. Ibid., p. 1252.

16. Miriam F. Hirsch, *Women and Violence* (New York: Van Nostrand Reinhold, 1981), p. 64.

17. Ibid.

18. Voice "M" in Kate Millett, "Prostitution: A Quartet for Female Voices," in *Woman in Sexist Society: Studies in Power and Powerlessness,* Vivian Gornick and Barbara K. Moran, eds. (New York: Basic Books, 1971), p. 25.

19. Hirsch, *Women and Violence,* p. 64.

20. Charles E. Silberman, *Criminal Violence, Criminal Justice* (New York: Random House, 1978), pp. 89–90.

21. Voice "M" in Millett, "Prostitution: A Quartet," in Gornick and Moran, eds., *Woman in Sexist Society,* p. 21.

22. Angela Davis, *Women, Race and Class* (New York: Random House, 1981), pp. 3–29.

23. Bev Eaton, interview with Kathleen Barry. "Of Human Bondage," *Valley Advocate* (Northampton, Mass.) November 10, 1982, p. 9.

24. Hirsch, *Women and Violence,* p. 58.

25. Joseph, "Styling, Profiling, and Pretending: The Games Before the Fall," in *Common Differences,* p. 181.

26. Ibid.

27. Ibid., p. 218.

28. Raymond M. Lane, "A Man's World: An Update on Sexual Harassment," *The Village Voice,* December 16–22, 1981, pp. 1, 15, 16.

29. Catherine A. MacKinnon, *Sexual Harassment of Working Women* (New Haven: Yale University Press, 1979), pp. 176–77.

30. Karen Lindsey, "Sexual Harassment on the Job," *Ms.,* November 1977, p. 48.

31. MacKinnon, *Sexual Harassment,* p. 30.

32. Ibid.

33. Seventy-five percent of white women are harassed by whites, and twenty-five percent of white women are harassed by blacks.

34. MacKinnon, *Sexual Harassment,* p. 31.

35. Davis, *Women, Race and Class,* p. 178.

36. Jean MacKellar, *Rape: The Bait and the Trap* (New York: Crown Publishers, 1975), p. 72.

37. Susan Brownmiller, *Against Our Will: Men, Women and Rape* (New York: Simon & Schuster, 1975), p. 213.

38. Diana Russell, *The Politics of Rape: The Victim's Pespective* (New York: Stein & Day, 1975), p. 163.

39. Brownmiller, *Against Our Will,* p. 194.

40. MacKellar, *Rape: The Bait,* p. 72.

41. Russell, *The Politics of Rape,* p. 163.

42. Davis, *Women, Race and Class,* p. 197.

43. Ibid.

44. Frederick Douglass, "The Lesson of the Hour" (pamphlet published in 1894). Reprinted under the title "Why is the Negro Lynched," in Philip S. Foner, *The Life and Writings of Frederick Douglass,* vol. 4 (New York: International Publishers, 1950), p. 501.

45. Jesse Daniel Ames, *The Changing Character of Lynching, 1931–1941* (New York: AMS Press, 1973).

46. Davis, *Women, Race & Class,* pp. 174–75.

47. Marvin E. Wolfgang and Marc Riedel, "Rape, Race, and the Death Penalty in Georgia," *American Journal of Orthopsychiatry* 45 (July 1975): 658–68.

48. Interview with Essie Green Williams conducted by Noreen Connnell and Cassandra Wilson in *Rape: The First Sourcebook for Women,* Noreen Connell and Cassandra Wilson, eds. (New York: New American Library, 1974), p. 242.

49. Ibid.

50. Ibid., p. 243.

51. Lenore E. Walker, *The Battered Woman* (New York: Harper & Row, 1979), p. 31.

52. Sue E. Eisenberg and Patricia L. Micklow, "The Assaulted Wife: 'Catch 22' Revisited," 3 *Women's Rights Law Reporter* (Spring/Summer 1977): 142.

53. Ibid.

54. Hearing on Violence Prevention Act, Formal Testimony, Harriet Tubman Women's Shelter presented by Kenyari Bellfield in U.S., Congress, House, Subcommittee on Select Education of the Committee on Education and Labor, *Domestic Violence: Hearing on H.R. 7297 and H.R. 8498,* 95th Cong. 2d sess., March 17, 1978, p. 521.

55. Davis, *Women, Race and Class,* pp. 181–82.

CHAPTER 7

LESBIAN PERSPECTIVES ON WOMEN, SEX, AND THE LAW

The lesbian perspective on sexuality has been the subject of much debate within the feminist community. At the risk of oversimplifying matters, there seem to be two types of lesbians: lesbian nonfeminists and lesbian feminists. A lesbian nonfeminist is a woman who is "instinctively" drawn to another woman because of her sexual desires and needs.[1] She is not particularly concerned about relating to her lover in ways that are markedly different from the ways in which heterosexual couples relate to each other, and she is not ideologically committed to promoting lesbianism as a way of life for anyone but herself and her lover. In contrast, a lesbian feminist may or may not be "instinctively" drawn to another woman because of her sexual desires and needs. She is, however, convinced that lesbian relations should be fostered among all women. The more that women engage in lesbian relations, the less hold will the institution of compulsory heterosexuality have over them.

Lesbian feminists are more or less adamant in their rejection of male-female sexual relations. Moderate lesbian feminists advance the view that lesbian sexual relations are better for women than heterosexual relations. That is, unlike heterosexual relations, lesbian relations are less bound by the pernicious role-playing that often characterizes male female sexual relations and which works to women's disadvantage. According to Simone de Beauvoir, for example, since lesbianism is regulated neither by an institution like marriage nor by conventions like romantic love, relations between lesbians can be especially free of restrictive stereotypes:

> Man and woman—even husband and wife—are in some degree playing a part before one another, and in particular woman, upon whom the male

always imposes some requirement: virtue beyond suspicions, charm, co-quettishness, childishness, or austerity. Never in the presence of husband or lover can she feel wholly herself; but with her woman friend she need not be on parade, need not pretend; they are too much of a kind not to show themselves frankly as they are.[2]

In sum, if a woman wants to escape the sex roles that society traditionally assigns her, then it is in her best interest to engage in lesbian relations. Significantly, moderate lesbian feminists do not castigate women who are unwilling and/or unable to discard heterosexual relations for lesbian sexual relations. As they see it, heterosexual preference is the product of a powerful combination of cultural imperatives and biological predispositions that are not easily transcended; and heterosexual relations are better than no sexual relations at all. Unlike moderate lesbian feminists, extreme lesbian feminists insist that if a woman is not willing or able to engage in lesbian relations, then she should refrain from all sexual relations rather than engage in hetero-sexual relations. Heterosexual relations are *per definiens* corrupt. They are elaborate erotizations of violence or domination on the man's part and pain or powerlessness on the woman's part. As such, they can only degrade, demean, and dehumanize women.

Recently lesbian feminists—moderate as well as extreme—have been chal-lenged on two accounts. First, critics have argued that lesbians play the same kind of sex roles that heterosexuals play. As these critics see it, most lesbian relations are butch-femme relationships in which one of the women plays the "male" role and the other woman plays the "female" role. Second, critics have pointed out that a growing number of lesbians—feminist as well as nonfeminist—are engaging in sadomasochistic sexual practices (S & M), and that if anything is an erotization of dominance and submission, S & M is.

The butch-femme criticism is one that has generated controversy within the feminist community. Originally, lesbian feminists disavowed butch-femme relations as aberrations. Currently, lesbian feminists are reconsider-ing butch-femme relations in a more favorable light. There is a growing sentiment among contemporary lesbian feminists that butch-femme sexual-ity does not necessitate the rigid role-playing that male-female sexuality does. In the 1950s, for example, lesbians joked about being a "butch fem" or a "femmy butch" or feeling "kiki" (going both ways). They also joked about reversal of expectations: "Get a butch home and she turns over on her back!"[3] Moreover, lesbian feminists who consistently favor either the butch role or the femme role maintain that the essential pleasure of butch femme sexuality consists in two women being themselves, not in two women mas-querading as something they are not. Commments one lesbian: "When a woman said 'Give it to me, baby!' . . . I never heard the voice of a man or of socially conditioned roles. I heard the call of a woman world-traveler, a brave woman, whose hands challenged every denial laid on a woman's life."[4]

Although the mainstream lesbian feminist community has largely made its peace with butch-femme sexuality, it remains divided on the issue of lesbian S & M. Opponents of lesbian S & M maintain that it is a gross parody of what is most objectionable about male-female sexual relations—that the male sadist does to the female masochist whatever *he* pleases in the name of *his* sexual pleasures. In a society that is characterized by disparities of social, economic, and political power between the genders, women's subordination to men subverts sexual relations into relations of male dominance and female powerlessness. In this conection Bat-Ami Bar On has argued that at least heterosexual S & M is morally objectionable:

1. All practices which violate the right of women to determine what can be done with and to our bodies are morally unacceptable.
2. The erotization of violence or dominance and pain or powerlessness necessarily involves a violation of the right to determine what can be done with and to one's body.
3. Therefore, sexual practices which are based on the erotization of violence or domination and of pain or powerlessness are morally unacceptable.
4. Sadomasochistic sexual practices are among the sexual practices which are based on the erotization of violence or domination and of pain or powerlessness.
5. Therefore, sadomasochistic sexual practices are among those sexual practices that are morally unacceptable.[5]

Proponents of lesbian S & M agree with Bat-Ami Bar On that *heterosexual* S & M is morally objectionable. However, they deny that *lesbian* S & M is morally objectionable. Some proponents of lesbian S & M claim that a distinction must be made between the erotizatioa of violence and pain on the one hand and the erotization of dominance and powerlessness on the other. Heterosexual S & M is an erotization of dominance and powerlessness. The male sadist's will negates the will of the female masochist, who becomes mere flesh: his sexual garbage pail, his punching bag. In contrast, lesbian S & M is the erotization of pain infliction (violence) and pain-reception (pain per se). The female sadist fulfills the expressed sexual wants and needs of the female masochist, who, in return, fulfills the expressed sexual wants and needs of the female sadist. Because the two women recognize each other as equals, neither the will of the one nor the other is negated; rather, they are both affirmed as sources of value.

Other proponents of lesbian S & M maintain that what distinguishes lesbian S & M from heterosexual S & M is that the masochist is in control of the former but not the latter.[6] Yet, the critics may in turn ask whether the masochist is really in control. There may be a rule in the lesbian S & M community according to which masochists, not sadists, determine the intensity and duration of a sexual exchange. Many sadists will respect this rule for their own sakes as well as the masochists'. If it became common knowledge, for example, that a sadistic lesbian routinely went too far, she would be hard pressed to find a masochist willing to have sex with her. But on any given occasion a masochist will run the risk of having her power usurped by a previously well-behaved sadist. And if this risk is nonexistent for a certain masochist—if she *knows* that she can always stay her sadist's hand—is she really enjoying the "pleasures" of masochism?

Conceding that a masochist cannot be in control during a sexual exchange and still be a masochist, still other proponents of lesbian S & M argue that the erotization of dominance and powerlessness is not necessarily morally objectionable. By playing at sadism (dominating) and masochism (being dominated) in one's private life, one can eventually overcome dominating and being dominated not only in one's private life, but in one's public life.

Unfortunately, if the testimony of many ex-lesbian masochists is accurate, then lesbian S & M is not always cathartic therapy, but rather behavior that reinforces the very tendencies which some lesbian feminists claim it eradicates.[7] The fact that so many lesbians who practice S & M scoff at the "vanilla," or affectional sex they used to enjoy, suggests that the more S & M one participates in, the more addicted one becomes. Audre Lorde comments:

> Those involved with sadomasochism are acting out the intolerance of differences which we all learn: superiority and thereby the right to dominate. The conflict is supposedly self-limiting because it happens behind bedroom doors. Can this be so, when the erotic empowers, nourishes and permeates all of our lives?[8]

If S & M helps lesbians get beyond domination and powerlessness in all their human relationships, including their sexual relationships, then there may be reason to endorse it. But if it merely adds new kinds of domination and powerlessness to old kinds of domination and powerlessness, then there is little to recommend it. Relations of domination and powerlessness between adults are morally objectionable to the degree that they erode the powerless party's will and/or brutalize the dominant party's will.

In any event, whether a lesbian is a feminist or not, a sadomasochist or not, she asks that she not be legally penalized simply because she is a lesbian. Although progress has been made in terms of gay rights, the rights of lesbians and male homosexuals are not as secure as those of blacks and other minorities. Twenty-six states still have antisodomy laws,[9] and Wisconsin is the only state with a comprehensive gay rights bill, which protects gays in housing, public accommodations, and government and private employment.[10] The Moral Majority and other similar organizations threaten to undo much of the progress that has been made toward the establishment of gay rights. Although legislation such as the Family Protection Act, which hopes to "encourage restoration of family unity, parental authority, and a climate of traditional morality"[11] by making federal funds *un*available "to any public or private individual, group, foundation, commission, corporation, association, or other entity which presents homosexuality, male or female, as an alternative lifestyle or suggests that it can be an acceptable lifestyle,"[12] has little chance of passing in Congress *in toto,* the mere possibility of its passage is ominous.

Were a strong Family Protection Act passed, it would probably affect the writing and publishing of books such as this one. Comment Larry Bush and Richard Goldstein:

> The chilling effect such a statute would have on politicians, journalists, researchers, and social activists who support gay rights is incalculable. A publisher or filmmaker who creates or distributes a realistic image of homosexuality might be subject to a denial of Social Security. A clinic with a gay outreach program might be ineligible for Medicaid. A church's concern for gay rights could cost it federal aid for refugee resettlement. A police liaison to the gay community might disqualify an entire department from federal funding.[13]

According to Bush and Goldstein, such speculations are not idle. Liberals are retreating on the gay rights issue. For example, fearing that their close identification with lesbian rights cost them votes during the E.R.A. campaign, the National Organization for Women recently soft-peddled its support for gay rights by asserting that the issue had regrettably been identified with "promiscuity, pornography, pederasty, and public sex."[14] Although many feminist lesbians agree that gay rights issues are confused and obscure in the public eye, they were upset when NOW failed to include a fact sheet on lesbian rights in a packet distributed on Women's Lobbying Day in early February 1981.

Given that lesbians have yet to be accepted by society at large, some lesbians fear that if they condemn any lesbian sexual practice whatsoever, they will play into the hands of those who would condemn any and all lesbian practices. Other lesbians insist that they must take this risk. As these women see it, unless lesbians condemn lesbian sexual practices that mimic objectionable, patriarchal sexual practices (such as rape), female sexuality will continue to be defined in terms of male sexuality.

Pornography

For some time lesbian feminists have been lamenting the fact that the porn industry portrays affectional lesbian relations—two women gently caressing and intimately touching one another—as inherently perverse. Exclaims Charlotte Bunch:

> Lesbians are tired of having our love, our culture, and our publications threatened by these labels of "perversion," and we will continue fighting for our right to proclaim and portray our love and our sexuality about the real perversions of pornography—the perpetrators of violence and hatred against women—by the fear that we will be called "pornographic" if we oppose them.[15]

Although the porn industry continues to denigrate affectional lesbian sex, in recent years it has begun to depict and describe lesbian S & M. Proponents of lesbian S & M find most of these portrayals unobjectionable with the exception of those depictions and descriptions in which the sadist rather than than the masochist is in control. In their estimation, these latter descriptions and depictions are gyno-thanatic or woman-degrading because they suggest that S & M between any two lesbians is just as nonconsensual as sex between Justine and the Marquis de Sade. Amy Hoffman comments: "Just as I'm sure that any woman who has been raped has no trouble telling the difference between her experience of a horrifying assault and consensual heterosexual sex, women who are involved in s/m know the difference between getting beaten up and an s/m scene."[16] Opponents of lesbian S & M insist that descriptions and depictions of one lesbian torturing another lesbian during a sexual encounter are gyno-thanatic. Indeed, as these lesbian feminists see it, it is especially inappropriate for the pornography industry to suggest that when two women make love they immediately eroticize domination and powerlessness. Such suggestions only add fuel to the fires of homophobia and detract from the fact that most lesbians, even those who practice S & M, are ostensibly trying to explode the game of sexual domination and powerlessness rather than to refine it further.

If group defamation suits are at all actionable—a remote possibility — lesbians could sue the pornography industry for making a series of films, for example, all of which suggested that lesbian "tops" (sadists) routinely snuff out lesbian "bottoms" (masochists). Presumably, most lesbians would join such a suit, either on the grounds that few lesbians engage in S & M or on the grounds that those lesbians who do know when the line between fantasy and reality is being crossed. Unfortunately, such a suit is unlikely to fare well in today's courts. Whereas a jury may be persuaded that heterosexual women as a class, are not, masochists who want and need to be sexually abused by sadistic men, it may not be as readily persuaded that lesbians as a class, are not, tough "butches" and tender "femmes" who need either to give or to receive sexual abuse. Until society as a whole understands lesbian sexuality better, the law will not be particularly cooperative when it comes to protecting a lesbian's reputation from the porn industry's apparent urge to degrade and defame the lesbian as she struggles to probe the meaning of woman-defined sexuality.

Prostitution

In large cities, there are just as many men and boys selling their bodies to men as there are women and girls selling their bodies to men. Statistics on the number of women who sell their sexual services to other women are not readily available. There is, however, empirical evidence that quite a few lesbians do sell their sexual services to men.[17] Some prostitutes claim that they became lesbians because constantly "turning tricks" with "johns" disillusioned them with respect to the male half of the species.[18] Other prostitutes claim that they were lesbians long before they entered "the life." Many of these prostitutes report that they couldn't "hustle" if they were "straight." Comments one lesbian: "How could I say, 'This is my old man, this is a trick'? Women are my personal life, and men are business."[19] Indeed, many lesbians who sell their sexual services to men insist that they are better off than their heterosexual counterparts. Asked to specify this "better off," one of these lesbians replied:

> Not having the need to depend on a pimp to keep you on the street, to fight your battles, to help you get tricks, to bail you out. Instead you depend on other women for that. Just a couple of phone calls and you get three or four other women there to help. This way you don't have to get beaten up so much, or put up with as much harassment, as I see in women who do not have other women to depend on. I don't think it would be a good thing to put down the prostitute-pimp relationship, but as an alternative I feel a lesbian relationship is better for me. I think the most ideal situation is to live in a collective with other lesbians, to exchange child care and tricks, to go to the hospital with each other when you have VD, or to help each other when you get arrested.[20]

Significantly, many feminists are more disturbed by lesbians who sell their sexual services to women than by those who sell their sexual services to men. Opponents of lesbian prostitution (women selling sexual services to women) maintain that it is defective because it parodies heterosexual prostitution. Proponents argue that lesbian prostitution is qualitatively different than either heterosexual or male homosexual prostitution, and that therefore it is not defective on the grounds that it mirrors those practices of heterosexual culture that are degrading. According to these lesbian feminists, neither the lesbian who sells her sexual services nor the lesbian who buys them is trying to make a power statement. The lesbian prostitute is simply providing another lesbian with an otherwise unattainable sexual experience. If this claim could be established empirically, opponents of lesbian prostitution would probably reconsider their objections to it. Unfortunately, no empirical research is being done in this area, and there is no way of telling whether lesbian prostitution in this society is any more sexually liberating than heterosexual or male homosexual prostitution. In any event, the main point of contention within the gay community is not whether lesbians should engage in prostitution, but whether lesbians should come out, as some male homosexuals have, and endorse cross-generational sex—that is, sex between adults and children.

Although many male homosexuals have reservations about cross-generational sex, they are not nearly as adamant in their opposition to it as most lesbians are. Indeed, recently many gay men and lesbians have found themselves increasingly divided on the issue of man-boy or woman-girl love. Most states continue to have strong laws against pedophilia (sexual experience between an adult and prepubertal child, regardless of gender or sexual orientation) and pederasty (sexual experience between male adults and male adolescents).[21] Although pedophilia and pederasty laws are generally enforced against men, there is nothing in the wording of pedophilia laws that suggests that they cannot be enforced against heterosexual women or lesbians. In the same way that women are not usually indicted and tried for incest and statutory rape, they are not usually indicted for pedophilia. Either women do not as a class abuse or misuse their proximity to children, or society as a whole prefers to believe that they do not. Given that women have been and still are the primary caretakers of children, it would distress many people to think, let alone believe, that women routinely engaged in sexual relations with the boys and girls entrusted to them during the day. Society finds it easier to think and to believe that sexual abuse and misuse of children is a male foible, and most feminists are convinced that this view accurately reflects reality.

Certain segments of the male homosexual community—for example, NAMBLA (North American Men/Boy Love Association)—have been pressing for the repeal or reform of pederasty and pedophilia statutes. As NAMBLA sees it, gay adolescents and even exceptionally mature gay children should not be denied the right to engage in consensual relations with gay adults. Children are developing sexual beings, and there is no more reason to restrict their sexual development completely than to restrict their intellectual development completely. Lesbians are very divided on the issue of cross-generational sex, both commercial and noncommercial. Like many mainstream male homosexuals, many liberal lesbian feminists try to dissociate themselves from organizations such as NAMBLA for political reasons. Society is already homophobic and it does not help to feed society's image of male homosexuals and, by parity of reasoning, of lesbians as child molesters. Talk of man-boy sex and of woman-girl sex is likely to make it that much harder for gay persons to adopt children or to be awarded custody of their own children.

NAMBLA's goals are not only politically embarrassing to some lesbian feminists, they are frequently morally unacceptable. According to Elaine Noble, for example, lesbians must as a matter of principle divorce themselves from pederasts and pedophiles:

> Gross personal abuse and affrontery of innocent children is a sacrilege of the highest order. Adults involved in the corruption of unprotected, impressionable children by drugs, alcohol and sex must be immediately halted and reprimanded. We will not tolerate nor in any way condone through lack of aggressive action the perpetuation of such deviant, defiant behavior.[22]

Noble's disavowal of gay adult/gay child love is rooted in the classical liberal position according to which only rational adults are able to give informed consent to decisions and actions that could possibly or do actually affect them negatively.[23] As a class, children have neither the store of knowledge nor the powers of control that adults as a class have. In general, children are more plagued by misinformation than adults, and they are more susceptible to coercion in both its negative (threats) and positive (favors) forms. It is likely that in any given instance the "consent" a child or even an adolescent gives to an adult's request for sexual relations will not be real, or informed, consent. Therefore, children should, as a class be protected, if necessary by law, from those adults who would take advantage of their unique vulnerabilities.

Like Elaine Noble, Robin Morgan also objects to cross-generational sex, but her reasons for her objection are those given by many radical feminists. As she sees it, children are capable of giving informed consent, but only to their peers. Children are sexual beings, admits Morgan, but "the only way that [their] sexuality [has] a way of flowering in any non-damaging, power-free relationship is with another child."[24] Man-boy sex is damaging to the child because it is not power free. Men frequently coerce boys into having sex with them, and in those cases where a boy supposedly enters willingly into sexual relations with a man, he does so, as Morgan sees it, not because he is sexually attracted to the man, but because "power is attractive and interesting, especially to the powerless."[25] Indeed, Morgan has nothing positive to say about cross-generational sex: "I think boy-love is a euphemism for rape, regardless of whether the victim seems to invite it. That is what has been said of the woman rape victim. When somebody relatively powerless is getting fucked, literally and figuratively, by somebody powerful, that is a rape situation."[26] Moreover, Morgan sees cross-generational sex as a male issue, not a female issue. With rare exception, women are not interested in having sexual relations with young or adolescent girls or boys. In fact, Morgan claims that because women raise children, they have an antierotic interest in them. Specifically, she mentions that diaper changing alone would prevent most women from being sexually attracted to the children they service.

Florence Rush lends support to Morgan's last point. The organization for which she frequently speaks, Lesbian Feminist Liberation of New York (LFL), is against any lowering of the age of consent because "the repeal of the age of consent laws presents greater dangers to young women as 97–99 percent of molested children and teenagers are girls who are raped or taken advantage of by *heterosexual* men."[27] Rush is convinced that the softening of pederasty and pedophilia statutes will not lead to the flourishing of genuine cases of man-boy and woman-girl love, but to the proliferation of girl molestation by unscrupulous men.[28]

In response to Noble, Morgan, and Rush, Pat Califia, who supports cross generational sex, offers several counterarguments. First, she argues against Noble that young persons are able to give informed consent and against Morgan that they are able to do this in instances that involve adults as well as instances that involve other young persons:

> Any child old enough to decide whether or not she or he wants to eat spinach, play with trucks or wear shoes is old enough to decide whether or not she or he wants to run around naked in the sun, masturbate, sit in somebody's lap or engage in sexual activity. We should be working to end the artificial state of sexual ignorance that children are kept in—not perpetuating or defending it.[29]

Second, Califia also disagrees with Morgan regarding the power differential issue. She argues that the power differential between adults and minors is much exaggerated, and that since all sexual relationships involve persons who have more or less economic or social power, there is no reason to single out man-boy sexual relations as somehow unique. According to Califia, Morgan makes too much of the power differential view, and her concept of rape comes close to suggesting that virtually all sexual relations—between men and women, between people of different races, between people of different socioeconomic classes, between able-bodied and handicapped people, and even between people of different size and sex—are "inherently nonconsensual."[30]

Third, Califia claims, in contrast to Rush, that lesbians do engage in woman-girl sex, and that the laws that supposedly protect heterosexual girls from male molesters also prevent homosexual girls from fully loving the women to whom they are sexually attracted. Observes one adolescent lesbian:

> I have had fully consensual sexual relationships with women (who happened to be over 21) since the age of 13. I could have been punished beyond my relationship being destroyed, cut-off, taken away . . . my lovers imprisoned . . . my being put through a trial and pressured to testify against them. . . . I could have been taken "into custody" by the state. I

could have been processed by a juvenile institution (a "home" or "school" or "camp") for an unlimited (until age 18) sentence as a status offender (for being involved in a sexual relationship and/or for being willfully and independently seeing a woman against my guardians' wishes—or for leaving their home).[31]

If statutory rape laws should be reformed on the grounds that most adolescent girls above the age of fifteen, say, are mature enough to decide whether or not to have sexual relations with men above the age of eighteen, say, then pedophilia and pederasty statutes should also be reformed.

Although Califia is to be commended for her support of children's rights, especially gay children's rights, it is doubtful that gay children's confusions, conflicts, and concerns will be assuaged by encouraging them to engage in sexual relations with gay adults who may or may not be willing and able to assist them in their growth toward sexual maturity. Perhaps gay children could be better assisted by organizations staffed by lesbians and male homosexuals who are unambiguously interested in gay children's rights rather than in their own sexual desires as gay adults. Just because a child is old enough to be aware that it likes candy but not spinach, trucks but not books, bare feet but not shoes, does not mean that she is ready completely to determine her diet, sources of entertainment, or wardrobe. The child must be able to provide an account for rejecting spinach more elaborate than an expression of disgust, and she must be able to defend her rejection of spinach with adequate reasons—"I can get the same vitamins from lettuce or a vitamin pill." Similarly, a child must be able to provide adequate reasons for consenting to an adult's sexual overtures—"I am attracted to x and I would very much like to explore my sexuality with her." But as Kate Millett, a major proponent of children's rights, points out, children in this society find it difficult to provide reasons for their decisions and actions, and this because they are not encouraged to develop their decision making powers at an early age.

> It's very hard to be free if you have no rights about anything, if you're subjected to endless violence—both physical and psychological, if you're not permitted to speak, if you have no money, if you're already governed by a whole state system which demands that you put in forced attendance in school whether you want to be there or not.[32]

In other words, unless children's rights are recognized across the board, it is going to be difficult for a child to choose freely an erotic relationship with an adult. There is no reason to believe that it is easier to be "free" about sex than any other aspect of human existence. Therefore, if NAMBLA and other related organizations are sincere about children's rights, they should work for a general strengthening of them rather than for the right of gay adults to engage in sex with gay adolescents and children. Age of consent laws need to be rethought not only regarding sexual relations, but regarding driving, drinking, and the draft. But age of consent laws should not be eliminated too quickly. Like it or not, society has to confront the fact that children are relatively powerless when compared to adults. The power children *essentially* lack is the power not of money, for example, but that of knowledge, self-knowledge, and self-control. Only their growth can remedy their lack, and the law has a responsibility to protect children until they are powerful enough—that is, sufficiently knowledgeable and self-controlled—to articulate for themselves their own wants and needs.

What this all suggests is that male homosexuals and lesbians are frequently caught in uncomfortable political binds. Some gays believe that unless they support all sexual minorities—prostitutes, pederasts, pedophiles, transvestites, sadomasochists, practitioners of sex in public parks and bathrooms—they will weaken their own cause. After all, male homosexuals and lesbians have been and still are described as deviants.

Other gays think that it is nonsense to endorse a sexual practice simply because it is the preferred practice of a minority. Each sexual practice must be examined on its own merits. If it leads to equality between persons (the liberal position), or to the overcoming of patterns of domination and submission in personal relations (the radical position), or to the overcoming of economic exploitation and social alienation (the Marxist position), then it is to be recommended. Otherwise not. Unless it can be established empirically that lesbian prostitution and cross-generational sex have morally desirable consequences, they should not be endorsed simply on the grounds that they are minority practices.

Sexual Harassment

Like their heterosexual counterparts, lesbians are subject to both nondiscriminatory (peer-on-peer harassment) and discriminatory (superordinate-on-subordinate harassment) sexual harassment. Lesbians can be subjected to nondiscriminatory sexual harassment either by heterosexual males or by lesbians. On occasion, heterosexual men will go out of their way to harass "dykes," taunting them on account of their sexual preference/sexuality. They will hurl slurs at these women, implying that they cannot be real women if they do not worship the male penis. And the law will not always rally to the defense of lesbians who are harassed by obnoxious men. For example, liquor licenses were revoked from two Greenwich Village bars, The Dutchess and Dejavu, which had an exclusively lesbian clientele. The State Liquor Authority took away the licenses on the grounds that the bars were discriminating against men. What the State Liquor Authority failed or refused to take into account was the reason for the bars' exclusionary policy. Until the "lesbian only" policies were adopted, heterosexual men routinely visited the bars for the sole purpose of harassing the lesbians there.[33] Similarly, lesbians can be sexually harassed by other lesbians. Some lesbians may foist sexual attentions upon other lesbians who already have lovers, for example. To a large extent, lesbians who are the victims of nondiscriminatory sexual harassment will be on their own. A lesbian will tend to reject any suggestion that she initiate a civil suit against her female harasser. Fearing that she will be laughed out of court, or doubting the wisdom of publicly proclaiming her sexual preference, the lesbian is apt to handle her problem in informal ways.

What lesbians find most distressing is discriminatory sexual harassment— the type of harassment that can deprive them of needed educational and occupational opportunities. To date, the problems of homosexual and lesbian sexual harassment have been closet issues. They have, however, been indirectly confronted under the rubric of bisexuality. Unfortunately, bisexual sexual harassment has been used more than a few times as an implicit *reductio ad absurdum* to defeat legal prohibitions of sexual harassment of women by men and of men by women. Catherine MacKinnon points out that in *Tomkins,* for example, the judge found that heterosexual harassment could not be sex-based because "gender lines might as easily have been reversed, or even not crossed at all."[34] Apparently the judge meant that if a male employer sexually harassed men as well as women or if a female employer sexually harassed women as well as men, no cause of action would lie in sex discrimination. But as MacKinnon observes, as "factual speculation," this line of reasoning is "irrelevant"; for "without an [actual] allegation of bisexual harassment, to conclude that this *possibility* disposes of the issue as a matter of law is simple error."[35]

What MacKinnon is getting at is that as a matter of law, no portion of discrimination doctrine has ever required "that because allegedly discriminatory treatment *could* be leveled equally against another group, when it is leveled against one, the reversed possibility destroys the group referent."[36] Indeed, what makes sexual harassment of women by men discriminatory is the arbitrary fact that although it *could* be directed against men, it happens to be directed against women. That is, were this another time and another place, men could find themselves in the position that women currently find themselves. But because this is the here and now, it is actual women and not possible men who bear the brunt of discriminatory sexual harassment.

Of course, that most sexual harassers are heterosexual men does not mean that the law should not sanction heterosexual women who sexually harass their male employees or students. Women who sexually harass men are no less blameworthy than men who sexually harass women. And that most sexual harassers are heterosexual persons does not mean that the law should overlook bisexual and gay sexual harassers. They also deserved to be sanctioned.

In this connection, it is important to note that if a bisexual employer or educator sexually harasses both men *and* women, then his or her practice probably does not constitute sex discrimination under Title VII or Title IX. These acts do not concern themselves with abuses of human sexuality per se. Rather they focus on any and all impermissible different consequences that flow from the gender distinction in the workplace or academy. In short, Titles VII and IX concern themselves only with those things that are done to females but not to males and/or those things that are done to males but not to females—where there are no work-related or school-related reasons for such differential treatment of men and women. So if a bisexual imposes his sexual attentions on both men and women, no matter how oppressive or odious his behavior is, it is not discriminatory in the relevant sense. He has treated his male and female employees or students equally.

If courts have been reluctant to scrutinize the behavior of *actual* bisexuals, they have been even more reluctant to consider the possibility, let alone the actuality, of male homosexual or lesbian sexual harassment. Unless a court is under a specific state or municipal gay rights' statute, it will not interpret sex discrimination under Title VII or Title IX to prohibit loss of occupational or educational opportunities because a person is gay. In other words, except in certain jurisdictions, Title VII, for example, fails to protect the lesbian who loses her job because her heterosexual employer does not want "dykes" around the office.[37] Were a national gay rights bill passed, however, lesbians would be protected from this type of discrimination—discrimination directed against them by those who do not approve of their sexual preference. Yet Titles VII and IX would have to be reinterpreted carefully before this bill could also protect lesbians from another type of discrimination— discrimination directed against them by those who wish to exploit their sexual preference by requiring them to perform sexual favors.

The term "sex" in Titles VII and IX is currently understood to denote gender status (male or female). Presented with a case of male homosexual sexual harassment, the EEOC stated that "in enacting Title VII Congress [did not intend] to include a person's sexual practices within the meaning of the term sex."[38] This understanding of "sex" may be too limited. According to Ethel Spector Person, for example, there are at least four legitimate denotations of the term "sex."

> Sex refers to four separate, but related, physical-psychological sets of data: (1) biological sex, defined by six anatomical and physiological characteristics: chromosomes, gonads, internal genitalia, external genitalia, hormones, and secondary sexual characteristics; (2) gender, composed of core gender identity (the sense, "I am female," "I am male") gender role identity (the sense "I am feminine," "I am masculine"), and gender role behavior; (3) sexual behavior, overt and fantasied, expressed both in choice of object and nature of activity; and (4) reproduction.[39]

Far from being mutually exclusive, these denotations are intimately related. As we come to understand these relationships better, it is to be hoped that the courts will reinterpret the term "sex" as it appears in Titles VII and IX to include sexual preference. Once this adjustment is made, lesbians will have no more to fear from their sexual harassers than heterosexual women have to fear from theirs.

Rape and Woman-Battering

In the same way that lesbians can be sexually harassed either by heterosexuals or by lesbians, they can be raped or battered either by heterosexuals or by lesbians. On occasion, heterosexual men try to "cure" lesbians by raping them. In her discussion of popular rape fiction by women, Lynne Farrow points out the elements of one type of classic rape fantasy:

> Big, strong, handsome soldier meets celibate lesbian woman who sees sex only as an instrument of brutality. But the man changes all that and makes her enjoy the experience against her will. He proceeds to make her, the sexually and socially aberrant female, normal. "All she needs is a good fuck" seems to be one of the cliches operating here.[40]

More recently, the parents of Stephanie Riethmiller paid $8,000 to a man in California to "deprogram" their daughter, who they believed was under a woman roommate's influence and had been forced into a lesbian relationship. According to Stephanie, she was raped by her deprogrammers, who hoped to break thereby the lesbian "spell" that had been cast over her.

Such occurrences are rare. So, too, are lesbian-on-lesbian rapes and lesbian-on-lesbian batteries. Although rape and woman-battering are by definition nonconsensual, in some lesbian S & M circles it is difficult to distinguish between nonconsensual sexual assaults and batteries and supposedly consensual assaults and batteries. For example, one noted lesbian advocate of S & M recently found herself in court, charging three other lesbians with aggravated assault and battery. During a sexual encounter she had cut a swastika into her lesbian partner's shoulder. Although she believed that her partner had consented to this carving, her partner felt otherwise. Two days after the sexual encounter, the woman into whose arm the swastika had been cut visited the lesbian activist's apartment. She brought with her two friends armed with a shotgun and a knife. The three of them then proceeded to beat up the lesbian activist, castigating her for her previous sexual excess.[41]

To be sure, such incidents are numerically small when compared to the number of husbands who beat, maim, or kill their wives. Nevertheless, if rape and woman-battering are unacceptable in heterosexual circles, they are unacceptable in lesbian circles.

Conclusion

Like black women and other minority women, lesbians are neglected by the law. Indeed, insofar as the law is concerned, they are virtually invisible. In large measure, this is because lesbians are forced to live on the fringes of society where the law does not reach. Although accounts of lesbians battering other lesbians are shocking, what is more shocking is that for them there are no official counseling programs and very few informal support groups. If a lesbian has a problem with another lesbian, she must handle it herself; unless her lover beats her to a pulp, the law lacks adequate categories to classify the physical and psychological harms perpetrated against her.

Unfortunately, society continues to ignore, trivialize, and even ridicule gay peoples' problems. Unless a gay rights bill is passed, the gay men and gay women will remain the law's stepchildren; and the heterosexual majority will fail to realize that crimes perpetrated against lesbians are just that: crimes. When a lesbian is harassed, raped, or beaten, society is harmed no more or less than when a heterosexual woman is harassed, raped, or beaten.

Like the nineteenth-century black woman, the twentieth-century lesbian cries out "Ain't I a woman, too?" It is hoped that twentieth-century power holders, especially lawmakers, will respond to the lesbian's complaint more quickly than nineteenth-century power-holders responded to the black woman's protest. The law owes its protection to every woman without exception.

Notes

1. There is much debate as to the roots of sexual desire and need. Some theorists claim that our sexual urges are rooted in biology; others insist that they are created by society, and still others maintain that "sexuality" is the result of the interactive processes that bridge the gulf between biology (nature) and society (culture). Whereas the "biological" view of sexuality limits our ability to change the status quo for the better, the latter two allows us to reconstruct gradually the meaning of human sexuality.

2. Simone de Beauvoir, *The Second Sex* (New York: Vintage Books, 1974), p. 468.

3. Joan Nestle, "Butch-Fem Relationships: Sexual Courage in the 1950s," *Heresies* 3, no. 4, issue 2 (1981):22.

4. Ibid.

5. Bat-Ami Bar On, "Feminism and Sadomasochism: Self-Critical Notes," in *Against Sadomasochism*, Robin Ruth Linden et al., eds. (East Palo Alto, Calif.: Frog in the Wall, 1982), p. 76.

6. Ibid., p. 78.

7. In a public letter, Marissa Janel, for instance, explains that for her and many other lesbians, S & M is a learning experience, not a cathartic experience. See Marissa Janel,

"Letter From a Former Masochist," in *Against Sadomasochism,* Linden et al., eds., pp. 16–22.

8. Audre Lorde and Susan Leigh Star, "Interview with Audre Lorde," in ibid., p. 69.

9. Richard Goldstein, "The Politics of Liberation: 'Gay People Are Different from Everyone Else—Except in Bed,'" *The Village Voice,* June 25/July 1, 1980, p. 19.

10. "1982: The Year in Review," *Gaylife: The Mainstream Gay Weekly,* December 30, 1982, p. 6.

11. Quoted by Larry Bush and Richard Goldstein, "The Anti-Gay Backlash," *The Village Voice,* April 8–14, 1981, p. 10.

12. Ibid.

13. Ibid.

14. Ibid., p. 12.

15. Charlotte Bunch, "Lesbianism and Erotica in Pornographic America," in *Take Back the Night,* Laura Lederer, ed. (New York: William Morrow, 1980), p. 92.

17. Amy Hoffman, "Politics, Pleasure, Pain: The Controversy Continues," book review, '*Gay Community News,* December 4, 1982, p. 7.

17. Rachel Weil, *Gay Community News,* December 2, 1978, p. 8–9.

18. Ibid., p. 9.

19. Ibid.

20. Ibid.

21. Pedophilia and pederasty laws are aimed at adults who engage in sexual relations with children who are not related to them. These statutes are to be contrasted with those prohibiting incest (sexual experience between an adult and a minor to whom he or she is related by blood).

22. John Paul Hudson, "The Gay Almanac: The Boston Boise Affair and the Censorship of Sexual Minorities," *Gaysweek,* March 6, 1978.

23. John Stuart Mill, *On Liberty* (New York: Liberal Arts Press, 1958), p. 117.

24. Jill Clark, "Interview with Robin Morgan," *Gay Community News,* January 20, 1979, pp. 11–12.

25. Ibid.

26. Ibid.

27. Lynne Shapiro, "Women Loving Women Denounce Men 'Loving' Boys," *Lesbian Tide* 9, no. 2 (September/October 1979):14.

28. Miriam F. Hirsch, *Women and Violence* (New York: Van Nostrand Reinhold, 1981), p. 58.

29. Pat Califia, "Man/Boy Love and the Lesbian/Gay Movements," in *The Age Taboo,* Daniel Tsang, ed. (Boston: Alyson Publications, 1981), pp. 138–39.

30. Ibid., p. 138.

31. "A Militant Young Dyke's Feminist Perspective on the Age of Consent Question," in ibid., pp. 130–31.

32. Mark Blasius interviews Kate Millett, "Sexual Revolution and the Liberation of Children," in ibid., p. 82.

33. "Demo in Support of Lesbian Bars," *News Midwest,* December 22, 1982, p. 3.

34. *Tomkins v. Public Service Electric & Gas Co.,* 422 F. Supp.553, 556 (D.N.J. 1976).

35. Catherine A. MacKinnon, *Sexual Harassment of Working Women* (New Haven: Yale University Press, 1979), p. 201.

36. Ibid.

37. In approximately 40 to 50 cities and counties a homosexual cannot be denied an apartment or a job on that basis alone.

38. 2 Empl. Prac. Guide (Commerce Clearing House) §6493 (1976).

39. Ethel Spector Person, "Sexuality as the Mainstream of Identity: Psychoanalytic

Perspectives," *Signs: Journal of Women in Culture and Society* 5 (Summer 1980):605–6.

40. Lynne Farrow, "That's All She Wrote: Popular Rape Fiction by Women," in *Rape: The First Sourcebook for Women,* Noreen Connnell and Cassandra Wilson, eds. (New York: A Plume Book, 1974), p. 101.

41. "Lesbian S & M Writer Attacked," *Gaylife: The Midwestern Gay Weekly,* December 30, 1982, p. 2.

CHAPTER 8

CONCLUSION

Common Connections

GOOD GIRL/BAD GIRL

The intention of this book has been to articulate connections between pornography, prostitution, sexual harassment, rape, and woman-battering. One such connection is that all of these phenomena embody Western culture's celebration of the "good" woman and its condemnation of the "bad" woman. To the degree that Western cultural history has praised the good, or spiritual woman, whose body is not for the viewing, feeling, or taking, it has castigated the bad, or sensual woman, whose body is for the viewing, feeling, and taking. Although this dualistic view of women is largely, if not exclusively, the product of male imagination, many women have nonetheless internalized it.

During the nineteenth-century, social-purity reformers (the good girls) stood in marked contrast to the free-love activists (the bad girls). The purity reformers were influenced by a remarkable confluence of medical scientific theory and religio-sentimental literature that claimed that women, as a group had moral, spiritual, and aesthetic sensitivities that were superior to those possessed by men. Concerned not only about men's souls but also about their crude, coarse, and competitive world, these early feminists proclaimed that women must carry their higher moral vision into the public realm by moral purification of man's world. As these women saw it, the world would never be a better (more "feminine") place unless an end were put to pornography, prostitution, and all other practices that gave direct offense to the "ideal of the delicate and frigid female."[1]

In contrast to these purity reformers, free love activists insisted that what the world needed was not men who were more spiritual, but women who were more sensual. They urged their contemporaries to achieve a transvaluation of their principles such that people would begin to equate goodness (not badness) with sensuality, the cult of Dionysius, adultery, polygamous relationships, loose women, and so on. Similarly, people should equate badness (not goodness) with spirituality, the cult of Apollo, fidelity, monogamous relationships, frigid women, and so on.

This nineteenth-century rift between diverging groups of feminists is largely reconstructed in twentieth-century arguments such as the one between Women Against Pornography (the good girls) and Samois, a support organization for lesbians who practice sadomasochism (the bad girls). WAP and other related organizations have initiated campaigns against pornography, especially gyno-thanatic pornography, on the grounds that it degrades and defames women. Implicit in the WAP campaign is the assumption that male sexuality is cruel, callous, and violent, whereas female sexuality is kind, sensitive, and gentle. In general, WAP constituents are convinced that sexual relations between heterosexuals would be much improved (characterized by equal respect and consideration) were women in charge of the sexual dynamic.

Although members of Samois do not necessarily disagree with WAP's indictment of male sexuality, they object to WAP's endorsement of "vanilla" sex (caring, cuddling, and caressing sex) as the paradigm for sex for all women and/or all people. According to Samois, women must be allowed to engage in any and all sexual experiences—violent or nonviolent—provided of course that this experimentation takes place in a lesbian environment. Not only does Samois object to WAP's "puritanism," it also objects to what it perceives as WAP's political naivete. As Samois sees it, the antipornography campaign is likely to result not so much in the restriction of women-degrading fantasies and activities as in the suppression of lesbian fantasies and activities by society as a whole.

Although the debate between pro- and antipornography forces is considerably more complex than these brief paragraphs suggest, more and more feminists are growing uncomfortable with monistic views of female sexuality, according to which all women must subscribe to a uniform code of sexual regulations and rituals in order to be worthy of the title "feminist." As these feminists see it, an institution of compulsory lesbianism is not better than an institution of compulsory heterosexuality. To tell a woman that she cannot be a feminist unless she is/or becomes a lesbian is just as objectionable as to tell a feminist that she cannot be a woman unless she is/or becomes male-identified. In other words, each woman must be free to discover and express her own sexual self, whether or not that sexual self is politically correct and socially acceptable.

As a result of this new openness in the feminist community, heterosexual feminists are coming out of their closets in the hope of finding women who wish to explore with them the advantages as well as the disadvantages of sexual relations with men. Likewise lesbian feminists are increasingly willing to admit that they enjoy role-playing from time to time. No longer is a feminist hissed and booed out of a room simply because she has a man in her life and wants to keep him there; and no longer is a lesbian feminist castigated simply because she enjoys butch-femme or thinks that it has some value. Indeed, as feminists become more trusting of each other, there is less emphasis on orthodoxy and more stress on individuality. Unfortunately, this celebration of sexual plurality will remain confined to the feminist community unless the categories of "good female sex" and "bad female sex" are not only transvaluated but also transcended by society as a whole.

WOMEN AND VIOLENCE

Pornography, prostitution, sexual harassment, rape, and woman-battering are frequently described as crimes of violence perpetrated by men against women. This is not to claim that men do not commit violent crimes against men. On the contrary, as Jean Bethke Elshtain has observed, most victims as well as most perpetrators of violent crimes are also males.[2] But even though most victims of crime are male, when women are violently victimized by men, it is usually simply *because* they are women. Dorie Klein comments: "Although violence and abuse have been no strangers to most dominated groups, in tracing the female experience through history and across cultures, one notices that women have often been injured *as women:* as childbearers, as sexual objects for men, and as nurturers."[3] Klein also points out that unlike male victims of violent crime, women are prone to blame themselves for their own victimization. An attractive woman may blame herself for being beautiful, thereby attracting the pornographer's, harasser's, or rapist's attention. Similarly, a wife may blame herself for being selfish, stubborn, or sassy, thereby meriting her batterer's angry words and hard blows. To be sure, there is something tragic about these unnecessarily repentant women, since they berate themselves for having a body and a will, and yet very few women totally escape these exercises in self-condemnation.

According to Dorothy Dinnerstein, there is an explanation for women's tendency to blame themselves for the violence men direct against them.[4] Humans as a whole feel ambivalent toward the flesh. We hate it because it limits our control and because we know that it is destined to die; yet we love it because it is a source of pleasure for us. To the degree that the flesh signifies mortality, human beings fight against it by engaging either in baby-making (a largely female project) or world-building (a largely male project). Both of these endeavors promise an immortality of sorts. However, a woman can make only so many babies and a man can build only so many worlds. From time to time each woman and each man will be forced to confront the destiny of her or his own flesh. On such occasions, the tendency will be either to bury oneself in the pleasures of the body, hoping to forget its limitations, or to lash out against the body, hoping to conquer its limitations. Because Western culture has come to identify woman with the "fleshy" dimensions of human existence, it is woman who is alternately treasured as the symbol of life (she is after all the bearer of future generations) and despised as the symbol of death (the future generations she bears will also perish). Therefore, it is woman's body that is alternately pampered or abused not only by men but also by women.

As Dinnerstein sees it, this state of affairs will continue as long as women are not only the bearers of babies, but the primary rearers of children. For the infant, the mother is at one and the same time the source of a child's feelings of plentitude and omnipotence ("She must be here for me alone") and of feelings of deprivation and depotentiation ("She wasn't here today when I needed her"). As a result, both male and female babies grow into adults who expect too much from women. If infants were reared by men and women equally, they would grow into adults who would be no more prone to blame women than men for the human condition. Dinnerstein speculates that children would grow into adults able to accept the limits of the human condition—limits that are imposed neither by men nor by women, but by factors beyond any human being's control. Consequently, neither men nor women would be any more celebratory or condemnatory of female flesh than male flesh. Men would be less likely to abuse women sexually, to blame them for continuing a "doomed" species; and women be less likely to blame themselves for not being able to conquer human suffering and death—to make all the "hurts" and "ouches" go away.[5]

THE DECONSTRUCTION OF SEXUALITY

Common to the issues of pornography, prostitution, sexual harassment, rape, and woman-battering is a set of confusions about what sexuality is. Traditionally, a person's sexuality was virtually equated with his or her biological sex. It was simply assumed that the other major manifestations of sexuality —gender, sexual identity/behavior, and reproductive capacities—necessarily flowed from one's biological sex.[6] Significantly, contemporary society is beginning to deny not only the primacy of biological sex but also the assumption that a person's gender, sexual identity/behavior and reproductive capacities automatically flow from his or her biological sex.

1. *The Separation of Gender from Biological Sex:* According to many feminist theorists, none of the interrelated *aspects* of gender—gender role behavior (female baby-making and male world-building), gender role identity (feminine and masculine characteristics), and gender identity (feminine and masculine self-concepts)—necessarily flows from biological sex. That is, just because person *x* is a biological female does not necessarily mean that person *x* will act like a female or think like a female. Similarly, just because person

y is a biological male does not necessarily mean that person *y* will act like a male or think like a male.

First, more and more females are engaging in world-building role behavior and more and more males are becoming involved in child-rearing. As the old boundaries between the public and private realms break down, it seems that one's biological sex has less and less to do with one's professional or familial role in society. Women make excellent police officers, physicians, and tree surgeons; men make excellent secretaries, cooks, and nurses.

Second, many contemporary females feel free to develop aspects of their personality traditionally labeled "masculine," and many contemporary males feel free to develop aspects of their personality traditionally labeled "feminine." Although feminists welcome this development, they do not necessarily advocate an androgynous society in which each and every human being would embody exactly the same combination of feminine and masculine characteristics. I am referring not to any natural set of feminine and masculine characteristics, but to that set of feminine and masculine characteristics Western culture has constructed. If the culturally constructed categories "feminine" and "masculine" are imperfect, it is unlikely that any androgynous composite of them will be perfect.[7] Third, some men are trying to understand what it means to have the gender identity of a woman in this society. Likewise some women are trying to understand what it means to have the gender identity of a man in this society. In this connection, consider the numerous current movies and theater productions in which a man tries to pass for a woman or vice versa. In *Tootsie* Dustin Hoffman plays a man (Michael Dorsey) disguised as a female (Dorothy Michaels), in *Victor/Victoria* Julie Andrews plays a woman disguised as a man employed as a female impersonator, and in the play "Torch Song Trilogy" Harvey Fierstein plays a homosexual male (Arnold) who performs as a drag queen. Throughout stage and screen history women have disguised themselves as men and vice versa. For example, in a bid for freedom, many Shakespearean women disguised themselves as men. Part of their message was that women are just as smart as men, as clever (if not more so), and as devious, but that femaleness does not provide the illusion of authority and credibility that maleness does. In a different vein, numerous male comedians have disguised themselves as women. Part of their message was and still is that a man will lose something if he becomes a woman; namely, dignity. Like she, he will be forced to wear silly clothes (padded bras, corsets, spike heels) and to engage in idle chatter.

Today, more than ever, writers are asking actors to pose as women, not simply to give spectators a good laugh as Jack Lemmon did in *Irma le Douce*, but to force spectators to wonder what life would be like if one had the gender identity of a member of the opposite sex. Carolyn Heilbrun, the author of *Toward a Recognition of Androgyny*, is particularly interested in the phenomenon of men playing women:

Men playing women, if they don't camp it, can be very moving, whereas women playing men is always a bid for freedom. . . . Now I think—it's a little like that book *Black Like Me* in which its white author disguised himself so as to know what it was to be black—that a man playing a woman really wants to have the experience. It's a real breakthrough, and it has a lot to do with a perception of the failure of patriarchy. One is given a different vantage point if one sees it both as the oppressed and the oppressor.[8]

Indeed, this is more or less what Dustin Hoffman had to say about his dual role as Michael Dorsey and Dorothy Michaels: "I'm telling you if you are a woman for a month, the world is a different experience in ways you would never imagine."[9] Although cross-dressing is by no means *the* solution to the problems that pervade male/female relationships, any strategy that introduces men to women's world and vice versa is probably to be recommended in the name of consciousness-raising.

2. *The Separation of Sexual Identity and Behavior from Biological Sex:* Feminists also argue that, like gender, sexual identify and behavior do not necessarily flow from biological sex. In general, Western culture has taught that men and women are made for each other—that man's sexual object is woman and vice versa. It has also taught that, no matter the cost, men and women must give up the polymorphous-perverse sexuality of their infancy for the genital sexuality of their adulthood. Thanks to Freud, each normal man and normal woman must accomplish this fear by weathering the stormy oedipal crisis. According to Freud, both boys and girls are said to pass through an oral and anal stage in early infancy during which they take pleasure in thumb-sucking and feces-producing, respectively. Then they both become more specifically sexual in their interests. The penis becomes an object of attention to the boy and the clitoris to the girls. The girl tires of her clitoris, disappointed in its size and function. She turns away from her mother (whom she holds responsible) and projects her love toward her father. From her father she hopes to obtain a penis; when it becomes apparent that no penis is forthcoming from her father, she translates this new disappointment into the desire to bear a child by a man. The male child's ordeal is less complex. Around the age of three the male child becomes intensely and sexually attached to his mother, a passion he soon gives up because of the fear that his father may take revenge on him by means of castration. The sexuality of both sexes then passes into a period of latency around the age of five, reemerging near puberty in recognizable masculine and feminine forms—that is, active and passive forms. Those who do not weather the oedipal crisis successfully become "abnormal"—male homosexuals or lesbians.

Currently, this Freudian view of reality is being challenged by persons who believe that each man and each woman should be able to choose his or her sexual object/sexual activity. An increasing number of men and women are rebelling against what Adrienne Rich calls the institution of *compulsory* heterosexuality, which teaches, like Freud, that heterosexuality is the paradigm for all human sexual relations. To be normal is to be heterosexual; to be abnormal is to be a homosexual man, a lesbian, or a bisexual.[10] In recent years however, gays and bisexuals have challenged this homophobic conception of sexual normalcy. As these men and women see it, homosexual men, lesbians, and bisexuals are no less normal than heterosexual men and women.

An increasing number of men and women are experimenting with new forms of sexual behavior. In general, men, but especially women, are belying the notion that women are sexually passive and that men are sexually active. Women are gradually becoming just as sexually assertive as men; and slowly, men are coming to enjoy the passive as well as the active dimensions of sexual exchanges. In particular, vaginal orgasm is no longer the quintessential sexual experience for women. Not only are women taking pleasure in clitoral orgasms, they are also engaging in oral and anal sex. Moreover, a growing number of women are maintaining that they prefer hugging, touching, kissing, rubbing, and cuddling to any form of sexual intercourse whatsoever. Likewise, the erect penis is no longer the *sine qua non* for male sexual experience. Oral and anal sex are growing in popularity, as are hot tubs, massages, and extended foreplay. Although polymorphous-perverse sexuality has yet to win the day, the varieties of contemporary sexual experience are blossoming as the institution of compulsory sexuality, which requires men to be sexuallly dominant and women to be sexually submissive, is shriveling.

3. *The Separation of Biological Sex from Reproductive Capacities:* Feminists argue that reproductive capacities do not necessarily flow from biological sex. As technology advances, it becomes clearer that females of the human species need not conceive, bear, or rear children. Since the introduction of reliable means of contraception and safe means of abortion, women need no longer conceive and bear a child they do not want. Indeed, if in vitro fertilization is developed so that children can not only be conceived but also grown outside human wombs, no woman will have to bear a child. As it stands, no woman need rear her biological child—at least she need not rear it alone. Depending on how much help she can solicit or purchase, a mother can spend as little or as much time with her progeny as she desires. Conversely, the new technology has generated talk of implanting wombs and milk-yielding breasts in men who wish to give birth to their children and/or to suckle them. In this connection, many men have already begun to assume the role of primary childrearer, debunking the truism that fathers cannot make good mothers.

Perhaps the result of sexuality's deconstruction—of the separation of biological sex from gender, sexual identity/behavior, and reproductive capacities—will be a rethinking of what is erotic, consensual, liberating, and life-affirming sex on the one hand, and what is thanatic, coercive, enslaving, and life-negating sex on the other. The latter qualities are certainly common to sexual harrassment, rape, and woman-battering. They are also common to much, though not all, of pornography and prostitution. Unfortunately, it is difficult to distinguish between liberating and enslaving prostitution and between nondegrading and degrading pornography. Until this period of deconstruction is lived through, our understanding of sexuality is bound to be partial and provisional. Indeed, we may never again achieve—or even desire to achieve—a unitary understanding of human sexuality. A plurality of voices celebrating a variety of sexual experiences may be the most effective defense against deforming sexual stereotypes whenever, wherever, and however they manifest themselves.

Differences of Perspective

Although biological differences exist between males and females, differences of perspective between men and women and the disputes caused by these differences stem primarily from socially created and maintained inequalities of knowledge and power. Socialized to take pride in their sexual prowess, men tend to interpret encounters with the opposite sex quite differently than do women, who have been taught to regard their sexual powers with some shame. This is not to suggest, however, that male pride is any less problematic than female shame. On the contrary, because male pride generally leads to sexual compulsion, it is just as repressive as female shame, which generally leads to sexual inhibition.

Male sexual compulsion is generated by the burden of being sexually adequate. In this society, sexual adequacy for men is specifically defined in terms of erection and penetration. Men spend considerable energy pursuing women as prey, trying to conquer, overwhelm, or exhaust them. When a man fails to "get it up" and "get it in," he feels depotentiated. In contrast, women are less burdened with a precise notion of female sexual adequacy. Unfortunately, this is a mixed blessing, for it leads to much confusion on women's part. Is the sexually adequate woman one who gives pleasure to a man or one who receives pleasure from a man? Or is the sexually adequate woman one who takes pleasure from a man?

The notion of taking pleasure is an unsettling one. It suggests not only autonomous activity, but ignoring, using, or abusing one's sexual partner. Although many men have tended to reduce women to things, to nonpersons who exist for male ends, objectification has not always been carried to such extremes by all men. Moreover, as the compilers of *Diary of a Conference on Sexuality* suggest, objectification may be an ineliminable feature not only of heterosexual relations, but of all sexual relations:

We agree that the other person must be recognized, but it is unlikely that one subject (yourself) can fully act for the interest of another subject (the other) simultaneously. The other is seen as a subject and as an object. To imagine that the other not be perceived as an object in any way be perceived as an object in any way is unrealistic. Perceiving the object as such (including subjecthood) may be necessary for eroticism. The anti-object school of thought leads to an attack on erotic representation as well. The point is that women have never had a chance to represent themselves, i.e., they've been forever objects, never subjects. The corrective is self-representation, the mutuality of being subject and object, not the elimination of objectification.[11]

The subject/object or self/other dichotomy cannot be transcended. This does not mean, however, that human beings should resign themselves merely to the transvaluation of these dichotomies. It is no better for women to be the selves (subjects) and men to be the others (objects) than it is for men to be the selves and women to be the others. The most desirable situation is one in which each man and woman has the choice of alternating between being subject and being object, between acting and being acted upon, between giving and receiving.

Having said this much, I wish to take note of the fact that the above paragraph was written by a white, middle-class, middle-aged, heterosexual woman who moves in circles that are largely—though by no means exclusively—white, middle-class, middle-aged, and heterosexual. Although I believe that many of my black, upper-class, lower-class, adolescent, seniorcitizen, or lesbian friends would agree with some of my observations, I know that they would not agree with all of my observations. Carole Vance, Academic Coordinator of the Barnard Women's Center comments:

> We base our theories on limited information about ourselves and, at best, a small number of other women. . . . Yet we wish to develop a framework inclusive of all women's experience. (Sexuality must not be a code word for heterosexuality, or women a code word for white women.) To do so we must make a renewed effort to talk with each other. . . . Such is the only way to remedy our ignorance and avoid a sexual theory circumscribed by the boundaries of individual lives and idiosyncracies.[12]

The diffences among women are just as important as the similarities among women. Unless attention is paid to what divides women's sexual perceptions as well as to what unites them, chances are that discussions of female sexuality—and male sexuality for that matter—will remain unilluminating.

Although a complete book on women, sex, and the law would have discussed differences of perspective that arise from a woman's age, appearance, ethnicity, education, and so on, this book focused on but three major set of differences: those that exist between black women and white women, those that exist between lower—class women and middle- or upper-class women, and those that exist between heterosexual women and lesbians. On the one hand, we read that the balance of power in the black community favors women. The black matriarch rules the roost and dispenses her sexual favors as she wishes, when she wishes, and to whom she wishes because the black patriarch has been depotentiated—suppressed, repressed, and oppressed—by the white patriarch. On the other hand, we read that the black woman is visually degraded, callously prostituted, sexually harassed, brutally raped, and mercilessly battered far more than her white counterpart. Further, we read that unlike today's liberated white women, black women remain willing to take much more in the way of abuse form their own men, either because their emotional, legal, and financial status is so much worse than that of comparatively abused white women, or because they can excuse black men's sometimes vicious behavior by blaming it on white society rather than on the black soul.

Yet of course not all black women are married to depotentiated black men, and not all black women belong to the lower class. Rich or relatively well-to-do black women may have more in common with the white women who share their class than with black women, who share their race. In other words, the differences in perspective between black and white women may not always be greater than the differences between poor and rich women regardless of race. Because middle- and upper-class women are usually more educated than lower-class women, they are not only more likely to have so-called liberated views about sexuality, they are less likely to take abuse from their own or anyone else's men. Convinced that her knowledge—and not some man's power—is the road to autonomy and social status, an educated woman may prefer no man in her life to an abusive man. In contrast, an uneducated woman, especially if she is poor, may be grateful for any emotional and economic support whatsoever—even if its source is an abusive man.

When it comes to sexuality, the differences between heterosexual women and lesbians, no matter their race or class, are particularly sharp. The reaction of heterosexual women to lesbians has been mixed. On the one hand, some heterosexual women feel inferior to lesbians. If men are as violent and women-hating as some radical feminists have suggested, then the only morally correct and politically appropriate thing for a self-respecting woman to do is to avoid men as much as possible. However, few heterosexual women are always able or willing to shun men. Even though she is committed to the overthrow of patriarchy, a heterosexual woman may find herself in the arms of a man. When this happens, she may feel obliged either to define her man as the exception—a nonoppressive, woman-loving man—or to castigate herself for her lack of resolve. On the other hand, some heterosexual women feel superior to lesbians. As they see it, lesbians are escapists who are afraid to confront men and to acknowledge that "sexuality is simultaneously a domain of restriction, repression, and danger as well as a domain of exploration, pleasure, and agency."[13]

Most heterosexual *feminists* claim that they are neither inferior nor superior to lesbians. But even these women may idealize sexual relations between lesbians as the epitome of nonoppressive sexual relations—sexual relations in which two human beings treat each other with equal respect and consideration. Unfortunately, such idealization may be premature. Lesbians as a group, like heterosexual women as a group, have yet to define female sexuality in ways that distinguish it adequately from male sexuality. Indeed, in recent years some feminists have considered the possibility that female sexuality is not essentially different from male sexuality. But whether or not male and female sexual desires and anxieties are essentially the same, the truth of the matter will remain hidden unless each woman tries to articulate the meaning of her sexuality by discovering those physical sensations that please her body and draw her psychically closer to other people. Until this happens, any comprehensive description of female sexuality is likely to remain unrepresentative of women's experiences, and any prescription for female sexuality is likely to remain idiosyncratic.

The Limits of the Law

Given that this is a pluralistic society, characterized by wide disagreements on everything, including female sexuality, the importance of the law as a vehicle of social and sexual control cannot be underestimated. In a melting-pot society such as ours, where racial, ethnic, and religious diversity prevail, law is what holds things together. By requiring all of us to abide by a uniform set of regulations or be punished, the law promises each one of us a measure of security. No person will be allowed to violate the legitimate rights of another person without suffering the negative consequences of his or her misconduct. But the law is a minimalist institution: It punishes only manifest or serious harms. It does not censor or sanction those hidden or less blatant harms that plague society more routinely. Nor does it, as a rule, reward positive behavior that benefits society. In short, the law is not a substitute for morality, and legal reformation is not the same as moral transformation. To pass laws prohibiting sexual abuse and gender discrimination is not automatically to eliminate "woman-hating" and to achieve sexual equality; it is, however, to protect the rights of those who need to be protected.

But even if the law is a minimalist institution, it has certain maximalist tendencies—tendencies to nip evil in the bud. Although Anglo-American legal theorists are concerned about these expansionist tendencies, they are not always opposed to them. Victor Li, for example, contrasts Anglo-American law's "falling-off-the-cliff" policy with Chinese law's "sliding-down-the-slope" policy and finds our law lacking. A "falling-off-the-cliff" policy maintains a hands-off attitude until a person commits a crime. The law stands by as a troubled body, for example, stews on the playground, slouches in school, and grouches at home. Only when the boy robs a liquor store will the forces of the law intervene; and then it will probably be too late to help him or his unlucky victim. In contrast, a "sliding-down-the-slope" policy allows the law to intervene at the first signs of misbehavior—at the stewing or slouching or grouching stage. In this way the troubled boy is simply not permitted to become a juvenile delinquent. He is not allowed to ruin his own life or that of anyone else. Unfortunately, the price of this policy is sometimes a subtle loss of freedom, an imperceptible gravitation toward a big-brother, if not a big-daddy, state.[14]

The point is simply this: When women encourage the law to be more active on their behalf, they tread a potentially perilous path. Support can mutate into control, and a gain on one front can represent a loss on another. For example, in her masterful study, *Prostitution and Victorian Society: Women, Class and the State,* Judith Walkowitz argues that if there is any lesson to be learned from the attempts of nineteenth-century feminists to "save" their prostitute sisters, it is that commercial sex (pornography as well as prostitution) is a dangerous issue for feminists:

> In their defense of prostitutes and concern to protect women from male sexual aggression, earlier generations of feminists were still limited by their own class bias and by their continued adherence to a "separate sphere" ideology that stressed women's purity, moral supremacy, and domestic virtues. Moreover, feminists lacked the cultural and political power to reshape the world according to their own image. Although they tried to set the standards of sexual conduct, they did not control the instruments of state that would ultimately enforce these norms. There were times, particularly during the anti-regulationist campaign, when feminists were able to dominate and structure the public discourse on sex and arouse popular female anger at male sexual license. Yet this anger was easily diverted into repressive campaigns against male vice and sexual variation, controlled by men and corporate interests whose goals were antithetical to the values and ideals of feminism.[15]

Walkowitz's cautionary notes are important for several reasons. First, feminists need to confront the fact that the law exists not to challenge but to protect the reigning socioeconomic order, which is largely maintained by prevailing race, gender, and class barriers. Until people decide to change the status quo, the law can do only so much for women—and, by parity of reasoning, only so much for racially and economically disadvantaged persons —because it is difficult for the law to change what it was designed to preserve and promote.

Second, feminists must remind themselves that their immediate goals have not always meshed with the immediate goals of racially and economically disadvantaged persons. For example, racial bias has detracted from otherwise laudable reforms in rape law. Strict rape laws seem to result in the arrest, prosecution, and imprisonment of many more minority men than white men, even though there is no airtight reason to believe that black and chicano rapists outnumber white rapists by any significant number. Similarly, strict woman-battering laws have a way of affecting lower-class men in ways that they do not affect middle- and upper-class men. Unlike rich men, poor men cannot hire the best lawyers or command the sympathy of judges. Consequently, unlike rich men, poor men are more likely to be incarcerated for their crimes, even though they are no more or less blameworthy than their wealthy counterparts. Of course, this is not to claim that weak rape and woman-battering laws are advisable. It is to suggest, however, that the ultimate goals of gender, race, and class reform are mutual goals. What feminists have in common with other social activists is a desire to break down barriers to social equality, to construct a society in which each person is provided with the concrete means to take advantage of bona fide educational and occupational opportunities, and the fostering of human relationships based on mutual respect, concern, and consideration. Given these goals, perhaps feminists ought to work as closely as possible with those who are working toward race and class equality.

Third, feminists should not simply assume either that women's perspectives on sexuality are automatically more good, true, and beautiful than men's perspectives on sexuality, or that the law should favor women in ways that it does not favor men. Instead, feminists should raise two open questions: (1) when it comes to sexuality, should the law trust women's perceptions more, less, or the same as men's perceptions? and (2) when it comes to crime, should the victim's physiological and physical injuries count more, less, or the same as the perpetrator's intentions and motives?

The current tendency within the feminist community is to focus on the harmful effects sustained by the victims of pornography, prostitution, sexual harassment, rape, and woman-battering rather than on the perpetrator's states of mind. This trend is good in that women probably need more legal protection than men, since our legal system is skewed in ways that favor men's interests and rights. This trend is also worrisome in that it represents a tendency toward a policy of strict liability. It took Anglo-American law centuries to move *away* from a system of strict liability, a system that accepted no excuses or justifications for the harms one inflicted, to a system that took into account a perpetrator's motives and intentions. "Did Mr. Z purposely, knowingly, recklessly, negligently, or inadvertently (accidentally) inflict x on Ms. Y?" is just as important a question as "How seriously was Ms. Y harmed by Mr. Z?" If Ms. Y's injuries are not weighed more heavily than Mr. Z's intentions, she will probably be left without much of a legal remedy, since society is structured in ways that discredit women, especially when it comes to sexual matters.

Unless the law takes this discrepancy into account, it will not be able adequately to address the interests and rights of women. To move too far in this direction is of course problematic: The rights of male defendants are just as important as those of female victims. But not to move far enough in this direction is equally problematic; it is not only to leave women unprotected but also to prompt them to vigilante tactics. Frustrated by the slow wheels of justice, women have from time to time taken the law into their own hands. In recent months women have picketed pornographers, harassed their harassers, and even killed their rapists, pimps, and batterers in preemptive acts of self-defense. When the law fails to address the rights of a vulnerable group, it courts desperate actions on its part.

Finally, and most important, women must realize that at best the law can curb sexual violence against women. It cannot promise to eliminate such conduct. For this reason legal remedies should be accompanied by extralegal remedies whenever possible. Indeed, assuming that extralegal remedies are less coercive than legal remedies, the former should be substituted for the latter if at all possible. This is precisely the approach many feminists favor. Having observed that the law is an "after-the-fact" strategy, many women are seeking ways to prevent the awful facts from ever happening or, should they happen, from repeating themselves. Several chapters of *Take Back the Night* suggest ways in which women can highlight the objectionable character of thanatic pornography without invoking the criminal sanction. Most of these means are consciousness-raising strategies like the tours WAP conducts on New York's porn strip. Likewise, insofar as sexual harassment is concerned, such organizations as the Working Women's United Institute in New York City and the Alliance Against Sexual Coercion in Boston stress the importance of establishing sexual-harassment crisis centers to provide counseling and advocacy for actual and potential sexual harassment victims. Women's organizations have also worked hard to establish rape prevention and crisis centers as well as battered women's shelters. To a lesser extent, prostitutes have attempted to throw off the yoke of exploitative pimps by organizing themselves into unions.

These efforts are likely to flounder unless they are supported financially and unless they are encouraged by powerful social institutions such as the law, education, medicine, and business. In particular, it is important that women's groups work together with representatives of the criminal justice system. Where police and prosecutors are in close contact with those who administer battered-women's shelters and rape-crisis centers, for example, sexually abused women tend to find the help they most want and need—psychological (counseling for them and perhaps also their families), economic, medical, and legal.

Predictably, sexual relations between men and women will not improve overnight, and tomorrow will not produce a definition of female sexuality that embodies the diverse perspectives of myriad women. No free society is reeducated or resocialized quickly, especially where something as "personal" as sexuality is involved. For quite some time women will remain vulnerable because of their sexuality and gender; and for quite some time, women will have to rely on the law to rectify those social inequities that retard their journey toward full personhood. But as woman creates for herself new sexual and gender identities, and as her social and economic lot improves, she will have less need to rely on the law for succor. Rather, woman will have every reason to rely on herself.

Notes

1. David A. J. Richards, "Commercial Sex and the Rights of the Person: A Moral Arguement for the Decriminalization of Prostitution," *University of Pennsylvania Law Review* 127, no. 5, (May 1979):1253.

2. Jean Bethke Elshtain, "The Victim Syndrome: A Troubling Turn in Feminism," *The Progressive* 46 (June 1982):43.

3. Dorie Klein, "Violence Against Women: Some Considerations Regarding Its Causes and Its Elimination," *Crime and Delinquency* 27, no. 1 (January 1981):64.

4. Dorothy Dinnerstein, *The Mermaid and the Minotaur* (New York: Harper & Row, 1976).

5. Even if Dinnerstein can help us understand not only why so many men sexually abuse women, but why so many women tolerate such abuse, her solution to this problem is not entirely satisfactory. Convinced that "massive psychological problems" lie at the heart of human sexual malaise, Dinnerstein insists that things will not change unless dual parenting and dual careers become the rule. Her solution has much to recommend it, but she fails to consider how social institutions (law, education, business, the arts, medicine) will also have to change if this massive process of resocialization is to succeed. Moreover, she fails to offer much hope to this generation of people, especially this generation of women, for whom resocialization is not a real possibility and who must rely instead on institutions like the law to protect their interests and rights as sexual beings.

6. Ethel Spector Person, "Sexuality as the Mainstay of Identity: Psychoanalytic Perspectives," *Signs: Journal of Women in Culture and Society* 5, no. 4 (Summer 1980):606.

7. For a complete discussion of androgyny, see *"Femininity," "Masculinity," and "Androgyny,"* Mary Vetterling-Braggin, ed. (Totowa, N.J.: Littlefield, Adams, 1982).

8. Carolyn Heilbrun quoted by Mary Cantwell, "The Sexual Masquerade Is Conveying a New Kind of Message," *The New York Times* January 16, 1983, section 2, p. 25.

9. Ibid.

10. Adrienne Rich, "Compulsory Heterosexuality and Lesbian Existence," *Signs: Journal of Women in Culture and Society* 5, no. 4 (Summer 1980):631–60.

11. Hannah Alderter, Meryl Altman, Kate Ellis, Beth Jaker, Marybeth Nelson, Esther Newton, Ann Snitow, and Carole S. Vance, eds., *Diary of a Conference on Sexuality* (Faculty Press, 1981), p. 33.

12. Carole S. Vance, "Concept Paper: Towards a Politics of Sexuality," in ibid., p. 40.

13. Ibid., p. 38.

14. Victor H. Li, *Law Without Lawyers: A Comparative View of Law in China and the United States* (Boulder, Colo.: Westview Press, 1978).

15. Judith R. Walkowitz, "The Politics of Prostitution," *Signs: Journal of Women in Culture and Society* 6, no. 11 (Autumn 1980):135.

INDEX

Abuse. *See* Rape; Sexual harassment;
   Woman-battering
Academia, sexual harassment in, 68–69,
   71–72, 83–86, 163–65
Acquaintance-on-acquaintance rape,
   103
Adequacy, male sexual, 200
Against Our Will: Men, Women, and Rape
   (Brownmiller), 166, 167
Aggravated assault, 113
Aggression, male, 16, 97–98, 149–50. *See
   also* Rape; Woman-battering
Alabama, chastisement rule in, 128
Alexander v. *Yale*, 80
Alliance Against Sexual Coercion, 206
Ames, J.D., 167, 173
Amir, M., 102, 121
Anal sex, 199
Anglo-American law: "falling-
   off-the-cliff" policy, 203–4;
   traditional concept of pornography
   in, 7–9; on woman-battering, 127–28
Anorexia, 86
Antidiscrimination law, 77–83
Anti-Lynching Crusaders, 167
Anti-Semitism, 29
Arrest-avoidance policy, 135–36
Assaultive behavior: degrees of, 112–13;
   types of, 125–26, 129. *See also*
   Woman-battering
Assault law: assimilation of rape law
   to, 112–19; sexual harassment and,
   73–74; woman-battering and, 133–41
Association of Southern Women for
   the Prevention of Lynching, 167
Augustine, 99–100

Ayletrides, 53

Backhouse, C., 86, 88
Balfour, V., 70, 88
Bard, M., 136
Barnes v. *Train (Costle)*, 79–80
Barry, K., 162, 173
Battering. *See* Woman-battering
Battery tort, 73
Bayles, M., 68–69, 88
Beauvoir, S. de, 38, 54–55, 62, 63, 120,
   175, 190
Bellfield, K., 171, 174
Bengali-Pakistani conflict, 92–93
Beuharnis v. *Illinois*, 21–22
Bias, against rape victim, 90, 101, 105,
   120, 205
Biological sex: separation of gender
   from, 196–98; separation from
   reproductive capacities of, 199–200;
   separation of sexual identity and
   behavior from, 198–99
Black perspectives, 153–74, 202;
   deemphasis on sex-exploitative
   issues, 153–55; on pornography,
   155–59; on prostitution, 159–62; on
   rape, 166–69; on sexual harassment,
   162–66; on woman-battering, 169–71
Blackstone, W., 127, 128, 148, 150
Blame, women victims' self-, 66, 195
Blitz rape, 103
Bloustein, J., 60, 64
Born Innocent (film), 17
Brecht, B., 19, 34
Brownmiller, S., 14, 17, 29, 33, 59, 63,
   97, 101, 120, 166, 173

Bruno v. *Codd*, 142
Bunch, C., 180, 191
Bush, L., 179, 191
Butch-femme sexuality, 176–78
Butler, J., 48, 110, 122

C.O.Y.O.T.E. (Cast Off Your Old Tired Ethics), 54–55, 58
Califia, P., 184–85, 191
Call girls, 52, 159. *See also* Prostitution
Campbell, G., 84
Capitalism, prostitution and, 49–50
Capitalist-patriarchy, 60–61
"Carnal knowledge," 92–94
Catharsis model, 15–16
Causation argument, 17–18
Cautionary instructions in rape law, 105–6
Censorship, 6–7, 14–15
Chastisement rule, 127–28
Chastity, female, 42, 93–94, 108
Childrearing, 196, 197, 199
Children: cross-generational sex with, 182–86; as prostitutes, 52–53; sexual exploitation of, 59–60
Christianity: influence on law, 98–104; on pornography and obscenity, 7; stance on prostitution, 38
Civil law: function of, 128; problems with approach of, 75–77; on sexual harassment, 72–74; on woman-battering, 128–33
Class, social, 49–51, 160, 202
Clear, T.R., 107, 112–13, 116, 118, 122
Clear-and-present-danger approach, 17, 27–28
Cleaver, E., 167
Coercion: individual and institutional, 60, 109–11, 159; in sexual harassment, 67, 68–69
Cohen, L., 86, 88
Commercial sex. *See* Prostitution
Commission on Obscenity and Pornography, 15
Compulsory heterosexuality, 2, 199
Comstock, A., 7–8
Conformity, moral, 40
Connell, N., 108, 121, 122
Consent: age of, 113–14, 184, 185–86; issue of, 75–76; prior sexual history and, 106–7
Consequences approach, 76

Continental Can Co. v. *Minnesota*, 80
Contract, marriage, 95
Corne v. *Bausch and Lomb, Inc.*, 78
Corroboration rules, 104–5, 113
Counseling, psychological, 144
Credibility, prior sexual history and, 107–9
Crime: defined, 129; as lower-class occupational option, 160; prostitution and, 44
Criminal-circumstances approach to rape law, 109–11
Criminalization of prostitution, 39–46
Criminal law: aim of, 128; on rape, 10–19, 205; for sexual harassment, 71–72; on woman-battering, 128–30, 133–41
Crisis centers, 206
Crisis helplines, 144
Crisis-intervention and conflict-management approach to woman-battering, 136–37
Cross-generational sex, 182–86
Culture, view of women in Western, 110, 119, 159, 193–200
"Curtain rule," 128

"Date-rape," 85
Dating ritual, black, 163
Davis, A., 5, 166–67, 173
Death penalty, racism and, 168
Decriminalization of prostitution, 56–60; black prostitution and, 160–62; laissez-faire, 47, 58–59, 60; with regulation or licensing, 46–47, 56–68
Deep Throat (film), 28
Defamation: group, 19–24, 28, 158, 180–81; law, 18–24, 35
Deferral of prosecution, 144
Degradation: pornography and, 9–13; prostitution and, 41–42, 60–61
Dejavu, The (lesbian bar), 186
Destruction of property, 126
Devil in Miss Jones, The (film), 28
Devlin, L.P., 40, 62
Diary of a Conference on Sexuality (Alderter et al.), 200
Dinnerstein, D., 195–96, 207
Discrimination: antidiscrimination laws, 77–83, 84, 87, 188; in laws against prostitution laws, 55–56

Discriminatory sexual harassment, 78–83; of blacks, 163–66; of lesbians, 187–89

Disparate-impact approach, 81–82

Disparate treatment approach, 80–81, 82

Divorce, 129, 130–33

Domestic violence. *See* Woman-battering

Dominance, erotization of, 177, 178, 180

Donnerstein, E., 16, 17

Double standard, 48

Douglas, A., 12

Drugs, prostitution and, 160

Due-process rights, 56

Dutchess, The (lesbian bar), 186

Dworkin, A., 19, 34

Eccles, D., 74–75

Echols, A., 6

Economics, prostitution and, 49–51

Education. *See* Academia

EEOC, 188

EFCS (Executive Financial Counseling Service), 84

Eisenberg, S.E., 151, 174

Elshtain, J.B., 10–11, 33, 150, 195, 207

Employer liability in discriminatory sexual harassment, 82–83, 87

Employment, sexual harassment in, 71–72, 78–83, 163–65

Engels, F., 49

English, D., 9, 19, 32, 36

Equal Employment Opportunity Commission, 188

Equal-protection clause, 142

Ericsson, L.O., 51, 61

Erotica, 9. *See also* Pornography

Evidentiary rules: lying temptress image of woman and, 100–102; in rape laws, 104–9

Excessive-force rule, 146–47

Existentialist feminists, 53–54

Extralegal remedies: for sexual harassment, 83–86; as supplement to legal, 206–7

Extramarital condition of rape, 94–96

Family, myth of ideal, 127

Family Court Act (N.Y. 1962), 142

Family Protection Act, 179

"Family Violence: The Prosecutor's Challenge" (Sich), 140

Fantasy, rape, 189

Farrow, L., 189, 192

Feinberg, J., 26, 33, 35, 45, 62

Felony, assault as, 112–13

Feminist(s): concepts of prostitution, 48–55; defining sexuality, 12–13, 31, 194–95, 203; existentialist, 53–54; on harm principle of pornography, 15–24; on legal approaches to prostitution, 55–59; on legal responses to sexual harassment, 77–83; lesbian, 175–78; Marxist, 49–50, 109, 111, 154; new openness among, 194–95; nineteenth-century, 48, 57, 193–94, 204; radical, 51–53, 154, 183–84; Socialist, 50–51; on women-degrading pornography, 9–13. *See also* Lesbian perspectives

Fierstein, H., 197

First Amendment, 17, 18, 25, 27

Foaski, L., 114, 122

Free love activists, 193–94

Freud, S., 3, 5, 28, 42, 198

Frye, M., 23, 25

Garcia, I., 119

Garden of Eden myth, 99

Gardner, T., 156, 158, 172

Gay, R., 145

Gay rights, 178–79, 188. *See also* Lesbian perspectives

Gender: differences of perspective due to, 1, 76–77, 200–203; harassment, 83, 84–85; separation from biological sex of, 196–98

Goldstein, R., 179, 191

Good-girl/bad-girl myth, 38–39, 193–200

Grievance procedures, for sexual harassment, 86

Griffin, S., 10, 33, 90, 120, 159, 172

Group defamation, 19–24, 28, 158, 180–81

Guilt, harassment and, 66

Gyno-erotic pornography, 10

Gyno-thanatica, 13–27; campaigns against, 156, 194; depiction of sex in, 10–11; harm principle arguments against, 15–24; offense principle arguments against, 24–27; privatization of, 29; racist, 158

Hale, M., 94, 121
Harassment. *See* Sexual harassment
Harm, sexual harassment and issue of, 77
Harm principle: defined, 13–14; against gyno-thanatica, 15–24; prostitution and, 43–44; sexual harassment and, 71–72
Harriet Tubman Women's Shelter, 171
Hefner, H., 28
Heilbrun, C., 197–98, 207
Helplines, crisis, 144
Hetairae, 53–54
Heterosexuality, compulsory, 2, 199
Hirsch, M.F., 62, 173, 191
Hoffman, A., 180, 191
Hoffman, D., 197
Hollibaugh, A., 30, 31, 36
Homicides, spouse, 145–49
Homosexuality. *See* Lesbian perspectives
Hughes, F., 145
Hughes, J.C., 68, 88
Husband: murder of, 128, 145–49; rape by, 94–95
Hustler (magazine), 13
Hypersensitivity, issue of, 76–77

Identity, sexual, 198–99
Images, misogynistic, 98–104
Imitation model, 15, 16
Imminent-danger rule, 147–49
Independence, woman-battering and, 149
Individual coercion, 60, 109, 111, 159
Injunctive orders, 130, 139, 143
Injuries, assaultive rape and, 115–16
Insanity, spouse murder and, 145–46
Institutional coercion, 60, 109–11, 159
Institutional liability, 87
Intention, issue of, 18–21
Intentional infliction, of mental or emotional disturbance tort, 74

Jennings, M.A., 44, 62, 173
Jiveboy (magazine), 156–57
Joseph, G.I., 163, 172
Judges: criminal remedies for woman-battering and, 141; racism and, 168

Kaminer, W., 17, 30, 33, 35
Kant, I., 42
"Kinder, kirche, kuche" theory of womanhood, 84
Klein, D., 5, 62, 152, 195, 207
Ku Klux Klan, 142

Lane, R.M., 89, 173
Law: age of consent, 185–86; battered black women's expectations of, 171; defamation, 18–24, 35; influence of Christianity on, 98–104; as instrument of social control, 4; limits of, 203–7; pedophilia and pederasty, 182–86; on prostitution, 55–56; on sexual harassment, 71–77; statutory rape, 113–14, 185. *See also* Anglo-American law; Civil law; Criminal law; Rape law
Lederer, L., 10, 33, 34, 63
Lesbian Feminist Liberation of New York, 184
Lesbian perspectives, 175–92; feminist, 175–78; on pornography, 179–81; on prostitution, 181–86; on rape and woman-battering, 189; on sexual harassment, 186–89; types of lesbians, 175
Lewis, J., 153, 172
Li, V.H., 203–4, 208
Liability: employer's, 82–83, 87; strict, 205–6; tort, 72–74
Liberated woman, prostitute as quintessential, 53–55
Liberty-limiting principles. *See* Harm principle; Moralism, principle of legal; Offense principle; Paternalism, principle of legal
Little, J., 168
Longino, H., 18, 34
Lorde, A., 154, 172
Lynching, of blacks, 167

"Macho" behavior, 15
MacKellar, J., 166–67, 173
MacKinnon, C., 5, 13, 33, 61, 64, 73–74, 76, 77, 83, 87, 88, 164–66, 173, 187, 191
"Madonna-prostitute complex," 38. *See also* Good-girl/bad-girl myth
Male prostitution, 58
Male sexual compulsion, 200

Marcus, M.L., 146, 147, 152
Marital-exception rule, 94–96, 114
Marital violence. *See* Rape;
  Woman-battering
Marriage: contract, 95; state's interest
  in preserving, 131–32. *See also* Spouse
  murder
Marxist feminists, 49–50, 109, 111, 154
Marx, K., 49–50, 63
Masochism: lesbian, 177–78;
  pornography and, 19–20. *See also*
  Sadomasochism (S & M)
Massachusetts, chastisement rule in,
  128
Masturbation, Victorian view of, 7–8
May, L., 68, 88
Mead, M., 78–79, 89
Medea, A., 65, 75, 88
Mediation agreements, woman-
  battering and, 138
Melani, L., 114, 122
Metcalf v. *Metcalf*, 133
Michigan Supreme Court, 131
Micklow, P.L., 151, 174
Mill, J.S., 24–25, 35, 62, 191
Miller v. *Bank of America*, 78–79
Miller v. *California*, 8–9
Millet, K., 60–61, 63, 173, 185, 191
Minors. *See* Children
Misdemeanor, assault as, 112
Misogynistic images, 98–104
Moralism, principle of legal, 14, 33,
  39–43
Morgan, R., 183–84
Mosher, D., 15–16, 33
Myths: Garden of Eden, 99;
  good-girl/bad-girl, 38–39, 193–200;
  of ideal family, 127; racist, 166–68,
  170, 172

NAMBLA (North American Men/Boy
  Love Association), 182–83, 185
National Black Feminist Organization,
  168
National Commission on the Causes
  and Prevention of Violence, 170
National Institute of Law Enforcement
  and Criminal Justice, 120
National Organization for Women
  (NOW), 179
National Socialist Party, 29
Nelson, M., 33, 207

Nervous shock, tort of intentional
  infliction of, 74–75
Nevada, regulation of prostitution in,
  47, 57
Newsweek (magazine), 65
New York City Police Department,
  136, 142–43
New York Times, 70
Noble, E., 183
No-fault divorces, 130
Noncoercive sexual harassment, 67,
  70–71
Nonconsensual intercourse, 96–98

Objectification, 200–201
Obscenity: law, contemporary, 17;
  pornography and, 7–8
Oedipal crisis, 198
Offense principle, 14, 24–29, 46
On, B-A.B., 177, 190
Oppression: perspectives on, 154–55;
  prostitution and, 49–53
Oral sex, 199
Orgasm, 199

Pain, erotization of, 177. *See also*
  Sadomasochism (S & M)
Paternalism, principle of legal, 14, 33,
  44–46
Paternity, issue of, in rape, 93
Patriarchy, 50, 60–61, 110
Peace bonds, 135, 139
Pederasty, 182–86
Pedophilia, 182–86
Peers, sexual harassment between,
  82–83, 85
People's Republic of China: legal policy
  in, 203–4; prostitution in, 51
Pepe, H.A., 139
Perception, issue of, 20–21
Person, E.S., 5, 188, 191–92, 207
Perspectives, differences due to gender,
  1, 76–77, 200–203. *See also* Black
  perspectives; Lesbian perspectives
Pimps, 57, 161–62
Playboy (magazine), 6, 13, 158
Plea-bargaining, woman-battering and,
  139, 140
Police officers: criminal remedies for
  woman-battering and, 134–38, 139;
  rape cases and, 102–3
Pomeroy, S.B., 54, 63

Pornai, 53
Pornographers, intentions of, 18–21
Pornography, 6–36; black perspectives
on, 155–59; as dangerous issue, 204;
defining women-degrading, 9–13;
gyno-thanatica, 13–27; lesbian
perspectives on, 179–81; offense
principle in, 24–27; racism in, 156–58;
traditional concept in Anglo-
American law of, 7–9
*Pornography and Silence: Culture's Revenge
Against Nature* (Griffin), 10
"Pornography Commission Revisited:
Aggressive-Erotica and Violence
Against Women" (Donnerstein), 16
Power: differential between adults and
minors, 183, 184; institutional control
and, 87; sexual harassment as issue
of, 77–78, 81
Powerlessness, erotization of, 177, 178,
180
President's Committee on Law
Enforcement and the Administration
of Justice, 44
Privacy, right to, 27, 56, 126, 128
Proarrest policy, 137–38
Procreational model, 41
Promiscuity, 106–7, 159–60
Property destruction, 126
Prosecution, deferral of, 144
Prosecutors: criminal remedies for
woman-battering and, 138–40;
litigation against, 142
Prostitution, 37–64; black perspectives
on, 159–62; children and, 52–53;
confusion over, 37; criminalization
arguments, 39–46; as dangerous issue,
204; decriminalization arguments,
46–47, 56–60, 160–62; degradation
and, 41–42, 60–61; feminist concepts
of, 48–55; feminist legal approaches
to, 55–59; lesbian perspectives on,
181–86; licensing of, 46–47, 56–58;
male, 58; traditional image of, 38–39
*Prostitution and Victorian Society: Women,
Class and the State* (Walkowitz), 204
Protection order, 143
Provocation, wife-battering and, 132–33
Psychiatric examinations, in rape cases,
106

Psychological injury: from battering,
125–26; from pornography, 22–23;
from rape, 115–16
Psychological counseling, 144
Public decency, offense principle and,
25–26
Purity reformers, 193

Racism: of black pimps, 161–62; black
priorities and, 153–55; myths,
166–68, 170, 172; in pornography,
156–58; sexual harassment and,
164–66
Radical feminists, 51–53, 154, 183–84
Raguz v. *Chandler,* 142
Rape, 90–123; as assault *sans phrase,*
117–19; bias against victim of, 90,
101, 105, 120, 205; black perspectives
on, 166–69; "date-rape," 85; defining,
91–98; effect of misogynistic images
on, 98–104; fantasy, 189; lesbian
perspectives on, 189; prostitution's
effect on, 58–59; psychological injury
from, 115–16; rate of reported, 11,
12; as sexual assault, 117, 118–19;
sex-specificity of, 91–92; types of,
102–3
Rape law, 100–119; assimilation to
assault law of, 112–19;
criminal-circumstances approach to,
109–11; effect of lying temptress
image on, 100–104; evidentiary rules,
104–9; penalties for, 114–15; racial
bias in, 205; recent reforms in,
104–19
Rape: The Bait and the Trap (MacKellar),
166
Redbook (magazine), harassment survey
of, 66
Regulation of prostitution, 46–47,
56–58
Reik, R., 19
Reisman, D., 22–23, 35
Reproduction, separation of biological
sex from, 199–200. *See also*
Childrearing
Resistance condition in rape, 96–98
Restraining orders, 135
Retaliatory violence, doctrine of, 26–27,
29
Retreat, self-defense plea and duty to,
147

Rich, A., 2, 5, 33, 199, 207
Rich, B.R., 20, 34
Richards, D.A.J., 7, 32, 42, 47, 62, 207
Richette, L., 149
Riethmiller, S., 189
Risk, reasonable assumption of, 45–46
Romantic love, 41
Rubin, G., 30–31, 36
Runaways, prostitution and, 60
Rush, F., 184
Russell, D., 34, 166, 167, 173
Russia, prostitution in, 51

Sadomasochism (S & M), lesbianism
    and, 176–78, 180, 189
Salmond, J., 21
Samms, M., 74–75
Samms v. *Eccles*, 75
Samois, 194
Schwartz, M.D., 107, 112–13, 116, 118,
    122
Scottsboro Nine Case, 102, 168
Seduction, as distinct from sexual
    harassment, 68–69
"Selective aggression," 16
Self-defense, spouse murder in, 145–48
Sex: biological, separation from,
    196–200; depiction in gyno-thanatica,
    10–11; legitimate denotations of
    term, 188–89; oral and anal, 199;
    roles, 175–76, 195–97
Sexism, black perspectives on, 153–55
Sexual adequacy, 200
Sexual harassment, 65–89; in academia,
    68–69, 71–72, 83–86, 163–65;
    antidiscrimination laws and, 77–83,
    84, 87, 188; bisexual, 187; black
    perspectives on, 162–66; coercive, 67,
    68–69; defined, 112; discriminatory,
    78–83, 163–66, 187–89; effects of,
    65–66; in employment, 71–72, 78–83,
    163–65; extralegal remedies, 83–86;
    feminist legal responses, 77–83;
    lesbian perspectives on, 186–89;
    noncoercive, 67, 70–71;
    nondiscriminatory, 162–63, 186–87;
    between peers, 82–83, 85; standard
    legal responses to, 71–77; syndrome,
    66; as ubiquitous phenomenon,
    67–71; verbal, 83–84
Sexual history, prior, 106–9, 114
Sexual identity, 198–99

Sexuality: Augustine's teachings on,
    99–100; butch-femme, 176–78;
    concept of, 2; deconstruction of,
    196–200; defining female, 12–13, 31,
    194–95, 203; functions of, 41;
    heterosexual vs. lesbian, 202–3; of
    infancy, 198; perspectives on, 205–6;
    rape as aggression against female,
    117
Shafer, C.M., 23, 35
Shame, harassment and, 66
Shelters, battered women's, 144, 171,
    206
Shoemaker (coal) Mine, 83–84
Sich, N., 140
Silberman, C.E., 123, 160, 173
Silhouette romances, 12
Sixth Amendment, 108
Skokie crisis, 28–29
Snuff (film), 17, 28
Social class, 49–51, 160, 202
Socialist feminists, 50–51
Socialization of women, 51–53, 75–76,
    155
Soft pornography, 11, 12
Solicitation for prostitution, public,
    46–47
Sontag, S., 31, 36
"Special protection" status of women,
    118
Speech, freedom of, 18
Spouse abuse. *See* Woman-battering
Spouse murder, 127, 145–49
Stanley v. *Georgia*, 27
State v. *Wanrow*, 146–47
Statutory rape laws, 113–14, 185
Stein, M.L., 52, 63
Steinem, G., 10, 33
"Stitch rule," 135
Streetwalkers, 159. *See also* Prostitution
Strict liability, 205-6
Students, harassment of, 80, 83–86
Students' rights movement, 85
Submission, female, 97–98, 150

Take Back the Night (Lederer), 10, 206
Take Back the Night (TBTN), 7, 11, 22
Talbert, M., 167
Talmadge, D., 139
Temptress image, 99–104
Terrell, M.C., 167
Tertullian, 99, 121

Theater, gender identity in, 197–98
Thompson, 65, 75, 88
Tibbs, D., 168
Title IX, 80, 83, 84, 87, 188
Title VII, 78, 79, 80, 83, 84, 188
Tomkins v. *Public Service Electric and Gas Co.*, 79
Tootsie (film), 197
"Torch Song Trilogy" (play), 197
Tort law. *See* Civil law
Toward a Recognition of Androgyny (Heilbrun), 197
Truninger, E., 139
Truth, S., 155

U.S. Supreme Court, 21, 25, 27
U.S. Task Force on Crime, 134
United States Civil Rights Commission Hearings on Domestic Violence, 149
Universality, standard of, 26, 27
Utah Supreme Court, 74–75

Vaginal penetration condition of rape, 92–94
Vance, C.S., 201, 207
Venereal disease, prostitution and, 43–44
Vetterling-Braggin, M., 5, 34, 207
Victimization of women, 195
Victim precipitated forcible rape, 102–3
Victor/Victoria (film), 197
Vietnam, 59
Violence, 195–96; cycle of, 132, 137, 149–50; erotization of, 177; rate of, against women, 11, 12; retaliatory, 26–27, 29. *See also* Rape; Woman-battering
Virginia, rape law in, 111
Virginity, female, 93, 100

Walker, A., 157, 172

Walker, L.E., 137, 150
Walkowitz, J.R., 32, 57, 63, 204, 208
Washington (State) Supreme Court, 146–47
Wells, I.B., 167
Wharton, F., 148, 152
Wife beating. *See* Woman-battering
Wigmore, J.H., 101, 105–6, 121
Williams, E.G., 168–69, 174
Woman, women: -as-victim theme, 118–19; images of, 2–3, 90–91, 98–104, 131; "special protection" status of, 118; Western culture's view of, 110, 119, 159, 193–200
Woman-battering, 124–52; black perspectives on, 169–71; civil remedies for, 128–33; criminal remedies, 128–30, 133–41; cycle of, 137, 149–50; definition and causes, 125–26; independence and, 149; lesbian perspectives on, 189; search for more effective legal remedies, 141–44; society's response to, 124; spouse murder and, 145–49; traditional legal doctrine, 127–28
Women, Race & Class (Davis), 166
Women Against Pornography (WAP), 6, 7, 11, 22, 194
Women Against Violence in Pornography and the Media (WAVPM), 7, 9, 11, 22, 30–31
Working Women's United Institute, 206
Workplace. *See* Employment
World-building role, 195, 197

Yale Law Journal, 90
Yale University, harassment suit at, 66

Zamora, R., 17–18